Children
and Material Culture

Each of us was once a child. As we grow older, many of us have children and grandchildren of our own. It is impossible to imagine a society without children. Yet children have been notably absent from archaeological narrative.

This is the first book to focus entirely on children and material culture. It makes children visible, and goes beyond this in addressing the theoretical and practical implications of studying children through material culture. The contributors ask:

- What is the relationship between children and the material world?
- How does the material culture of children vary across time and space?
- How can we access the actions and identities of children in the material record?

The collection spans the Palaeolithic to the late twentieth century, and uses data from across Europe, Scandinavia, the Americas and Asia. The international contributors are from a wide range of disciplines including archaeology, cultural and biological anthropology, psychology and museum studies. All skilfully integrate theory and data to illustrate fully the significance and potential of studying children.

Joanna Sofaer Derevenski is a Research Fellow at Fitzwilliam College, Cambridge.

Children
and Material Culture

Edited by
Joanna Sofaer Derevenski

London and New York

First published 2000
by Routledge
11 New Fetter Lane, London EC4P 4EE

Simultaneously published in the USA and Canada
by Routledge
29 West 35th Street, New York, NY 10001

Routledge is an imprint of the Taylor & Francis Group

Selection and editorial matter © 2000 Joanna Sofaer
Derevenski
Individual chapters © 2000 individual contributors

Typeset in Garamond by Taylor & Francis Books Ltd
Printed and bound in Great Britain by TJ International Ltd,
Padstow, Cornwall

British Library Cataloguing in Publication Data
A catalogue record for this book is available from the British
Library

Library of Congress Cataloging-in-Publication Data
Children and material culture
1. Children, Prehistoric. 2. Children–History. 3. Material
culture. 4. Industries, Prehistoric. 5. Archaeology and history.
6. Civilization, Ancient. 7. Civilization, Medieval.
GN799.C38 C55 2000
305.23'09–dc21   99-089569

ISBN 0–415–18897–0 (hbk)
ISBN 0–415–18898–9 (pbk)

The child is familiar to us and yet strange, she inhabits our worlds and yet seems to answer to another, she is essentially of ourselves and yet appears to display a different order of being.

(Jenks 1982: 9)

Childhood is our own first historical era, an era we know first hand, not vicariously, as we know so much of the past.

(Schlereth 1990: 90)

Contents

PART III
The transmission of knowledge   51

Chapter Five
APPRENTICE FLINTKNAPPING: RELATING MATERIAL CULTURE AND SOCIAL PRACTICE IN THE UPPER PALAEOLITHIC   53
Linda Grimm

Chapter Six
CHILDREN, MATERIAL CULTURE AND WEAVING: HISTORICAL CHANGE AND DEVELOPMENTAL CHANGE   72
Patricia Greenfield

PART IV
Childhood lives   87

Chapter Seven
NEANDERTHAL COGNITIVE LIFE HISTORY AND ITS IMPLICATIONS FOR MATERIAL CULTURE   89
Jennie Hawcroft and Robin Dennell

Chapter Eight
NOT MERELY CHILD'S PLAY: CREATING A HISTORICAL ARCHAEOLOGY OF CHILDREN AND CHILDHOOD   100
Laurie Wilkie

PART V
Children and relationships   115

Chapter Nine
THE CONSTRUCTION OF THE INDIVIDUAL AMONG NORTH EUROPEAN FISHER-GATHERER-HUNTERS IN THE EARLY AND MID-HOLOCENE   117
Liliana Janik

Chapter Ten
CHILDREN, GENDER AND THE MATERIAL CULTURE OF DOMESTIC ABANDONMENT IN THE LATE TWENTIETH CENTURY   131
Victor Buchli and Gavin Lucas

PART VI

Geographies of children   139

PART VII

Children and value   167

PART VIII

Demography and growth of children   191

Illustrations

Contributors

Lesley Beaumont, Lecturer in Classical Archaeology, Department of Classical Archaeology, University of Sydney, NSW 2006, Australia.
E-mail: lesley.beaumont@archaeology.usyd.edu.au

Victor Buchli, Lecturer, Department of Anthropology, University College London, Gower Street, London, WC1E 6BT, UK.
E-mail: v.buchli@ucl.ac.uk

Andrew Chamberlain, Senior Lecturer in Biological Anthropology, Department of Archaeology and Prehistory, University of Sheffield, Northgate House, West Street, Sheffield S1 4ET, UK.
E-mail: a.chamberlain@shef.ac.uk

Sally Crawford, Lecturer in Mediaeval Archaeology, Department of Ancient History and Archaeology, University of Birmingham, Edgbaston, Birmingham, B15 2TT, UK.
E-mail: S.E.E.Crawford@bham.ac.uk

Robin Dennell, Professor of Archaeology and Prehistory, Department of Archaeology and Prehistory, University of Sheffield, Northgate House, West Street, Sheffield S1 4ET, UK.
E-mail: R.Dennell@shef.ac.uk

Patricia Greenfield, Professor of Psychology, Department of Psychology, University of California, Los Angeles, 1282A Franz Hall, 405 Hilgard Avenue, Los Angeles, CA 90095–1563, USA.
E-mail: greenfield@psych.ucla.edu

Linda Grimm, Associate Professor of Anthropology, Department of Anthropology, Oberlin College, Oberlin, OH 44074, USA.
E-mail: linda.grimm@oberlin.edu

Jennie Hawcroft, Doctoral student, Department of Archaeology and Prehistory, University of Sheffield, Northgate House, West Street, Sheffield S1 4ET, UK. *E-mail*: J.E.Hawcroft@shef.ac.uk

Sanne Houby-Nielsen, Assistant Professor, Department of Classics, Museum of Classical Antiquities, University of Lund, Sölvegatan 2, S–223 62 Lund, Sweden. *E-mail*: sanne.houby-nielsen@klass.lu.se

Louise Humphrey, Researcher, Human Origins Group, Department of Palaeontology, The Natural History Museum, Cromwell Road, London, SW7 5BD, UK. *E-mail*: L.Humphrey@nhm.ac.uk

Liliana Janik, Affiliated Lecturer, Department of Archaeology, University of Cambridge, Downing Street, Cambridge, CB2 3DZ, UK. *E-mail*: lj102@hermes.cam.ac.uk

Grete Lillehammer, Curator, Museum of Archaeology Stavanger, National Research Centre for Paleostudies and Conservation, Boks 478, N–4001 Stavanger, Norway. *E-mail*: gli@ark.museum.no

Gavin Lucas, Project Officer, Cambridge Archaeological Unit, Department of Archaeology, University of Cambridge, Downing Street, Cambridge, CB2 3DZ, UK. *E-mail*: gml15@hermes.cam.ac.uk

Simon Mays, Human Skeletal Biologist, Ancient Monuments Laboratory, English Heritage, Fort Cumberland Road, Eastney, Portsmouth, Hampshire, PO4 9LD, UK. *E-mail*: simon.mays@english-heritage.org.uk

Koji Mizoguchi, Lecturer in Japanese Archaeology, The Institute of Archaeology, University College London, 31–34 Gordon Square, London, WC1H 0PY, UK. *E-mail*: k.mizoguchi@ucl.ac.uk

Blythe Roveland, University Archivist, St John's University, Jamaica, NY 11439, USA. *E-mail*: roveland@aol.com

Joanna Sofaer Derevenski, Research Fellow, Fitzwilliam College, Cambridge, CB3 0DG, UK. *E-mail*: jrs35@cam.ac.uk

Laurie Wilkie, Assistant Professor of Anthropology, Department of Anthropology, University of California, 232 Kroeber Hall, Berkeley, CA 94720–3710, USA. *E-mail*: wilkie@sscl.berkeley.edu

Preface

From the very moment of birth we are surrounded by the material world. Engagement with the world comes through interaction with that materiality and through material expression. Children perceive, react and add to the world through material culture as objects guide the child's experience. Images of children are materially presented and perceived. Even in death, children may be surrounded by material expressions of grief. Children are not removed from the material world, but are critical to it. Whenever we walk down the street, go to the supermarket, or switch on the TV we see and hear children. Debates surrounding children and childhood in modern European and Anglo-American life are increasingly voracious. Many of us have children or grandchildren of our own. Each of us was once a child.

The importance of material culture to children, and the centrality of children to our own lives, ensures their validity as subjects of study. Yet the importance of the relationship between children and material culture goes further than this. This book was inspired by the need not only to highlight children as a category and make them visible, but to go beyond this in addressing the theoretical and practical implications of studying children through material culture. What constitutes a material culture of the child? Do all children have something in common that unites them as a category and which also generates that category through material culture? Is there a cross-cultural material culture of the child or is it historically and contextually contingent? How are children perceived and constructed? To what extent are interpretations affected by relatively recent understandings of what children and childhood 'ought to be', as well as our own childhood experiences? Since the concept of 'child' is intimately bound up with a notion of timed life course change, how does this relate to other categorisations such as 'adolescent', 'adult' or 'elderly'? How is knowledge transmitted and how can we use the categories 'children' and 'child' to explore questions of social and technological production and reproduction vital to an understanding of continuity and change in, and through, material culture?

In seeking to access and explore the materiality of children, contributors to this volume come from a number of different disciplinary backgrounds, work with a variety of data and present a range of theoretical and practical approaches. In this, the book reflects the increasingly fragmented and diverse nature of modern archaeology. Yet, all writers place the child at the centre of their interpretations, illustrating the way that a focus on children can radically reconfigure and enhance understandings of the world in which people live. A book of this nature can never hope to be comprhrehensive, nor does it aim to be. However, the deliberately wide-ranging nature of this volume and broad definition of material culture to include skeletal remains as well as artefacts, serve to illustrate the promise of studying children.

Some of the papers in this book were first presented at the 1996 *Theoretical Archaeology Group* session on 'Children in the past', but more than half were written specifically for this volume. The book is ordered thematically and begins by touching on 'Theoretical perspectives' in the study of children and material culture. Sofaer Derevenski scrutinises presentist expectations of a material culture of children. Lillehammer analyses why children have been infrequently addressed within mainstream archaeology and advocates the development of theory and method specific to the archaeology of children. In the following section, 'Representing and perceiving children', Roveland finds that, in contrast to archaeological literature, children in juvenile fiction are often presented as innovators and inventors who provide inspiring models to today's child readers. The apparent audacity of these images provides real challenges to those involved in interpreting material culture. Beaumont is concerned with defining the boundaries between childhood, adolescence and adulthood. Concentrating on adolescence as a key transition, she presents an iconographic study of these stages, exploring the sociological realities of how they were perceived and experienced in fifth century Athenian society. The transmission of knowledge is a key issue within archaeology and material culture studies and is one for which the study of children has great potential. Contributors to this section offer two different studies of apprenticeship. Grimm's is a detailed case study of a single Palaeolithic apprentice flintknapper, identified through technological variability and understood through the development of a social practice theory of learning. Greenfield takes a sociohistorical approach, exploring changes in how girls learn to weave by following two generations of Zinacantec women. She examines the impact of changes in the economic environment on learning, teaching and innovation. The dynamic nature of child life is considered in the section 'Childhood lives', which focuses on the material expression of childhood. Hawcroft and Dennell compare patterns of childhood and development in Neanderthals and modern humans, arguing that these led to differences manifest in their lithic technologies. By contrast, through her examination of toys in nineteenth and twentieth century American society, Wilkie exposes the childhood experiences of individual children who were independent social actors in dialogues of race, class and gender.

Relations between children and adults are the main theme of 'Children and relationships'. Janik explores variation in the mortuary categorisation of children among Early and Mid-Holocene fisher-gatherer-hunter communities. Differences are interpreted in terms of distinct communal perceptions of the relationship between adults and children. Buchli and Lucas examine the construction of childhood and gender identity by a single mother and her children within a late twentieth century British context. In the section 'Geographies of children', Mizoguchi addresses how changes in the spatial patterning of child burials in Yayoi cemeteries located the deceased within a web of relationships between the living and the ancestors, reflecting social perceptions of the category 'child'. Houby-Nielsen looks at the way that changing patterns of child burial fundamentally affected the development and plan of the city of Athens. 'Children and value' illustrates the fluid nature of attitudes towards children. Crawford suggests that the relative absence of children within pagan Anglo-Saxon cemeteries does not reflect the unimportance of children. Instead, ideas regarding what constituted a child and how this was expressed were vastly different to those prevailing today. Mays' study of infanticide in Britain considers changing perceptions of personhood and traces variations in attitudes from the Roman period until the late twentieth century. Finally, the section 'Demography and growth of children' considers the information that can be gained from the physical remains of children themselves. Humphrey investigates methodological issues associated with growth studies and how comparative studies of the growth of children from archaeological assemblages can be used to examine wider social issues such as changing subsistence strategies or social inequality. Chamberlain explores the implications of demographic analysis for reconstructions of past populations of which children were a part.

It is perhaps a sign of increasing interest in the topic of children that, although this volume took time to develop, it was nurtured without too many growing pains! Throughout this project, the contributors have stressed their excitement and enthusiasm for a book on children and material culture. I thank them warmly for this and hope that some of the enjoyment for their subject comes through to the reader. Special thanks are due to Jessica Pearson for her invaluable assistance and friendship. Lastly, this book owes much to Kiri.

Joanna Sofaer Derevenski

Part I

Theoretical perspectives

Chapter 1

Material culture shock

Confronting expectations in the material culture of children

Joanna Sofaer Derevenski

CHILDREN AND CONTEXTUAL CONTINGENCY

Sometime after the end of apartheid in South Africa, a photograph of a young girl dressed in an oversized camouflage shirt and shorts and holding a handgun appeared in the British press (Figure 1.1). Next to the picture, an accompanying article described how some Afrikaner children were being given military training. It also expressed shock and concern. The photograph and article provoked further comment in editorials and in the letters page. Why does the image and idea of a child with a gun have such a powerful effect upon the observer?

Figure 1.1   A week in the life of the 'new' South Africa

Source: Photograph: Ian Berry, Magnum Photos

The photograph is a record of a real contemporary event, rather than the fiction of a book or film. The child is not playing; the gun is a lethal weapon, the girl is being trained to kill. The photograph creates a disjunction between the encultured expectations of the modern Western reader and material reality. Connections which we hold with concepts of 'child' (innocent, passive, protected, happy and young) and 'weapon' (worldly, aggressive, violent, suffering and adult) are mutually exclusive oppositions. The juxtaposition of a child with a lethal weapon creates incongruity; the material culture of the gun ought to be held in a different hand, the uniform of battle should be worn by another body. Further disruption is caused by a female holding the gun as weapons are deemed male objects (McKellar 1996). We conceive of children as apolitical, yet here the girl appears involved in adult intrigue. For all these reasons, conceptual associations between the child and the material culture do not match.

Figure 1.2   Child playing

Source: Photograph: Joanna Sofaer Derevenski

Yet, ultimately this photograph conveys very little about the child as an individual person. No autobiography or description of her daily life is attached to the image. We know nothing of her personal history and will almost certainly never meet her face to face. Our perception of the child and her life is formed through the relationship between the child and the material culture in the photograph, itself a form of material expression. Our knowledge about the events leading up to the photograph and those that followed it is constructed through the accompanying text rather than through the image. In highlighting the gap between expectation and reality, this photograph confronts us with our own expectations regarding children and material culture and forces reconsideration of what it means to be a child.

Perceptions of children and the particular forms of material culture with which they may be observed are deeply affected by context and the wider material environment in which they are situated. Ostensibly similar forms of material culture to that used by the Afrikaner child in a military setting are readily provided for children in a domestic milieu (Figure 1.2). Guns sold in the local toy shop are often made of similar materials (metal and plastic) and are of comparable size to their deadly counterparts. Without detailed inspection of the object, the cellophane and cardboard packaging are often the primary clues that the former should be presented as toys. Yet, within the home, perceptions of the child and the material culture of the gun seem less disturbing. In this context the child conforms to our expectations: children, rather than adults, ought to use toys. The threat of genuine violence is removed. If a male holds the gun then gender expectations are confirmed. The child's interaction with the object is classified as play, an activity to which no political motivation is attributed. The understanding of the material culture is closer to our own experience and conceptual associations between the child and the material world seem appropriate.

Children have often been sentimentalised (Cox 1996; James *et al.* 1998). Research like that of Opie and Opie (1959, 1969, 1993) on nursery rhymes and games has become the popular face of child life. In researching the material imagery of the life course in photographic libraries and archives, I found searches under the heading 'children' overwhelmingly yielded images of smiling children playing with dolls, blocks or other toys, children in parks or naturalistic settings, children with pets, naked children, gurgling babies or humorous pictures of children posed growing in flowerpots or on the toilet. The classification of these pictures clearly draws on conceptualisations of the child as happy, innocent, natural, immature, uninhibited, amusing and sweet. Less pleasant images of children were often classified according to the country in which the photograph was taken. Thus, while a child may be the primary subject of a photograph, if the picture lacks 'cute factor' the child is reduced to an ethnographic curiosity.

Ennew (1986) argues that Western childhood has become a period in the life course characterised by social dependency, asexuality and the obligation to be happy, with children having the right to protection and training but not to social or personal autonomy. The corollary to this is that power relations are weighted in favour of adults (James *et al.* 1998; Qvortrup *et al.* 1994). Being a child is to have a particular place in the social order. To step outside those relational boundaries and be a child outside adult supervision is to be out of place (Connolly and Ennew 1996). The Afrikaner child appears to have reversed the social order, even to the extent of posing a threat to adults through the possession of a weapon. She has obtained power through the materiality of the gun.

In popular and academic circles, there is growing concern that children are losing their childhood (Scraton 1997a; Cox 1996; Winn 1984). High-profile cases of paedophilia or the murder of children by other children, such as the murder of 2 year old James Bulger by two 10 year old boys in Britain, and a spate of school shootings in the United States, have dismayed and bewildered (Hay 1995; Egan 1998). How could adults do such repellent things to defenceless children? How could children commit such crimes? There is at once a need to protect children yet simultaneously to demonise them (Davis and Bourhill 1997). Thus, being a child is not simply defined by age and power relations, but is also experiential.

Experience is also defined by materiality (Cole *et al.* 1971; Sofaer Derevenski 1994, 1997a). Recent research on the impact of the war in the former Yugoslavia in which children were invited to write life-history essays (Povrzanovic 1997) reveals within the repeated theme of loss of childhood an acute awareness of how being a child is affected by the material environment. Similarly, an 11 year old caught up in the siege of Sarajevo wrote in her diary of her fear, loss of innocence and despair, and of her life without school, fun, games, friends, nature and sweets (Filipovic 1994). These she perceived to be the material ingredients of childhood (Cunningham 1995). Deprived of them she and her friends can't be children (Filipovic 1994; Cunningham 1995). For her, 'a child was not simply someone aged between, say, birth and fourteen; a child could be a real child only if he or she had a "childhood"' (Cunningham 1995: 1). In the case of Croatian children, the material culture of war was employed in the reproduction of their lived realities, providing a form of catharsis (Povrzanovic 1997; Korkiakangas 1992).

If being a child is constructed through material experience then, returning to the image of the Afrikaner child with a gun, one is suddenly faced with a series of questions: She looks physiologically like a child, but is she a child? Are her experiences those of a child? Does she have a childhood? Is she a child because she has no control over her actions and is being indoctrinated or manipulated? The social and moral issues raised by this picture are paralleled by important questions from an archaeological point of view: Given that the gun is clearly being used by the child and is part of her material reality, is it then a material culture of children? If so, does it also form part of a material culture of childhood or does the weapon represent its loss? Is a toy gun the real material culture of children? Is it the material culture of childhood? Is there more than one way of being a child and more than one childhood, each of which are equally as valid, if perhaps not as pleasurable, as another?

CHILDREN AND ARCHAEOLOGICAL CONTINGENCY

Given the importance of context in constructing the materiality of children's lives and in determining the ways in which children and material culture are perceived, how are artefacts and more particularly weapons, interpreted when found with children in the past? The clearest examples of associations between children and weapons are in mortuary contexts. Furthermore, some of the boldest and most influential statements concerning the interpretation of children and material culture have been made regarding these settings.

Weapons are frequently identified as symbols of power and masculinity (Bradley 1990; Treherne 1995). In cases where such artefacts are deposited with both selected children and adults, or where they are given similar forms of burial, this is construed as strong evidence for inherited status and wealth (e.g. Peebles and Kus 1977; Whittle 1996; Lillie 1997; Welinder 1998); 'it is usually suggested that as the children died too young to have actually earned the right to the objects on their own merit, the objects must have been placed there by the parents whose positions the children would have inherited had they lived' (Pader 1982: 57 cited in Crawford 1991: 18). Brown (1981) identified the mortuary treatment of children as a key indicator of the relationship between social and demographic variables; 'as the hierarchical aspects increase, children will be accorded more elaborate attention in proportion to the decline in the opportunity for replacement of the following generation' (ibid.: 29). In cases where children are exclusively buried with particular artefacts, or conversely, are the only individuals deposited without them, this is understood in terms of horizontal differentiation and the construction of difference between age groups (Chapman and Randsborg 1981; O'Shea 1984; Richards 1987; Morris 1992).

These principles have often been key to the analysis of children and material culture in archaeological contexts. For example, O'Shea (1981) studied the distribution of artefacts in two Arikara sites in the central plains of North America – the mid-eighteenth century Larson cemetery and the early nineteenth century Leavenworth cemetery. Along with other artefacts, the occurrence of gun parts in the graves of sub-adults at Larson was identified as evidence for the ritual expression of social differentiation between adults and sub-adults, as well as ranking within the sub-adult category. By contrast, at Leavenworth the distribution of gun parts was less restricted. This change in artefact distribution was understood in terms of a temporal de-ritualisation of mortuary practice with a shift towards increased emphasis on individual and family economic power (ibid.). In this case, weapons with children are first understood as mediators of ritual and then as an index of the wealth of older individuals who, by association, transfer their power to younger ones. Simply by virtue of being 'children', the young cannot be identified as powerful in their own right. Objects in child graves are interpreted in a fundamentally different way to the same artefacts with adults.

The graves of Anglo-Saxon 'warrior children' (Gilchrist 1997: 47) contain weapons including arrowheads, spearheads, swords and shields. However, not all Anglo-Saxon children were buried with such artefacts; in a sample of forty-seven fifth to seventh century English cemeteries, Härke (1992a: 183, figure 33) found that only sixty out of 382 graves classified as neonates, infants I or II and juveniles on the basis of skeletal immaturity were weapon burials. A far higher proportion of adults were buried with weapons; 231 out of a total of 511 graves. The frequency of child graves containing weapons, the number and type of weapon deposited, and the length of spears and knives appear to be related to age at death (Härke 1992a, 1989). The data derived from the study of the children's graves forms an important strand of evidence in Härke's interpretation of Anglo-Saxon mortuary practice. He suggests that the deposition of weapons in both child and adult burials was primarily a symbolic act which recognised the social or ideological hereditary 'warrior status' of an individual, independent of the experience or ability to fight (Härke 1990, 1992a, 1992b; Gilchrist 1997). The inclusion of arms in the burial may have been partly dependent on the completion of rites of passage (Härke 1992a; Pader 1982). Crawford (1991) points out that 10 years was the legal age of adult responsibility in the seventh century. However, Härke (1990, 1992a) suggests that the primary determinant of weapon burial was descent and ethnicity. Thus, the graves of children with weapons are used to explore the broader social structure of the Anglo-Saxon period.

Such far-reaching interpretations of children and material culture often seem to dissolve when small or miniature weapons are found with children. For example, the miniature spearhead found in the grave of an infant at the La Tene I site of Vrigny, France (Champion 1994) has been interpreted as a toy (Chossenot *et al.* 1981). Similarly, a sword, spear and frying-pan from a Vendel grave in Leirol, Norway (Selboe 1965; Linderoth 1990), and miniature daggers and a spearhead from Birka (Gräslund 1973) have been reported as toys. Indeed, in cases when osteological analysis cannot be carried out, small objects are sometimes used to infer the presence of a child (Gräslund 1973; Hodson 1977).

These interpretations are based on the assumption that since children are by definition smaller than adults, only children interact with small objects. Furthermore, in modern Western society, children are implicitly regarded as passive; people who play rather than contribute socially or economically to society. Hence the archaeological value ascribed to a miniature object is minimised and its identification as a toy relegates the significance of the artefact to the level of curiosity. The identification of an object as a toy is rarely related to social significance or meaning. It is rather a morphological description constructed on the basis of the artefact's size and material (Lillehammer 1989) which presupposes the same cultural values as those held in our society. However, the functional identification of an object as a purpose-built toy is a complex task (ibid.; Egan 1996). We often forget that children constantly interact with the everyday objects that surround them (Schlereth 1990; Sofaer Derevenski 1994) and that their material realities are just as complex as those of adults. The use of both miniature and full-size objects to understand issues of learning (Lillehammer 1989; Sofaer Derevenski 1997a) or socialisation (Sillar 1994; Park 1998) are only just starting to be explored.

CHILDREN AND EPISTEMOLOGICAL CONTINGENCY

There seems to be a fundamental epistemological difference between how we regard modern children and how we understand children in the past. These reactions not only reflect the contextual and archaeological contingency of interpretation, but also temporal frameworks and concerns around which those interpretations are constructed.

Modern concerns focus on the living child as a subject, either of love or of vilification. Children are romanticised and intrinsically valued as the epitome of innocence and good (Zelizer 1985). Youth is privileged over experience and children held up as examples to society through events such as the annual 'Children of Courage Awards' in Britain. At the other extreme, as in the James Bulger case, children are portrayed as irredeemably corrupt and evil (Davis and Bourhill 1997; Scraton 1997b). In the fields of social work and child protection, a 'child-centred' approach is increasingly becoming the norm (Morrow and

Richards 1996; Bates *et al.* 1997). Thus, the preoccupation is *with and about children themselves*.

By contrast, archaeological children are rarely a focus of attention in their own right but used in a fairly narrow way in efforts to understand the construction of what is implicitly regarded as an 'adult' society. In other words, archaeology views society *through the child* but does not investigate it in terms of being about children as individuals with social identities. Objects with children are interpreted in an altogether different way to those in adult graves. In a similar way that the material expression of women was once understood only through association with men (Arnold 1991), the material culture of children is only interpreted by reference to adults.

These profound contrasts in the way in which children are perceived in present and past are mirrored in the way that children are identified. Living children are likely to be recognised as variable and culturally constructed (Jenks 1982; James and Prout 1990; Qvortrup *et al.* 1994). They are identified in terms of social relations and there is, therefore, no universal child (James *et al.* 1998). Although this perspective has gained increasing currency within archaeology (Sofaer Derevenski 1994; Johnsen and Welinder 1995; Welinder 1998), archaeological children are primarily located through the identification of the body. Children are defined as a developmental age group and categorised according to the conventions of physical anthropology. The archaeological meaning of the term 'child' is above all physiological, although it is frequently linked to chronological age (Ginn and Arber 1995). Children are therefore identified in a naturalised and reductionist manner as a universal biological category, rather than as social beings whose categorisation is a relative concept negotiated through context and the materiality of experience.

Even in a developmental sense, the age categories commonly described within physical anthropology are problematic. Biologically accurate assessments of skeletal development form somewhat artificial divisions in terms of social and mental development (Burman 1994; Morss 1990; Sofaer Derevenski 1994). Yet, the biological basis for the identification of children is frequently transformed into a social unit as a series of ethnocentric assumptions about the link between biological development and social involvement are imposed. Modern, Western attitudes to children are extrapolated back into the past. Social relations are read as epiphenomena of nature (James *et al.* 1998).

Through the primacy attached to biological identification, archaeology has by default created an 'embodied child' (c.f. James 1993), but one whose life, experience and identity remain unexplored and inaccessible. The child is embodied but vacuous, devoid of agency and action. The study of the child from a purely developmental perspective prioritises the adult as complete and fully formed while relegating the child – the incomplete and therefore lacking sub-adult (James *et al.* 1998). As long as the child is defined solely through the body as a universal developmental phenomenon, it lacks elements of social or cultural difference upon which to hook a contextually specific and culturally constructed child. Archaeology is therefore forced to fall back on potentially misleading ethnocentric cross-cultural principles of interpretation.

CHILDREN, BODIES AND MATERIALITY

We cannot see full-blown social constructionism as an antidote to the body problem. Viewing the child as completely culturally constructed simply replaces one reductionism with another (James *et al.* 1998). Dispensing with the material reality of children by failing to acknowledge the skeleton as a person, fundamentally challenges the basis of archaeology as a discipline since archaeology relies on making inferences from material remains. Furthermore, removing the physicality of the child from view negates the potential ways in which social relations and the lives of children may be shaped by their bodies (Turner 1996; James 1993; James *et al.* 1998), and vice versa.

The skeleton is a site of articulation between biology and culture (Sofaer Derevenski 1998). Physiological changes occur throughout the life course as individuals grow, mature and senesce (Crews and Garruto 1994). Through a process of cultural negotiation, these biological changes become incorporated into social life (Sofaer Derevenski 1997b). In this respect, the physical reality of the child within the archaeological record is particularly powerful because of the sheer number of physiological changes in the skeletally immature and the speed at which they take place. 'The body in childhood is a crucial resource for making and breaking identity precisely because of its unstable materiality' (James *et al.* 1998: 156). Bodies and differences between bodies become signifiers of identity (James 1993). 'The issue of embodiment as a cultural process surfaces most poignantly at key points in the life cycle: the trajectory of the body is given symbolic and moral value: bodily forms are paradigmatic of social transition' (Prendergast 1992: 1 cited in James *et al.* 1998: 162).

If the bodies of children are historically and socially situated (Toren 1993) and different types of bodies are culturally meaningful, how can archaeology access social life through the body? Left with only the skeleton, we are unable to observe the behaviour of the fleshed living being and have only our own socio-historically specific, modern biomedical understanding of skeletal data (Armstrong 1987; Laqueur 1990; Foucault 1974). How can we attribute social meaning to the body in practice, without falling back on our own preconceptions? How can we understand the body in relation to material culture rather than privileging either as the primary focus of analysis? Perhaps we need to look at the distribution of material resources that shape the structure of practice (James *et al.* 1998: 166).

Social life is not a pure construction of meaning, but mutually constructed from 'heterogeneous materials' including bodies, technology, material culture and minds, each of which enrols and orders the others in fluid and shifting combinations (Latour 1993; James *et al.* 1998). In doing so, the boundaries between bodies and other materials become blurred and the body is extended through its association with material culture. While this general understanding of the relationship between bodies and material culture may be applicable to all individuals, no matter what their biological or social categorisation, it is particularly useful in exploring the complex conundrum of the relationship between culture and biology which lies at the heart of the study of children.

James *et al.* (1998) identify the work of Place (1997) as an example of the way in which this approach can be used to explore the relationship between bodies and objects. In an ethnographic study of a paediatric ward, Place (1997) describes the way in which the bodies of children are intimately combined with material culture through tubes and other equipment connecting the body to medical apparatus. These enable detailed examination of the internal organs, which are symbolically monitored through signals or traces. 'The boundary of the body is extended and circumscribed by both corporeal (human) and non-corporeal (technological) elements. The body is, in this sense, "technomorphic", revisable by connection to technological artifacts' (Place 1997 cited in James *et al.* 1998: 167). The boundary of the body is unclear. Is it enclosed by the skin or bounded by the technologies used to treat and monitor it? (James *et al.* 1998).

Modern children continually make associations with machines. James *et al.* (1998) cite as examples bicycles, computers, toys, videos and televisions. Children interact with the world around them (Sofaer Derevenski 1994, 1997a) and similar connections with other forms of material culture may also have existed in the past. It is therefore possible to draw a conceptual parallel in terms of the ethnographic links between living children and material culture, and the relationship between the bodies of dead children and their associated artefacts.

The body of a child lies in intimate contact with artefacts in a grave. The grave constructs and restricts, forcing the person and objects into association. It envelops the body and, as a human creation, is itself a form of material culture. In this setting one is once again forced to question where the boundary between the child and material culture lies. The association between artefacts and individuals can be used to actively create, manipulate and convey individual identity (Sørensen 1991, 1997), blurring the physical and conceptual boundaries between body and artefact. Furthermore, as the skeletal body lacks the skin and flesh of the living, it becomes difficult to draw a unique line around it, sealing it off from the material world; the internal core of the body, itself composed of many separate bones and unfused epiphyses, becomes exposed and externalised. The issue becomes even more complex if corporate or secondary burial is considered. Here one starts to ask not only about the boundary of a single body, but about the location of boundaries between mingled and perhaps dispersed bodies.

In analysing the relationship between the body and the material world, Place (1997) makes a distinction between 'child data' (what happens within the corporeal body) and 'data child' (the visible manifestation of that corporeality through its connection to surrounding technological artefacts) (James *et al.* 1998; Prout forthcoming). Understanding the ambiguity surrounding the archaeological child may be aided by employing a modified form of this distinction.

'Child data' can be regarded as the information derived from the study of the skeleton (the internal remains of the corporeal body). In other words, that physiological data generated through the study of the child as an artefact. Thus, physical anthropology is given its own distinct role in the study of the child. By contrast, 'data child' is the recognition of the physical and social corporeality of the child – living and dead – through the construction of the grave and the artefacts deposited in association with the child. 'Data child' can therefore be regarded as the material manifestation of the interaction between child and society.

The consonance of 'data child' and 'child data' cannot be taken for granted (Place 1997; Prout forthcoming). Just as the paediatrician in Place's study constantly maintains the relationship between the two forms by monitoring the patient and interpreting the symbols and signs produced by the medical technology, the archaeologist has to maintain the relationship between 'data child' and 'child data' through the study of the skeleton and the interpretation of symbolic elements of material culture. 'Data child' and 'child data' mutually explicate each other (James *et al.* 1998). 'They are conjoined, mutually explicating only when juxtaposed. When the two forms do separate, one becomes a set of meaningless symbols, the other a disordered mass of flesh and blood' (Place 1997 cited in James *et al.* 1998: 168). However, the relationship between 'child data' and 'data child' can potentially take many forms and a variety of associations be created. 'The issue becomes not whether there exists a "real" body as distinct from social constructions of it – because this would be taken for granted – but how many different claims to "speak for" this body and enrol it in the service of intentional social action are made' (James *et al.* 1998: 168).

CHILDREN AND CHILDHOOD

Place's (1997) distinction between 'data child' and 'child data' suggests that there is more than one child as a subject of study. If there are many different children, notions of child-hood also become problematised since they can no longer be seen as congruent with a homogeneous 'ideal' child. The body may have varying importance in different construc-tions of childhood and the ideology of childhood cannot be mapped directly onto the body. It may therefore be useful to further fracture the study of children by consciously sepa-rating notions of the child (incorporating 'child data' and 'data child') from those of childhood.

Childhood is often perceived as a structural category that can be compared with other structural forms or life periods in society such as youth, adulthood and old age (Qvortrup 1994). In contrast to notions of the child, in which the physical body can be seen, touched and identified in social discourse and archaeological practice, the very intangibility of child-hood lends it a more obvious relativism, particularly within archaeological contexts. 'To account for childhood ... calls for analyses of ... broad social processes that in their interac-tion come to constitute ... the social practices that define childhood' (Alanen 1988: 64). Children live their lives under a variety of conditions (Qvortrup *et al.* 1994) and, since material culture plays an active role in social practice (Hodder 1982, 1987; Shanks and Tilley 1987), '[d]ifferent children in different circumstances may be associated with different material resources – producing ... many competing versions of childhood' (James *et al.* 1998: 168). Indeed, Bourdieu (1977: 91) talks of 'the mind born of the world of objects'. Just as there are many different children, there is diversity in childhood experience and ideology (Munday 1979; Davin 1990; Stafford 1995; James *et al.* 1998; Helleiner 1998).

The modern, Western perception of childhood as a prolonged period of dependence on an adult has led archaeologists to construct interpretations that reduce children to passive, inert automatons. Yet, children are actors and constructors of their own lives who act not simply intuitively, but initiate action by choice (Wartofsky 1983). There is a wealth of ethnographic evidence from both traditional and modern societies documenting their participation in social and economic life (e.g. Bray 1911; Draper 1975; Cain 1977; Qvortrup 1985; Bambi and Berti 1988; Gullestad 1988; Morrow 1994). In this sense, it is difficult to attribute to childhood and adulthood different ontological statuses (Qvortrup 1994). Even if one suggests that adults are more effective in elaborating the material world, this does not itself constitute ontological difference (ibid.), but is merely a question of scale.

If there is no fundamental ontological distinction between childhood and adulthood then, from an archaeological perspective, we cannot ascribe to artefacts found with chil-dren a fundamentally different status to those found with adults. Furthermore, children are situated within the same cultural milieu as adults (Sofaer Derevenski 1994). Individual societies may have material cultures of the child, but this does not necessarily imply either separate or homogeneous material cultures of childhood (James 1993). If childhood is a period of life distinct from that of adulthood, then the origins of this difference must be located elsewhere (Qvortrup 1994).

Instead of defining children through preconceived notions of social life, we need to try and understand the social situation of children in the past through an exploration of their social and individually constructed identities *as children*. We need to identify the implications of what it meant to *be* a child, using the same forms of inference as we might do when studying the social identity of other members of society. This would allow children to be treated as active agents and enable us to take more account of the contexts in which artefacts appear. We could then use the relationship between children and material culture to construct interpretations, rather than subjecting children to a series of cross-cultural assumptions regarding who they are and what they do.

CONCLUSION

This chapter began with two photographs – one of a girl with a handgun at an Afrikaner training camp, the other of a boy with a toy gun in a domestic environment. As a form of material culture, these photographs parallel archaeological evidence from more distant antiquity and highlight similar questions regarding how we interpret children and artefacts: What do we do when associations between children and objects present a disjunction between expectation and reality? What is the role of the body in identifying children as children? How are children, childhood and material culture related in different sociocultural, historical and epistemological settings?

The study of children and material culture straddles past and present. It is unique in having direct access to children who lived in the past through the study of their corporeal and material remains. Yet, understandings of children and childhood past are inevitably embedded within modern, Western contemporary discourse. Rather than simply replicating this discourse in studies of other communities, we need to analyse its nature and be aware of the extent to which it affects interpretations.

The explicit study of children as a category of person assumes some kind of unity to that category which allows individuals belonging to it to be identified. However, while notions of 'the child' may be unified through the body, 'children' are culturally specific since the body may be translated in contrasting ways. 'Children' and 'childhood' are not interchangeable as neither can be mapped directly onto the other. Furthermore, being a child is an individual, as well as social, experience.

At first, the many layers within the study of children seem contradictory, generating fundamental tensions between each other. The great challenge is that children are at once universal, culturally specific and individual. Investigating the materiality of children plays a vital role in comprehending this complexity. 'Children are people. This is a step to feel proud of. We have begun to ask ourselves: "What is a child after?" The question complicates life, but it is a sign of our decency that we have begun to ask it' (Hymes 1955: 139).

REFERENCES

Alanen, L. (1988) 'Rethinking childhood', *Acta Sociologica* 31(1): 53–67.
Armstrong, D. (1987) 'Bodies of knowledge: Foucault and the problem of human anatomy', in G. Scambler (ed.) *Sociological Theory and Medical Sociology*, London: Tavistock, pp. 59–76.
Arnold, B. (1991) 'The deposed princess of Vix: the need for an engendered European prehistory', in D. Walde and D.E. Willows (eds), *The Archaeology of Gender. Proceedings of the*

22nd Annual Chacmool Conference, Calgary: Archaeological Association of the University of Calgary, pp. 366–74.

Bambi, A.S. and Berti, A.S. (1988) *The Child's Construction of Economics*, Cambridge: Cambridge University Press.

Bates, J., Pugh, R. and Thompson, N. (eds) (1997) *Protecting Children: Challenges and Change*, Aldershot: Arena.

Bourdieu, P. (1977) *Outline of a Theory of Practice*, Cambridge: Cambridge University Press.

Bradley, R. (1990) *The Passage of Arms: An Archaeological Analysis of Prehistoric Hoards and Votive Deposits*, Cambridge: Cambridge University Press.

Bray, R.A. (1911) *Boy Labour and Apprenticeship*, London: Constable Press.

Brown, J.A. (1981) 'The search for rank in prehistoric burials', in R. Chapman, I. Kinnes and K. Randsborg (eds) *The Archaeology of Death*, Cambridge: Cambridge University Press, pp. 25–37.

Burman, E. (1994) *Deconstructing Developmental Psychology*, London: Routledge.

Cain, M. (1977) 'The economic activities of children in a village in Bangladesh', *Population and Development Review* 3: 201–27.

Champion, S. (1994) 'Regional Studies: a question of scale', in K. Kristiansen and J. Jensen (eds) *Europe in the First Millenium B.C.*, Sheffield: J.R. Collis, pp. 145–50.

Chapman, R. and Randsborg, K. (1981) 'Approaches to the archaeology of death', in R. Chapman, I. Kinnes and K. Randsborg (eds) *The Archaeology of Death*, Cambridge: Cambridge University Press, pp. 1–24.

Chossenot, D., Neiss, R. and Sauget, J.M. (1981) 'Fouille de sauvetage d'une nécropole de La Tàne I à Vrigny (Marne)', *Mémoires de la Société Archéologique Champenoise* 2: 131–49.

Cole, M., Gay, J., Glick, J.A. and Sharp, D.W. (1971), *The Cultural Context of Learning and Thinking: An Exploration in Experimental Anthropology*, New York: Basic Books.

Connolly, M. and Ennew, J. (1996) 'Introduction: children out of place', *Childhood* 3(2): 131–47.

Cox, R. (1996) *Shaping Childhood. Themes of Uncertainty in the History of Adult–Child Relationships*, London: Routledge.

Crawford, S. (1991) 'When do Anglo-Saxon children count?', *Journal of Theoretical Archaeology* 2: 17–24.

Crews, D.E. and Garruto, R.M. (eds) (1994) *Biological Anthropology and Ageing: Perspectives on Human Variation Over the Life Span*, Oxford: Oxford University Press.

Cunningham, H. (1995) *Children and Childhood in Western Society since 1500*, London: Longman.

Davin, A. (1990) 'When is a child not a child?', in H. Corr and L. Jamieson (eds), *Politics of Everyday Life: Continuity and Change in Work and the Family*, Basingstoke: Macmillan, pp. 37–61.

Davis, H. and Bourhill, M. (1997) ' "Crisis": the demonization of children and young people', in P. Scraton (ed.) *'Childhood' in 'Crisis'?*, London: UCL Press, pp. 28–57.

Draper, P. (1975) '!Kung women: contrasts in sexual egalitarianism in foraging and sedentary contexts', in R.R. Reiter (ed.) *Toward an Anthropology of Women*, London: Monthly Review Press, pp. 77–109.

Egan, G. (1996) *Playthings from the Past. Lead Alloy Miniature Artefacts c.1300–1800*, London: Jonathan Horne.

Egan, T. (1998) 'Analysis: school killings: fatal games children play', *Guardian*, 16th June 1998: 15.

Ennew, J. (1986) *The Sexual Exploitation of Children*, London: Polity Press.

Filipovic, Z. (1994) *Zlata's Diary: A Child's Life in Sarajevo*, London: Viking.

Foucault, M. (1974) *The Archaeology of Knowledge*, London: Tavistock.

Gilchrist, R. (1997) 'Ambivalent bodies: gender and medieval archaeology', in J. Moore and E. Scott (eds) *Invisible People and Processes: Writing Gender and Childhood into European Archaeology*, London: Leicester University Press, pp. 42–58.

Ginn, J. and Arber, S. (1995) ' "Only connect": gender relations and ageing', in S. Arber and J. Ginn (eds) *Connecting Gender and Ageing: A Sociological Approach*, Buckingham: Open University Press, pp. 1–14.

Gräslund, A.-S. (1973) 'Barn i Birka', *Tor* 15: 161–79.

Gullestad, M. (1988) 'Agents of modernity: children's care for children in urban Norway', *Social Analysis* 23: 38–52.

Härke, H. (1989) 'Knives in early Saxon burials: blade length and age at death', *Medieval Archaeology* 33: 144–8.

—— (1990) 'Warrior graves? The background of the Anglo-Saxon weapon burial rite', *Past and Present* 126: 22–43.

—— (1992a) *Angelsächsische Waffengräber des 5. bis 7. Jahrhunderts*, Köln: Rheinland-Verlag.

—— (1992b) 'Changing symbols in a changing society: the Anglo-Saxon weapon burial rite in the seventh century', in M. Carver (ed.) *The Age of Sutton Hoo: The Seventh Century in North-Western Europe*, Woodbridge: Boydell, pp. 149–62

Hay, C. (1995) 'Mobilization through interpellation: James Bulger, juvenile crime and the construction of a moral panic', *Social and Legal Studies* 4: 197–223.

Helleiner, J. (1998) 'Contested childhood: the discourse and politics of traveller childhood in Ireland', *Childhood* 5(3): 303–24.

Hodder, I. (ed.) (1982) *Symbolic and Structural Archaeology*, Cambridge: Cambridge University Press.

—— (1987) 'The contextual analysis of symbolic meanings', in I. Hodder (ed.) *The Archaeology of Contextual Meanings*, Cambridge: Cambridge University Press, pp. 1–10.

Hodson, F. R. (1977) 'Quantifying Hallstatt: some initial results', *American Antiquity* 42: 394–412.

Hymes, J. (1955) *A Child Development Point of View*, Englewood Cliffs, NJ: Prentice-Hall.

James, A. (1993) *Childhood Identities. Self and Social Relationships in the Experience of the Child*, Edinburgh: Edinburgh University Press.

James, A. and Prout, A. (1990) (eds) *Constructing and Reconstructing Childhood*, Basingstoke: Falmer.

James, A., Jenks, C. and Prout, A. (1998) *Theorizing Childhood*, Cambridge: Polity Press.

Jenks, C. (1982) 'Constituting the child', in C. Jenks (ed.) *The Sociology of Childhood: Essential Readings*, London: Batsford, pp. 9–24.

Johnsen, B. and Welinder, S. (eds) (1995) *Arkeologi om Barn*, Occasional Papers in Archaeology 10, Societas Archaeologica Upsaliensis: Uppsala.

Korkiakangas, P. (1992) 'The games children may not play', *Ethnologia Scandinavica* 22: 95–104.

Laqueur, T. (1990) *Making Sex: Body and Gender from the Greeks to Freud*, Cambridge, Mass.: Harvard University Press.

Latour, B. (1993) *We Have Never Been Modern*, Hemel Hempstead: Harvester/Wheatsheaf.

Lillehammer, G. (1989) 'A child is born: the child's world in an archaeological perspective', *Norwegian Archaeological Review* 22(2): 89–105.

Lillie, M. C. (1997) 'Women and children in prehistory: resource sharing and social stratification at the Mesolithic-Neolithic transition in Ukraine', in J. Moore and E. Scott (eds) *Invisible People and Processes: Writing Gender and Childhood into European Archaeology*, London: Leicester University Press, pp. 213–28.

Linderoth, T. (1990) 'Vart Har Alla Barnen Tagit Vägen?', *Popular Arkeologi* 8(3): 14–16.

McKellar, S. (1996) 'Guns: the "last frontier on the road to equality"?' in P. Kirkham (ed.) *The Gendered Object*, Manchester: Manchester University Press, pp. 70–9.

Morris, I. (1992) *Death-ritual and Social structure in Classical Antiquity*, Cambridge: Cambridge University Press.

Morrow, V. (1994) 'Responsible children? Aspects of children's work and employment outside school in contemporary UK', in B. Mayall (ed.) *Children's Childhoods: Observed and Experienced*, London: Falmer, pp. 128–43.

Morrow, V. and Richards, M. (1996) 'The ethics of social research with children: an overview', *Children and Society* 10(2): 90–105.

Morss, J. (1990) *The Biologising of Childhood: Developmental Psychology and the Darwinian Myth*, London: Lawrence Erlbaum.

Munday, E. (1979) 'When is a child a "child"? Alternative systems and classification', *Journal of the Anthropological Society of Oxford* 10(3): 161–72.

Opie, I. and Opie, P. (1959) *The Lore and Language of Schoolchildren*, Oxford: Oxford University Press.

—— (1969) *Children's Games in Street and Playground*, Oxford: Oxford University Press.

—— (1993) *The People in the Playground*, Oxford: Oxford University Press.

O'Shea, J. (1981) 'Social Configurations and the Archaeological Study of Mortuary Practices', in R. Chapman, I. Kinnes and K. Randsborg (eds) *The Archaeology of Death*, Cambridge: Cambridge University Press, pp. 39–52.

—— (1984) *Mortuary Variability: An Archaeological Investigation*, New York: Academic Press.

Pader, E.-J. (1982) *Symbolism, Social Relations and the Interpretation of Mortuary Remains*, British Archaeological Reports, International Series 130, Oxford.

Park, R.W. (1998) 'Size counts: the miniature archaeology of childhood in Inuit societies', *Antiquity* 72: 269–81.

Peebles, C.S. and Kus, S.M. (1977) 'Some archaeological correlates of ranked societies', *American Antiquity* 42: 421–48.

Place, B. (1997) 'The constructing of bodies of critically ill children: an ethnography of intensive care', draft of paper in A. Prout (ed.) (2000) *The Body, Childhood and Society*, London, Macmillan.

Povrzanovic, M. (1997) 'Children, war and nation: Croatia 1991–4', *Childhood* 4(1): 81–102.

Prendergast, S. (1992) *This is the Time to Grow Up: Girls' Experiences of Menstruation in School*, Cambridge: Health Promotion Trust.

Prout, A. (2000) 'Childhood bodies: construction, agency and hybridity', in A. Prout (ed.) *The Body, Childhood and Society*, London: Macmillan, pp.1–18.

Qvortrup, J. (1985) 'Placing children in the division of labour', in P. Close and R. Collins (eds) *Family and Economy in Modern Society*, London: Macmillan, pp. 129–45.

—— (1994) 'Childhood matters: an introduction', in J. Qvortrup, M. Bardy, G. Sgritta, and H. Wintersberger (eds) *Childhood Matters. Social Theory, Practice and Politics*, Aldershot: Avebury, 1–23.

Qvortrup, J., Bardy, M., Sgritta, G. and Wintersberger, H. (eds) (1994) *Childhood Matters. Social Theory, Practice and Politics*, Aldershot: Avebury.

Richards, J.D. (1987) *The Significance of Form and Decoration of Anglo-Saxon Cremation Urns*, British Archaeological Reports, British Series 166, Oxford.

Schlereth, T.J. (1990) *Cultural History and Material Culture. Everyday Life, Landscapes, Museums*, Ann Arbor: UMI Research Press.

Scraton, P. (ed.) (1997a) *Childhood in 'Crisis'?*, London: UCL Press.

—— (1997b) 'Whose "Childhood"? What "Crisis"?', in *Childhood in 'Crisis'?*, London: UCL Press, pp. 163–86.

Selboe, A.-C. (1965) 'Leketøy', *Kulturhistorisk Leksikon for Nordisk Middelalder*: 487–95.

Shanks, M. and Tilley, C. (1987) *Social Theory and Archaeology*, Cambridge: Polity Press.

Sillar, B. (1994) 'Playing with God: cultural perceptions of children, play and miniatures in the Andes', *Archaeological Review from Cambridge* 13(2): 47–63.

Sofaer Derevenski, J. (1994) 'Where are the children? Accessing children in the past', *Archaeological Review from Cambridge* 13(2): 7–20.

—— (1997a) 'Engendering children, engendering archaeology', in J. Moore and E. Scott (eds) *Invisible People and Processes: Writing Gender and Childhood into European Archaeology*, London: Leicester University Press, pp. 192–202.

—— (1997b) 'Linking age and gender as social variables', *Ethnographisch-Archäologische Zeitschrift* 3–4: 485–93.

—— (1998) 'Gender archaeology as contextual archaeology: a critical examination of the tensions between method and theory in the archaeology of gender', unpublished doctoral dissertation, University of Cambridge.

Sørensen, M.L.S. (1991) 'The construction of gender through appearance', in D. Walde and D.E. Willows (eds) *The Archaeology of Gender. Proceedings of the 22nd Annual Chacmool Conference*, Calgary: Archaeological Association of the University of Calgary, pp. 121–9.

—— (1997) 'Reading dress: the construction of social categories and identities in Bronze Age Europe', *Journal of European Archaeology* 5(1): 93–114.

Stafford, C. (1995) *The Roads of Chinese Childhood: Learning and Identification in Angang*, Cambridge: Cambridge University Press.

Toren, C. (1993) 'Making history: the significance of childhood cognition for a comparative anthropology of mind', *Man* 28(3): 461–78.

Treherne, P. (1995) 'The warrior's beauty: the masculine body and self-identity in Bronze Age Europe', *Journal of European Archaeology* 3(1): 105–44.

Turner, B. S. (1996) *The Body and Society: Explorations in Social Theory*, 2nd edn, London: Sage.

Wartofsky, M. (1983) 'The child's construction of the world and the world's construction of the child: from historical epistemology to historical psychology', in F.S. Kessel and A.W. Siegel (eds) *The Child and Other Cultural Inventions*, Houston Symposium 4 (1981), New York: Praeger, pp. 188–215.

Welinder, S. (1998) 'The cultural construction of childhood in Scandinavia 3500 BC–1350 AD', *Current Swedish Archaeology* 6: 185–204.

Whittle, A. (1996) *Europe in the Neolithic*, Cambridge: Cambridge University Press.

Winn, M. (1984) *Children Without Childhood: Growing Up Too Fast in the World of Sex and Drugs*, Harmondsworth: Penguin.

Zelizer, V.A. (1985) *Pricing the Priceless Child: The Changing Social Value of Children*, New York: Basic Books.

Chapter 2

The world of children

Grete Lillehammer

> We used to see the parents shaping the child, but now we see the child helping to shape the parents.
>
> (Friedrich 1983: 57)

WARMING UP THE WORLD OF CHILDREN

Given both the political nature of present archaeological debate and the fact that we are now entering a new millennium, it is a real challenge to embark on a discussion of the archaeology of children at the end of what Ellen Key called 'the child's century' (Key 1902). In order to further develop work that I began in the late 1970s (Lillehammer 1979, 1982, 1986, 1987, 1989, 1990), I tried to launch a project on the small-scale archaeology of children from Scandinavian shores. However, finding funds proved difficult and I found myself in a similar position to that of the child who asks for the moon! Children remain peripheral and difficult to assimilate into archaeological discussion.

The marginal position of children within the discipline has been pointed out elsewhere (Sofaer Derevenski 1994; Moore and Scott 1997) and stands in sharp contrast to the position of women's studies and gender research. As a by-product of the feminist movement, feminist critique (Mandt and Næss 1986; Dommasnes 1987; Sørensen 1988; Schanche 1989; Engelstad 1991; Damm 1994) is now incorporated within theoretical archaeology (Olsen 1997; Myhre 1991). Thus, although feminist perspectives cannot be said to have revolutionised archaeological theory, the critique has been accepted into the mainstream of the discipline and therefore into the accumulating process of archaeological knowledge production.

While an increased focus on children is partly a result of this trend (Myhre 1991), it has played little role in critiques of archaeological approaches and explanation. The archaeological child is placed in the space that children conventionally occupy in Western history, namely one often restricted to its relationship with its mother (Olsen 1997: 248–50; Dommasnes 1987: 17–18; Hodder 1984). Children are implicitly relegated to passive appendages to women. The nature of the relationship between women and children is rarely considered.

In a wider context, such perceptions of the minor place of children in society can be identified as symptomatic of how Western culture fails to respect women as makers of men. This denial of the reality of female experience (Greer 1997) might also be seen as a denial of children. An archaeology of children could therefore be seen as part of a strategy in women's resistance to domination (Brooke 1997). Given that childcare is often regarded as a primarily female burden (Bolen 1992: 49–62), perhaps we ought to lighten mother's load by seeing children as worthy subjects of study in relation to material culture.

In this chapter I therefore explore the possibilities for a social archaeology of children in terms of the links between theory and method in the highly prestigious and elitist universe of the archaeological production of knowledge. Without treating the present as lost modernity, my approach to the subject of children in current archaeology is the perspective of supermodernity: the individualisation of references (excess of ego), spatial overabundance (excess of space) and overabundance of events (excess of time) (Augé 1995: 1–41). My aim is to find out how the subject could form part of supermodernity.

LIGHTENING MOTHER'S LOAD

The adoption of child-centred analyses of the archaeological record has been a slow process. Such analyses have not yet been fully accepted as one of several to approach theoretical archaeology, but are rather seen as optional supplements to archaeological epistemology. The focus on children's archaeology forms a small part of the general emancipating strategy of modernity in which questions of the basis of authority in general (Giddens 1990), or the empowering of the academic establishment in particular, are relevant issues. From a feminist perspective, archaeological discourse consists of men thinking, commenting, writing and publishing theoretical texts about other men (Engelstad 1991). The post-modern man, himself being the world of his study (Augé 1995: 36), does not write about children of the past, because archaeology is not supposed to be about children. In his belief that archaeology is about something new – new discoveries, new projects, new information – it is not clear to him how an interest in children could contribute to the production of knowledge. Consequently, few studies stand out as extraordinary events of individual reference in the academy (Augé 1995). The archaeological effort has not resulted in the overabundance of information and over-investment in meaning which characterises the use of supermodernity to understand the whole of the present, because it is looking elsewhere (Augé 1995: 28–31), namely to the remote past of things in the creation of the archaeological artefact.

In Western culture the infant child is linked with the thought of the primitive (Lévi-Strauss 1969: 84–97). It would seem that archaeology is aware of the child, but is not primarily interested in the unprivileged position of the primitive, as the infant can neither empower archaeology, nor the archaeologist. In other words, the power of understanding children could not emancipate humanity or turn archaeology upside down. The status and prestige associated with the subject in the present academy is the consequence of the ambitious and antagonistic power strategies of that academy. Even to critically discuss this topic tends to result in an endless going round of the mulberry bush! The subject of children is brought out by feminist strategies and therefore associated with gender archaeology. It then takes on a critical form resembling gender archaeology, and is left lingering behind or in a position similar to it. Comforting or provoking as that may be, this does not bring us any further towards finding the answers that might provide interpretations of the archaeological data. The intentional and unintentional complexities of archaeological knowledge production make the search for the world of children highly problematic.

Given that archaeological theory and practice are deeply embedded in modernity and engaged in the pursuit of innovation, current archaeology appears full of contradictions.

On one hand there is the public desire to transform the past by creating meaning and identity in the present (Hodder 1996: 278). On the other, the archaeologist has to consider the recognition of a past (or pasts) which may diverge from anything we know in the present (Wylie 1993: 85). The day-to-day routines of archaeology require the application of theory, method and practical techniques in order to survey, excavate, record, preserve and protect archaeological data and prepare it for analysis. In order to understand the potentials and limitations of archaeological data, we must question both the deconstruction of the archaeological data and the subsequent construction or reconstruction of the data as archaeological artefact. This is particularly important when the archaeologist approaches the study of children.

The absence of archaeological awareness of children is integral to the 'practical consciousness' (Giddens 1984: xxiii) of routine in established ways of doing archaeology. A highly complex relationship exists between formal and informal processing of archaeological data in theory and practice and the final results. Data may not have been collected with children in mind. The person analysing the data may not be the person who excavated it. Furthermore, what is actually communicated in written form in reports and articles represents only a small and selective part of the process of archaeological analysis. These texts exclude the history of extensive informal discussions of theory and method and the whole range of questions and answers which go into the preparation of data and its collection from landscapes, monuments or museums. During this social process of partly improvised and intuitively planned collaboration, the archaeologist may forget ever having been a child. Conversely, the archaeologist's own relationship to his or her mother or father (Harding 1986: 126–35), the social construction of sexuality and gender and other childhood experiences, might consciously or unconsciously prevent practical initiatives to explore children as an issue. The study of children as a project therefore represents both the potential subversion of archaeology as a discipline as well as a potential threat to the individual.

Yet, given the fact that the academy is a social space in which innovation and difference constitute the most central and dynamic core of knowledge production, an archaeological focus on children as vehicles of the new is highly appropriate. The child is literally a new member of society and we might therefore ask in what way children contribute to innovations that lead to change as well as to continuity and cultural transference within the society (Lillehammer 1989). This raises the archaeological need for the development and application of social theory in order to understand society's recognition or rejection of the new, both in terms of the birth of the individual and his or her subsequent behaviour and achievements within that society. Since children are a vital element of society and society cannot be perpetuated without children, there can be no mature archaeology without recognising the importance of the link between children and change. But, does the theoretical literature adequately reflect the importance of this link?

The discourse of grand archaeological meta-theory focuses on abstract concepts of universality, relativity, objectivity and subjectivity in the interpretation of archaeological data (Preucel and Hodder 1996: 667–79). However important, a feature of such theorising is that children are made invisible through the abstracting process involved in the representation of ideas in the archaeological text. Even humanistic archaeology, which places people at the centre of discussion and considers culture as a model of, and for, action (Vinsrygg 1988) may regard children as part of the cultural context of change, but does not address their attitudes to temporality. Archaeology may be engaged in recognising difference in order to challenge the legitimacy of present social relations, categorisations and value systems (Tilley 1988) and may thus have the theoretical ability to view children as social actors embodying conflicts of interest, but does not regard them as properly representative of change. It is therefore a matter of some concern to explicitly address the world of children in archaeological theory.

THE 'CHILD'S WORLD' REVISITED

In 1989 I used the concept of the 'child's world' (Lillehammer 1989) to explore an archaeology in which the child is placed in an idealised position at the world's centre (Wordsworth 1827a: 293, 1827b: 3). In using it, I aimed for a definition that comprised the experience and relationship of being in the world as children. The approach was stimulated by the belief that children are 'active theorists' who constantly reconstruct their 'structure of thought' in order to make sense of the world (White and Notkin White 1980: 53). Children's psychology and experiential reality are different from that of adults, and a young child is therefore distinct from an adult, because of his or her lack of experience, social interaction and development into a functioning member of society (Meyrowitz 1985: 234–5).

However, the category 'child' is not homogeneous as individuals have diverse experiences of being a child. Recent psychological research indicates that chronological age is becoming a poorer and poorer indicator of the way people live (Neugarten 1981: 809–25), prompting rejection of the myth of age determinism. Historical changes in age-related behaviour and role-conceptions among both the young and elderly today permit less restricted behaviour and encourage fluidity between the lifestyles of old and young (Meyrowitz 1985: 235). Thus, for the concept of the 'child's world' to be adaptable to material culture and adjusted to archaeology, requires an approach that links the child collectively to aspects of time, space, culture and identity and includes the diversity of children. It may therefore be appropriate to replace the concept of the 'child's world' with that of the '*world of children*'.

The world of children comprises the interconnected relationships between being children in mind and action and the diverse spheres in which children actively move. Given these relationships, the cultural inventions of space and place form important clues in analysing the world of children. The world of children therefore differs from the traditional concept of childhood which is chronologically, biologically, or socially defined as a period of human ageing (Kanvall 1995: 7–12). Childhood relates passively to the state or period of being a child and as such is restrictive, since the use of childhood or other stages in human development including infancy, adolescence, adulthood and old age, tends to overlook the many factors that might bring about wide-scale change in definitions of child and adult roles. The processes by which changes in conceptions of the categories adult and child take place point beyond individual development towards the existence of more general social variables that influence the behaviour and status of all people regardless of age and stage of development (Meyrowitz 1985: 231–2).

In contrast to the notion of childhood, the theoretical scope of the world of children allows the adaptive or creative process of learning and coping in the world to be linked to the biological and cultural development of children by focusing on cultural transference and innovation in the production and reproduction of material culture. This notion highlights the active role of children since the material culture which children produce, or with which they interact, links the child to the environment, adults and other children and to the social basis of cultural tradition. The world of children is therefore partly linked to a separate notion of the world of adults (Lillehammer 1989). These worlds are regarded as related since one may feed or starve the other, and each therefore cannot be perceived without the other. Nevertheless, the two worlds are distinct in that while the child–adult relationship is such that children imitate the actions of adults (Bourdieu 1997: 87), in the world of children separated from that of adults, children imitate children. This later relationship contains a potentiality which differs from the child–adult relationship. Relationships between children create particular social identities which relate to interactions within or between particular age or social groups. Thus, while the socialisation of children has often been explored in the archaeological record through the division of labour, games and play (Lillehammer 1986,1989) and has previously been understood and categorised in terms of the way that children imitate adults, this interpretation presupposes behavioural conformity between children and adults in archaeological contexts. It fails to acknowledge the existence of different child-specific forms of interaction between children in which they form their own identities and in which adults do not always participate or provide an outside impetus. As such, it remains decentred from children themselves.

An approach which focuses on children's creation of themselves has implications for cultural transference, innovation and spatial differences between children and adults in patterns of material culture. The autonomy or restricted cultural control of children in the past (Claassen 1992: 5–6), the expectancy of conformity or autonomous behaviour, reflect the cultural perception of children as potential members of society. Yet to increase knowledge of children themselves, we need to find that separate world of children where children are explicitly revealed. We need to look for the spaces in which children learn to behave outside the adult world. For example, the creation of separate spaces in Palaeolithic cave art for the young (Guthrie, personal communication) functions to create places which are less controlled by adults. Are these then places where youngsters are inventing their own cultural identity or recreating in their own space adult mastery of the cultural and natural environment?

LOCATING THE WORLD OF CHILDREN

The archaeological examination of the world of ancient children both has potential and faces unsolved problems (Lillehammer 1986, 1989) which require continuous critical reconsideration and re-examination. However, in order to find the places where children 'model' children and examine the way in which children conform or diverge from the adult world, we first have to locate potential contextual evidence for the world of children

Direct evidence for children is found in contexts with human remains: skeletal or other organic material intentionally or unintentionally deposited in graves, dwellings, buildings, middens, bogs, lakes or sea. Indirect evidence can be found in archaeological data associated with the time, space and place of daily life: inside and around settlements, habitation camps and work places. Children can be found in every locale in the environment in which they live and die.

In order to further develop knowledge of the world of children we can discuss the archaeological context, source critique and interpretive problems which influence the retrieval of archaeological data specific to the analysis of children (Lillehammer 1986; Sellevold *et al.* 1984: 208–13; Gräslund 1973: 162). In this approach, the study of archaeological formation processes and the loss of archaeological information as a result of ancient and modern behaviours, soil conditions and disturbances, and archaeological sampling form the focus of discussion, making this approach similar to that of other research areas.

A more radical approach is to develop the contrast between the world of adults and world of children as a method for exploring the archaeological record. Thus we can draw analogies from other disciplines with specific relevance to the upbringing, learning, living conditions and health of children. In using such a comparative method to specifically examine relationships of time, space and place between the world of adults and the world of children, contextual analysis becomes more complex and an important focus for further debate. We have to consider and reconsider children in the context of known and expected archaeological source material. Nonetheless, in the field of archaeological practice we may also find the unexpected, and openly admit this does not fit a hypothetico-deductive view of science (Hodder 1996: 238).

THE POTENTIALITY OF THE WORLD OF CHILDREN

It is not therefore that it is especially difficult to create children in archaeological data, but if we were to ask which parts of the landscape of cultural heritage are representative of ancient children, could we look in ways other than by examining skeletons or artefacts stored in museums?

In exploring the world of children it is particularly important to understand the potentialities of children, from as early as conception or birth. Thus, insofar as potentiality is the essence of social relationships, the elaboration of aspects of potentiality may be an important theoretical tool in the study of children. However, for this to be fruitful, it is necessary to employ a cultural theory of ageing adapted to archaeological analysis.

In modern culture, the effects of technology and electronic media have resulted in a sense of social dislocation. Previously distinct roles of children and adults have become blurred, as for example, in the case of the crossing of traditional lines between the generations in matters of dress (Meyrowitz 1985: 315–17). Meyrowitz compares the lack of sense of social place with the Weberian 'ideal' of nomadic hunters and gatherers who are deemed to have no loyal relationship to territory. He regards changes in people's views of different generations as a potential threat to children's culture, which stands in danger of being conquered by adult modes of behaviour as children are increasingly treated as little adults and adults begin to act like overgrown children.

Although one might not agree entirely with Meyrowitz's analogy between nomadic attitudes to space and loss of social place, examinations of behavioural change can be used to explore potential shifts in spatial relationships within the world of children. Could the blurring of age roles have developed in small-scale societies of the past? Could age and gender constructions be affected by environmental or cultural changes such as climatic or ecological crises, cultural innovations, conflicts, migration and wars? Could shifts in individual and social location have effected changes in sense of place and altered the view of children in past societies?

Such shifts might account for why it is not always easy to distinguish children from adults in archaeological contexts. A study of childhood among early herders in Sweden in the middle Neolithic (Andersson *et al.* 1995) suggests that relatively few social distinctions were made between children and adults in middle Neolithic graves; only the smallest children appear to be recognised as different from adults. Similarly, among established farmers in the Bronze and Iron Ages in Sweden (Björkhager 1995; Lundin and Skoglund 1995), both children and adults were dressed in similar costumes.

This very similarity can be interpreted in terms of the perceived life potential of children among these groups. In a relatively young population with a high mortality rate (Welinder 1995, 1979) there is only a brief overlap between generations in which cultural transference and innovation can take place. Thus, age roles may be differently constructed, negotiated and renegotiated across time and space. In such a young population children could be raised in a world of children, take care of other children and contribute to society through child labour. The nature of the artefacts associated with burials might therefore represent the recognition of social and practical skills by society, and the similarities between child and adult in burial could reflect the idealisation of adulthood.

CONCLUSION

In order to understand the complex connections between power and contradiction in children's situation in life and in death, analyses of the world of children in the past implicitly call for the development of theory and method specific to the archaeology of children. This undertaking requires the establishment of working hypotheses and frameworks with specific reference to children (Kanvall 1995). Yet, a gap exists between the awareness of children in archaeology and the practice of the archaeologist who seems removed from the study of children. Just as supermodern children are users of non-places, the subject of children in archaeology is itself a 'non-place' in the supermodern flux of creating meaning for the world in general (Augé 1995: 53, 83–85). Although the subject has been turned into a 'museum piece' for exhibitions (Lillehammer 1979), culture heritage specific to children is still largely unknown in the archaeological literature. The subject is only gradually being absorbed into the supermodern universe of meaning in which the whole is understood in the present (Augé 1995).

I therefore suggest that we regard childhood as a state of passage which is then left to memories (Lillehammer 1989: 90). The children and adults of past societies are mute subjects who do not speak their mind regarding their face-to-face experience of living in their once real world. The outsider in the present is left with undertaking an archaeological construction or reconstruction of their past world on the basis of fragments from material culture. To the archaeologist, this process can resemble the subject–object relationship of the adult in which the child is regarded as part of the other, a different 'model' from oneself, but the child is also part of oneself, since the archaeologist has also been a child. In this relationship we may find ourselves trapped in memories which can create obstacles to the interpretation of a world of children; we may see images of adults, and not children, or children only in relationship to adults. This trap of cultural memory is linked both with the understanding of time, and individual or collective memory (Le Goff 1992: 3–4), and also with the thought of having a forward-looking, backward-looking or present-centred view of children (Takanishi 1978: 8–28; Babenroth 1922). Thus, the children who are themselves the focus of study may easily be appropriated by the experience of the archaeologist and turned into ideal objects of adult interest and exploration. The method proposed here is to use our experience from the study of remote places, read not through the ethnocentric grid of our own customary behaviour, but rather through a de-centring of our way of looking, through relearning how to think about space (Augé 1995:

35). In the study of remote places, in which the archaeologist is a human being studying human beings (Gustafsson 1996: 14) we cannot exclude ourselves from the subject of study (Shanks and Tilley 1987a, 1987b). Nonetheless, this should not permit us to overlook the 'other' (Engelstad 1991) and ignore cultural realities other than our own (Olsen 1991: 211–17).

In this chapter, my initial concept of the 'child's world' (Lillehammer 1989) has been developed into the concept of the 'world of children'. This latter concept includes a specifically spatial dimension of activity which distinguishes it from the concept of childhood, which is seen as passively and temporally constructed. The discussion has focused on methodological approaches to the understanding of time and space in relation to children's and adults' worlds, cultural memory and changes in perceptions of children. The relationship between children and adults may be fluid and complex. It is therefore essential to develop a cultural theory of ageing in archaeological theory in order to analyse children in the past. A primary element of this archaeological analysis of children should focus on notions of potentiality and discuss cultural transference and innovation by seeing children as human beings in their own right, albeit ones on small feet! Hence the need to search for a separate world of children in all spheres of social and material life. Rather than creating barriers and misleading interpretations, ultimately we may find that it is the very indistinctness of the boundaries between the world of children and the world of adults that makes this undertaking highly stimulating.

ACKNOWLEDGEMENTS

Thanks to the staff at the Haddon Library and Cambridge University Library, and my colleagues Liv Bakke, Ragnar Børsheim and Arnvid Lillehammer at the Museum of Archaeology, Stavanger for helping out with references. Finally, thanks to Hallvard Lillehammer for correcting my awkward English, which became a learning process for me. In the end, all other weaknesses and mistakes are my own.

REFERENCES

Andersson, G., Welinder, S., and Westeson, Å. (1995) 'Barndommens Gränser i Mellanneolitikum', in B. Johnsen and S. Welinder (eds) *Arkeologi om Barn*, Occasional Papers in 10, Societas Archaeologica Upsaliensis: Uppsala, pp. 9–28.

Augé, M. (1995) *Non-Places: Introduction to an Anthropology of Supermodernity*, London and New York: Verso.

Babenroth, C.A. (1922) *English Childhood*, New York: Columbia University Press.

Björkhager, V. (1995) 'Gravskicket under Barnåren. En Studie av Östgötska Gravar från Övergången mellan Bronsålder och Järnålder', in B. Johnsen and S. Welinder (eds) (1995) *Arkeologi om Barn*, Occasional Papers in Archaeology 10, Societas Archaeologica Upsaliensis: Uppsala, pp. 43–56.

Bolen, K.M. (1992) 'Prehistoric construction of mothering', in C. Claassen (ed.) *Exploring Gender Through Archaeology*, Monographs in World Archaeology 11, Madison, Wisconsin: Prehistoric Press, pp. 5–62.

Bourdieu, P. (1997) *Outline of a Theory of Practice*, Cambridge: Cambridge University Press.

Brooke, A. (1997) *Postfeminism, Feminism, Cultural Theory and Cultural Forms*, London and New York: Routledge.

Claassen, C. (1992) 'Questioning gender: an introduction', in C. Claassen (ed.) *Exploring Gender Through Archaeology*, Selected Papers from the 1991 Boone Conference, Monographs in World Archaeology 11, Madison, Wisconsin: Prehistoric Press, pp. 1–9.

Damm, C. (1994) 'Arkeologisk Materiale i et Feministisk Perspektiv: Hvorfor og Hvordan?', *K.A.N.* 17–18: 28–51.

Dommasnes, L. H. (1987) 'Tanker rundt et Program for Arkeologisk Kvinneforskning', *K.A.N.* 5: 3–26.

Engelstad, E. (1991) 'Images of power and contradiction: feminist theory and post-processual archaeology', *Antiquity* 65: 502–14.

Friedrich, O. (1983) 'What do babies know?', *Time* 15, August: 52–3.

Giddens, A. (1984) *The Constitution of Society*, Cambridge: Cambridge University Press.

—— (1990) *The Consequences of Modernity*, Stanford: Polity Press.

Gräslund, A.-S. (1973) 'Barn i Birka', *Tor* 15: 161–79.

Greer, G. (1997) 'She thinks she's on top. He knows better', *Observer Review* 19 October: 3–4.

Gustafsson, A. (1996) *Arkeologiens Egna Historier. Reflexioner kring Arkeologihistoria, dess Historiografi och Anvöndingar*, Gotarc Serie C. Arkeologiske Skrifter No 12, Göteborgs Universitet.

Harding, S. (1986) *The Science Question in Feminism*, Milton Keynes: Open University Press.

Hodder, I. (1984) 'Burials, houses, women and men in the European Neolithic', in D. Miller and C. Tilley (eds) *Ideology, Power and Prehistory*, Cambridge: Cambridge University Press, pp. 51–68.

—— (1996) *Theory and Practice in Archaeology*, London and New York: Routledge.

Kanvall, P. (1995) 'Barn i Förhistorisk Tid. En Teorisk Diskusjon kring Begreppet "Barn"', in B. Johnsen and S. Welinder (eds) *Arkeologi om Barn*, Occasional Papers in Archaeology 10, Societas Archaeologica Upsaliensis: Uppsala, pp. 7–12.

Key, E. (1902) *Barnets Aarhundrede*, Copenhagen: Gyldendalske Boghandel.

Le Goff, J. (1992) *History and Memory*, New York: Columbia University Press.

Lévi-Strauss, C. (1969) *The Elementary Structures of Kinship*, Boston: Beacon Press.

Lillehammer, G. (1979) 'Gjemt og glemt – Barn i Fortiden', *AmS-Småtrykk* 5: 4–7.

—— (1982) 'Med Barnet på Vei inn i Forhistorien', *AmS-Skrifter* 9: 97–102.

—— (1986) 'Barna i Nordens Forhistorie. Drøft Metodegrunnlaget og Kildenes Bærekraft', *K.A.N.* 2: 3–21.

—— (1987) 'Small-scale archaeology', in R. Bertelsen, A. Lillehammer, and J.-R. Næss (eds) *Were They All Men?*, AmS-Varia 17, pp. 33–4.

—— (1989) 'A child is born: the child's world in an archaeological perspective', *Norwegian Archaeological Review* 22(2): 89–105.

—— (1990) 'Barn av Sin Tid', *Arkeo* 1: 9–12.

Lundin, I. and Skoglund, M. (1995) 'Gravfältens Minsta. Om Barngravar under Förromersk Järnålder', in B. Johnsen and S. Welinder (eds) *Arkeologi om Barn*, Occasional Papers in Archaeology 10, Societas Archaeologica Upsaliensis: Uppsala, pp. 57–68.

Mandt, G. and Næss, J.-R. (1986) 'Hvem skapte og gjenskaper Vår fjerne Fortid? Struktur og Innhold i Norsk Arkeologi i Perspektivet: Hvor Mannlig er Vitenskapen?', *K.A.N.* 3: 3–28.

Meyrowitz, J. (1985) *No Sense of Place: The Impact of the Media on Social Behaviour*, Oxford: Oxford University Press.

Moore, J. and Scott, E. (eds) (1997) *Invisible People and Processes: Writing Gender and Childhood into European Archaeology*, London: Leicester University Press.

Myhre, B. (1991) 'Theory in Scandinavian Archaeology since 1969: A View from Norway', in I. Hodder (ed.) *Archaeological Theory in Europe*, London: Routledge, pp. 161–86.

Neugarten, B. L. (1981) *Age Distinctions and Their Social Functions*, Chicago Kent Law Review 57: 809–25.

Olsen, B. (1991) 'Metropolis and satellites in archaeology: on power and assymmetry in global archaeological research', in R.W. Preucel (ed.) *Processual and Post-processual Archaeologies. Multiple Ways of Knowing the Past*, Occasional Papers No 10, Southern Illinois University at Carbondale, pp. 211–24.

—— (1997) *Fra Ting til Tekst. Teoretiske Perspektiv i Arkeologisk Forskning*, Oslo: Universitetsforlaget.

Preucel, R. and Hodder, I. (eds) (1996) *Contemporary Archaeology in Theory: A Reader*, Oxford: Blackwell Publishers.

Schanche, K. (1989) 'Arkeologi og Feminisme', *K.A.N.* 8: 13–33.

Sellevold, B. J., Lund-Hansen, U. and Balslev Jørgensen, J. (1984) *Iron Age Man in Denmark*, Prehistoric Man in Denmark 3, Nordiske Fortidsminder Bind 8, Copenhagen.

Shanks, M. and Tilley, C. (1987a) *Re-Constructing Archaeology: Theory and Practice*, Cambridge: Cambridge University Press.

—— (1987b) *Social Theory and Archaeology*, Cambridge: Polity Press.

Sofaer Derevenski, J. (1994) 'Where are the children? Accessing children in the past', *Archaeological Review from Cambridge*, 13(2): 7–20.

Sørensen, M. L. S. (1988) 'Is there a feminist contribution to archaeology?', *Archaeological Review from Cambridge* 7(1): 31–50.

Takanishi, R. (1978) 'Childhood as social issue: historical roots of contemporary child advocacy movements', *Journal of Social Issues* 34(2): 8–28.

Tilley, C. (1988) 'Comments on archaeology: as if people mattered', *Norwegian Archaeological Review* 21(1): 12–17.

Vinsrygg, S. (1988) 'Archaeology: as if people mattered. A discussion of humanistic archaeology', *Norwegian Archaeological Review* 21(1): 1–12, 17–20.

Welinder, S. (1979) *Prehistoric Demography*, Bonn: Rudolf Habelt Verlag.

—— (1995) 'Barnens Demografi', in B. Johnsen and S. Welinder (eds) *Arkeologi om Barn*, Occasional Papers in Archaeology 10, Societas Archaeologica Upsaliensis: Uppsala, pp. 13–18.

White, S. and Notkin White, B. (1980) *Childhood: Pathways of Discovery*, London: Harper & Row.

Wordsworth, W. (1827a) *The Poetical Works of William Wordsworth*, Vol. I, London: Longman, Rees, Orme, Brown & Green.

—— (1827b) *The Poetical Works of William Wordsworth*, Vol. II, London: Longman, Rees, Orme, Brown & Green.

Wylie, A. (1993) 'Comments on analogy in Danish prehistoric studies', *Norwegian Archaeological Review* 26(2): 82–5.

Part II

Representing and perceiving children

Chapter 3

Footprints in the clay

Upper Palaeolithic children in ritual and secular contexts

Blythe Roveland

Presently the Shaman and his two companions rejoined the initiates, who were waiting for them. In the little low chamber which they had just left their feet trod upon the ritualistic signs which the Shaman had traced in the clay.

(Bégouën 1926: 190)

INTRODUCTION

Children, no doubt, were significant members of Upper Palaeolithic societies. Yet, while they have populated artist's reconstructions, museum dioramas and works of fiction, they are rarely encountered in the archaeological literature. One of my interests has been in children's fiction and non-fiction books with prehistoric themes through which present-day young people glean messages about the past (Roveland 1993, 1994, 1997a). More recently, I have begun to consider the implications of including children in archaeological interpretations about the Eurasian Palaeolithic (Roveland 1997b). The following is an initial attempt to articulate some of my thoughts on these seemingly disparate topics and to advance a dialogue on children in the Upper Palaeolithic. In order to launch such discussions, thousands of years of prehistory and vast areas are conveniently collapsed. In the future more fine-grained analyses which employ specific bodies of data should be developed.

In this chapter, I discuss several issues that may lead to understandings of Upper Palaeolithic children in various secular and ritual contexts. I begin by a short overview of children's books set in Palaeolithic times. Reading these stories, I argue, is a means by which we as archaeologists may begin to imagine the place of children as well as adults in our versions of the past. I then turn to a handful of ethnographic cases to examine what they may offer to considerations about Palaeolithic children. Following that discussion, attention is directed to archaeological research that has allowed for the presence of children in the Upper Palaeolithic including studies of art, burials and flintknapping. Finally, by way of conclusion, I explore a series of issues with which scholars from other disciplines have already been grappling for some time and propose their relevance to archaeology.

WHAT THE CHILDREN'S BOOKS SAY

Fictional works in English set in the Palaeolithic and written expressly for young people have been around for about a century. Perhaps the Palaeolithic has captured the attention of both writers and juvenile readers because it represents a remote time that is at once real and imaginary. Many of these books have featured children or adolescents in active roles. However, there are certainly also works of fiction of a didactic nature in which children are little more than passive characters, learning from adults to become obedient members of society. A few books do not portray children at all. One such book (Crowell 1976) describes a community made up of five men and a dog – a rather short-lived society I would imagine. It is not surprising that even in books in which children are the featured protagonists, adults are almost always in positions of power and authority. Nevertheless, children play significant roles in many of these stories and are often pictured facilitating technological and societal change.

A number of fictional Stone Age accounts, especially from the first three decades of this century, portray children in the active role of innovator and inventor. The basic formula of children as implementers of ideas and inventors of material culture is found in a variety of tales about the first fish spear, flint saw, bow and arrow, boat, taming of fire and cooking meat, and so forth. Another common theme in Palaeolithic fiction is children successfully domesticating animals; most often wolves and horses (see Roveland 1993). Frequently the act of taming leads to more significant contributions such as helping a struggling people find food or hunt animals in new ways. For instance, in *Malu's Wolf* (Craig 1995) the main character tames a wolf who later finds an elusive herd of mammoths upon which the group depends (Figure 3.1). The interesting twist in this story is the fact that Malu is a girl, which is quite rare. Like the boys, she is allowed to use a spear thrower and participate in an initiation ceremony in the painted cave.

Figure 3.1 Children in fictional accounts are often portrayed as innovators who introduce new ideas and items of material culture. In rare instances the child is a girl. Here Malu is pictured with Kono, the wolf she has tamed

Source: Redrawn from the jacket illustration by M.H. Donnelly in Craig 1995

A great many stories feature children with special artistic and spiritual talents. Sometimes these children are challenged in some way, either by a physical disability or by being outsiders or orphans. In *Turi of the Magic Fingers* (Williams 1939), for example, Turi, who was lamed by a cave bear attack, turns his attention to drawing on cave walls. His talents prompt his group to select him as their sorcerer (Figure 3.2). It should also be mentioned that he too tames a wild dog! Other child protagonists refuse to accept the limitations placed on them by their gender or by the fact that they are not adults. They nonetheless find a niche for themselves and contribute to society in some way.

It is no surprise that, unlike archaeologists,

writers and illustrators have had little difficulty in reconstructing a past that includes
children. Even though some have tried to use
ethnographically – and archaeologically –
derived data, they are not constrained by these
data. They also serve a very different audience.
I am certainly not advocating archaeological
stories that mirror the fictional variety. There
are numerous pitfalls in works of fiction such
as the perpetuation of gender stereotypes which
one hopes will be avoided in archaeological
reconstructions. There is no need to dream up
archaeological counterparts to Malu and Turi.
On the other hand, the fictional accounts do
suggest to us past worlds in which children
were active participants. Palaeolithic children
no doubt came upon ideas and inventions
through work and play. It is not difficult to
imagine that past children could have had
influence and could have effected real change.
They bring into our consciousness the richness
that is gained by adding not only gender and
age to archaeological reconstructions, but also
other social divisions (for instance, those based
upon mental, physical or spiritual attributes).
The use of ethnographic models may also help
in imagining the place of Palaeolithic children.

Figure 3.2   The protagonists in children's books
frequently have special artistic talents that are recognised
by their society. In this case 'Turi the Lame One' is made
the next sorcerer because of his accomplishments

Source: Redrawn from an illustration by H. Daugherty in Williams
1939: 91

ETHNOGRAPHIC CASES

While, of course, caution must be used when
drawing ethnographic parallels, an examination
of children cross-culturally may help free us
from a narrow Western view of children. It can aid in the evaluation of the conditions that
may affect children's activities and contributions. It also attunes us to the interconnections
and overlap between the worlds of adults and children among hunter-gatherers and other
'traditional' societies.

Draper (1976) noted several points about !Kung children that may influence archaeological thinking about hunter-gatherer children. First, she proposed that constraints on
child life were imposed by the nature of adult work and the organisation of people in
space. We might also look at this from another angle and assume that the presence of children significantly affected the organisation of adult tasks. A whole range of decisions
about the timing and location of activities is predicated on the existence of children. In
addition, Draper called attention to the fact that there were neither distinct play areas for
children nor were there areas for adults only. Children were most often in the company of
one or more adults rather than exclusively with other children. These issues regarding the
organisation and use of space have direct implications for archaeological interpretations.

Studies have also shown that !Kung children contributed little in terms of subsistence, child care and other tasks until they were fairly old (14 years for girls and 16 years for boys; Draper 1976: 210). Draper has suggested that this was due to the relative ease and predictability of obtaining resources. Other researchers believe that the !Kung scenario has, in fact, led to a commonly held, but misleading assumption that all hunter-gatherer children do not provide much to their own subsistence. Hawkes *et al.* (1995) evaluated both Hadza and !Kung children's participation in foraging in terms of costs and benefits. They concluded that Hadza children, who frequently accompanied women on long-distance foraging trips for berries, raised the combined rates of nutrient returns for women and children. On the other hand, the combined or 'team' rates among the Dobe !Kung are increased when children do *not* join foraging parties. The younger children may impede foraging activities and older children can contribute more by staying at base camps and cracking mongongo nuts which the adults gather.

Zeller (1987) compiled research on children's contributive activities in foraging and horticultural groups and found that children have diverse roles in work-related pursuits. In certain groups, such as among the Alaskan Inuit, children may supply a large portion of their own diets (ibid.: 545). In others, children's involvement is negligible. She proposed that children in hunter-gatherer and horticultural societies could reduce the economic demands on their mothers through a variety of direct contributions (such as providing their own food) as well as indirect ones (such as caring for younger children and going on errands) (ibid.: 542), which in turn would influence reproductive rates. Her survey found a positive correlation between levels of completed fertility and levels of contributions by children.

No doubt, the explanations given to account for differential economic roles of children in various contexts should be interrogated and debated further. However, by using these cases as models perhaps we can begin to use data routinely compiled by archaeologists concerning resource availability and reliability, and fertility rates to infer children's economic contributions.

ARCHAEOLOGICAL IMPRESSIONS OF PALAEOLITHIC CHILDREN

Just as adults, children are and were engaged in more than mere economic pursuits. Other realms of children's involvement have sometimes been discussed and it would not be accurate to assert that children have been completely absent from all archaeological interpretations regarding the Palaeolithic. In fact, sometimes it has been quite impossible for archaeologists to avoid 'seeing' children in the Palaeolithic. One of the most common contexts in which Palaeolithic youth have been acknowledged and considered is in discussions about small-sized footprints found preserved in the clay and sand of cave floors. They have been found both in areas associated and unassociated with parietal art (Ucko and Rosenfeld 1967: 225). In what has become a cliché (Conkey 1997: 355), initiation rites are frequently posited to explain the presence of children's prints in caves.

The discovery by the Bégouën family and the subsequent interpretations of the art and footprints at Le Tuc d'Audoubert early in the century certainly bolstered this view (Ucko and Rosenfeld 1967: 177). The lines of small heel prints in an adjoining low chamber 25 m from the famous clay bison led to the bizarre imagery of adolescent boys marching or dancing on their heels with toes pointed in the air in some sort of ceremony. Count Henri

Bégouën was convinced 'that the chamber had been used for the ritual initiation of adolescents' (Hadingham 1979: 181). His son also conjured such a scene in his novel *Bison of Clay* based on the site (Bégouën 1926). Other possible children's footprints have been found at L'Aldène, Fontanet, Pech Merle, Montespan, and the Réseau Clastres, a gallery in the Niaux cave complex (Bahn and Vertut 1988: 13–15; Leroi-Gourhan 1967: 181). Pfeiffer (1982) has argued that essential information transmitted in the depths of dark caves during ceremonies would have been more likely to remain imprinted on the minds of the participants.

If the estimates of the age of the individuals who made the prints are at all reliable, some intriguing implications can be drawn from those found thus far. Several researchers have noted that whenever there are several sets of footprints found together, groups of children or children and adults are represented rather than adults alone. Leroi-Gourhan (1967: 181) claimed that this fact 'argues strongly in favor of some sort of initiation ceremony'. Pfeiffer (1982: 184) stated that '[t]here is little doubt for whom at least some of the presumed ceremonies were devised'. He proposed this might mean that '[i]f ceremonies were continued at later stages of life, they may have been held elsewhere with caves used mainly for children' (Pfeiffer 1982: 184). Recently, Owens and Hayden (1997) have also sought to explain the presence of children in caves. They first analysed a sample of the ethnographically documented 'transegalitarian' (i.e. complex) hunter-gatherers in terms of the costs and exclusiveness associated with various maturation events. Such events included growth payments, puberty ceremonies, initiations and training. The authors then concluded that decorated Upper Palaeolithic caves were locales in which initiations of elite adolescents into secret societies took place.

Alternatively, we can perhaps conjecture that, as with many ethnographically documented cultures, children's and adult's activities overlapped in time and space to a great degree. Children were not necessarily there only if they were being initiated. Nor is it inevitably the case that they were just playing on the 'sidelines' while adults carried out rituals or other occupations. Children may have gone there 'as they would have gone elsewhere' (Ucko and Rosenfeld 1967: 225) and they may have been integral to the activities that went on there.

A handful of archaeologists has called attention to the possibility that some Palaeolithic art may have indeed been rendered by young people. While Bosinski and Fischer (1974: 116) surmised that children were excluded from the creation of engravings at Gönnersdorf, Russell (1989: 242) proposed that children may very well have incised images on slate and limestone plaques. In their comments on Lewis-Williams and Dowson's (1988) article about entoptic images in parietal art, Consens (1988) and Turner (1988) intimated that children may have participated in the execution of such images. Initially Lewis-Williams and Dowson (1988: 236) asserted that there was little evidence to suggest that Upper Palaeolithic geometric signs had been the work of children. However, in a later reply they did concede that they had no problem in believing that older children were involved in the ritual creation of some of the art (Lewis-Williams and Dowson 1990: 81). Other researchers have pointed to the fact that contemporary hunter-gatherer children take part in creating artistic imagery. For example, Australian Aboriginal children 'have developed considerable skill in the arts, especially engravings on clay floors' (Ucko and Rosenfeld 1967: 225). It would not be difficult to imagine Upper Palaeolithic children engaged in similar pursuits. Perhaps in Upper Palaeolithic societies, like in San communities, anyone was allowed and encouraged to attempt anything (Garlake 1995: 27).

One telltale sign that children joined in the production of 'art' can be found in their hand stencils on some rock faces. For instance, a small black, possibly gloved, handprint has been documented from a gallery of Altamira, the 'Cola de Caballo' (Freeman *et al.* 1987: 200–2). The best evidence, however, has come from Gargas where investigators have identified hand stencils deriving from adults, children and babies (Bahn and Vertut 1988: 105). In the latter case, an adult or older child must have placed the baby's hand on the wall to create the image. Therefore, such painted hands may be viewed more as representations of children (ibid.: 163) than as products of children.

Other depictions of children in artistic images are rare, or at least they have not been routinely recognised. One strong candidate comes from the open-air site of Gönnersdorf in Germany. Engraved plaquettes found at the site include representations of rows of abstract figures. They have been interpreted as portraying a procession of women or girls possibly engaged in dance (Bosinski and Fischer 1974: 116). One of these 'processions' seems to show a small figure facing in the other direction and strapped to the back of one of the females. That small figure may be an infant (ibid.: 45). The German researchers suggested that perhaps initiation rites involving girls entering womanhood were being portrayed (ibid.: 117). Other potential images of adolescents have been identified at Laussel and Laugerie-Basse (White 1986: 131, 153).

It is curious that the archaeologists who have insisted that the ubiquitous female imagery may symbolise and celebrate fertility have not taken up the issue of the ostensible absence of children. One could suggest that portrayals of small children who had survived the critical first years of life would make equally suitable fertility symbols. On the other hand, it may be that we have not recognised children in artistic representations. Parkington and Manhire (1997: 310) have discussed the lack of well-substantiated depictions of children on the rock paintings from the western Cape of South Africa. They suggest that part of the reason for the perceived absence of children may be that there have not been adequate studies on the use of scale. This insight may obtain for European Upper Palaeolithic imagery as well and might be pursued in the future. It is also conceivable that children were portrayed symbolically rather than 'realistically'.

Burials are another line of evidence that has made it difficult to completely ignore children in the Palaeolithic. In a sample of ninety-six Upper Palaeolithic burials, Harrold (1980: 202) found that there was no differentiation between adults and juveniles in terms of the distribution of grave goods. Some young individuals as well as some adults were buried with few if any grave goods while others were supplied with a substantial amount. At La Madeleine, Rocher de la Peine, and Grottes des Enfants, for example, children had been buried with clusters of shell beads and pierced teeth which had probably decorated their clothing (Pfeiffer 1982: 67–8; White 1986: 91–3). At Kostenki XV a child's burial was also furnished with various tools (Soffer 1985: 455). In addition, there are the burials at Sungir of two adolescents placed head-to-head with bone spears, shaft straighteners, animal carvings, stone and bone pendants and thousands of ivory beads (Gamble 1986: 188; Soffer 1985: 455). It may be argued that this kind of attention to children's graves indicates the existence of ascribed rather than achieved status. In such cases, the graves may simply provide another window onto the adult world rather than that of the child. Nevertheless, the fact that elaborate grave goods were bestowed on certain young individuals forces an examination of the diversity and importance of children's roles in Palaeolithic societies.

More recently, others have suggested that technological studies may reveal the work of child apprentices through indications of unskilled flintknapping. At the site of Etiolles, researchers have found not only what they believe to be evidence for children's production, but also that these activity areas were spatially distinct. Pigeot (1990) points to bounded clusters of debitage at the site that she proposes represented episodes in 'lithic education' at different levels of competency. She suggests that '[t]he organisation of youth education among traditional societies is probably more complex than previously realised' (ibid.: 136). In a similar study, researchers felt it necessary to rethink their interpretations of unit 27 M.89 at Pincevent, which was originally described as representing a 'specialized hunting camp created by a purely masculine group', when they concluded that young apprentices were present (Bodu *et al.* 1990: 156). In light of the new evidence they suggested that a nuclear family occupied the site. Of course, their original conclusion begs the question of why a specialised hunting camp constituted by men, women and children had been discounted initially.

An entire suite of issues can be addressed through such technological studies. Examination of the technical dimensions of the learning process may lead to new insights into change and innovation rather than simply cultural continuity. However, I am uneasy with some of the implications of the studies and interpretations discussed above. The focus of much of the research on the presence of children in secular and ritual contexts has been on the process of becoming adults. In other words, the child has been studied in terms of 'what she is subsequently *going to be* rather than what she presently *is*' (Goodwin 1997: 1).

THOUGHTS FROM OTHER FIELDS

While socialisation is certainly a significant element of children's lives, it is not the only dimension. Specialists in other fields such as social history, developmental psychology, linguistics and cultural anthropology have contemplated these other dimensions. Social historians and developmental psychologists have come to recognise the great diversity of children in time and space. Cahan *et al.* (1993: 195) have recommended to historians and psychologists some conditions that shape, limit and empower 'the social practice of children's lives'. These include the interaction of the child with '(1) the physical environment [including technology], (2) the social environment [including social relations and values], (3) the "imperial" practices of adults, and (4) the "native" practices of the child's social group'. Indeed, Lillehammer (1989: 102–3) discussed similar aspects of the child's world and submitted that the archaeological child could best be accessed through exploring the relationship of past children with the environment and the adult world. However, as White (1983: 20) has put forth, although artefacts and the constructed and natural world give shape to children's activities, they 'pick and choose among the universe of objects adults set before them'. It can be added that children modify and create some of the objects themselves (Bonnichsen 1973).

Attention to children in socio-cultural anthropology and linguistic anthropology has been uneven and sporadic. Children have infrequently been included in studies of social systems, systems of production, or religion and ritual except those involving initiation rites (Gottlieb 1998: 122; Schildkrout 1978: 110). Anthropologists have rarely given sufficient attention to the interaction of children with other children (Goodwin 1997: 1). For many years, the focus remained on socialisation in the fairly limited sense of children passively absorbing and internalising cultural norms and mores from information provided by adults. Schildkrout (1978: 110) stated that the emphasis on socialisation 'trivialized childhood as a social status' and that a great deal could be learned about a society if children were examined as children, rather than as adults of the next generation. More recently, anthropologists, particularly linguistic anthropologists involved in language socialisation studies, have assumed a more active role for children in the socialisation process. According to Schieffelin (1990: 17) '[s]ocialization is an interactive process between knowledgeable members and novices (children) who are themselves active contributors to the meanings and outcomes of interactions with others'. Children are agents in their own construction rather than purely imitative (Wartofsky 1983: 199).

It is probable that children in Palaeolithic societies, like those in other past societies, constituted the largest group of individuals in a population (Chamberlain 1997: 250). For his simulation of Palaeolithic populations, Wobst (1974) employed model life tables based on northern hunter-gatherer groups (Weiss 1973) in which young people under 15 years old accounted for over 40 per cent of the population. If in fact this is an accurate reflection of Upper Palaeolithic populations, then accounting for children in the archaeological record is far from irrelevant. We must set out by formulating research designs that are sensitive to the presence of children. Conkey (1991) has recommended that a place to begin investigating age and sex as axes of social differentiation might be in contexts beyond the household such as at aggregation sites. Whatever the future directions of discourse on Palaeolithic children may be, it would seem that archaeologists must allow for children as active participants. This would mean not only anticipating that children had a hand in rearranging the configuration of artefacts at a site (Hammond and Hammond 1981), but that they were intimately involved in their spatial organisation from the start. It would imply that children were engaged in learning activities and training, but also had original ideas themselves and did not mechanically reproduce the work of previous generations. It might indicate too that young people were regularly involved in rituals and ceremonies besides those of initiation into adulthood. Indeed, I suspect that following small footprints in the clay will lead to more than just the adult world.

ACKNOWLEDGMENTS

I wish to express my gratitude to Jo Sofaer Derevenski for asking me to participate in the TAG session and the present volume and for her encouragement. Earlier collaboration with Sheila Brennan and Martin Wobst for conferences in 1993 and 1994 led to some of the ideas presented here. However, no one but me can be blamed for any errors, omissions or flaws in logic. Appreciation is also due to my husband, Barrett Brenton, for sharing in my obsession with children's books about the Palaeolithic and helping me find them. Finally, I would like to thank my mother, Marilyn Roveland, for drawing the accompanying illustrations.

REFERENCES

Bahn, P. and Vertut, J. (1988) *Images of the Ice Age*, Leicester: Windward.

Bégouën, M. (1926) *Bison of Clay*, trans. R. L. Duffus, New York and London: Longmans & Green.

Bodu, P., Karlin, C. and Ploux, S. (1990) 'Who's who? The Magdalenian flintknappers of Pincevent, France', in E. Cziesla, S. Eickhoff, N. Arts and D. Winter (eds) *The Big Puzzle: International Symposium on Refitting Stone Artefacts*, Bonn: Holos, pp. 143–63.

Bonnichsen, R. (1973) 'Millie's Camp; an experiment in archaeology', *World Archaeology* 4(3): 277–91.

Bosinski, G. and Fischer, G. (1974) *Die Menschendarstellungen von Gönnersdorf der Ausgrabung von 1968*, Wiesbaden: Franz Steiner.

Cahan, E., Mechling, J., Sutton-Smith, B. and White, S.H. (1993) 'The elusive historical child: ways of knowing the child of history and psychology', in G.H. Elder, Jr., J. Modell, and R.D. Parke (eds) *Children in Time and Place: Developmental and Historical Insights*, New York: Cambridge University Press, pp. 192–223.

Chamberlain, A.T. (1997) 'Commentary: missing stages of life – towards the perception of children in archaeology', in J. Moore and E. Scott (eds) *Invisible People and Processes: Writing Gender and Childhood into European Archaeology*, London: Leicester University Press, pp. 248–50.

Conkey, M.W. (1991) 'Contexts of action, contexts of power: material culture and gender in the Magdalenian', in J.M. Gero and M.W. Conkey (eds) *Engendering Archaeology: Women and Prehistory*, Oxford: Blackwell, pp. 57–92.

—— (1997) 'Beyond art and between the caves: thinking about context in the interpretive process', in M.W. Conkey, O. Soffer, D. Stratmann and N.G. Jablonski (eds) *Beyond Art: Pleistocene Image and Symbol*, Memoirs of the California Academy of Sciences 23, pp. 343–67.

Consens, M. (1988) 'Comment', *Current Anthropology* 29(2): 221–2.

Craig, R. (1995) *Malu's Wolf*, New York: Orchard Books.

Crowell, P. (1976) *King Moo the Wordmaker*, Caldwell, Idaho: Caxton Printers.

Draper, P. (1976) 'Social and economic constraints on child life', in R.B. Lee and I. DeVore (eds) *Kalahari Hunter-Gatherers: Studies of the !Kung San and Their Neighbors*, Cambridge, Mass. and London: Harvard University Press, pp. 200–17.

Freeman, L. G., Bernaldo de Quirós, F. and Ogden, J. (1987) 'Animals, faces and space at Altamira: a restudy of the final gallery ("Cola de Caballo")', in L.G. Freeman (ed.) *Altamira Revisited and Other Essays on Early Art*, Chicago and Santander: Institute for Prehistoric Investigations, pp. 179–247.

Gamble, C. (1986) *The Palaeolithic Settlement of Europe*, Cambridge: Cambridge University Press.

Garlake, P. (1995) *The Hunter's Vision: The Prehistoric Art of Zimbabwe*, Seattle: University of Washington Press.

Goodwin, M.H. (1997) 'Children's linguistic and social worlds', *Anthropology Newsletter* 38(4): 1, 4–5.

Gottlieb, A. (1998) 'Do infants have religion? The spiritual lives of Beng babies', *American Anthropologist* 100(1): 122–35.

Hadingham, E. (1979) *Secrets of the Ice Age: The World of the Cave Artists*, New York: Walker.

Hammond, G. and Hammond, N. (1981) 'Child's play: a distorting factor in archaeological distribution', *American Antiquity* 46(3): 634–6.

Harrold, F. (1980) 'A comparative analysis of Eurasian palaeolithic burials', *World Archaeology* 12(2): 195–211.

Hawkes, K., O'Connell, J.F., and Blurton Jones, N.G. (1995) 'Hadza children's foraging: juvenile dependency, social arrangements, and mobility among hunter-gatherers', *Current Anthropology* 36(4): 688–700.

Leroi-Gourhan, A. (1967) *Treasures of Prehistoric Art*, trans. N. Guterman, New York: Harry N. Abrams.

Lewis-Williams, J.D. and Dowson, T.A. (1988) 'The signs of all times: entoptic phenomena in Upper Palaeolithic art', *Current Anthropology* 29(2): 201–45.

—— (1990) 'Reply', *Current Anthropology* 31(1): 80–4.

Lillehammer, G. (1989) 'A child is born: the child's world in an archaeological perspective', *Norwegian Archaeological Review* 22(2): 89–105.

Owens, D. and Hayden, B. (1997) 'Prehistoric rites of passage: a comparative study of transegalitarian hunter-gatherers', *Journal of Anthropological Archaeology* 16(2): 121–61.

Parkington, J. and Manhire, A. (1997) 'Processions and groups: human figures, ritual occasions and social categories in the rock paintings of the western Cape, South Africa', in M.W. Conkey, O. Soffer, D. Stratmann and N.G. Jablonski (eds) *Beyond Art: Pleistocene Image and Symbol*, Memoirs of the California Academy of Sciences 23, pp. 301–20.

Pfeiffer, J.E. (1982) *The Creative Explosion*, Ithaca: Cornell University Press.

Pigeot, N. (1990) 'Technical and Social Actors: Flintknapping specialists and apprentices at Magdalenian Etoilles', *Archaeological Review from Cambridge* 9(1): 126–41.

Roveland, B.E. (1993) 'Child the creator: children as agents of change in juvenile prehistoric literature', *Visual Anthropology Review* 9(1): 147–53.

—— (1994) 'Children confront the other: portrayals of Neanderthals in juvenile non-fiction books', *Archaeological Review from Cambridge* 13(2): 113–27.

—— (1997a) 'Reading about cave people: dispelling stereotypes and imagining the possibilities', *Archaeology and Public Education* 7(1): 11.

—— (1997b) 'Archaeology of children', *Anthropology Newsletter* 38(4): 14.

Russell, P. (1989) 'Who and why in Palaeolithic art', *Oxford Journal of Archaeology* 8(3): 237–49.

Schieffelin, B.B. (1990) *The Give and Take of Everyday Life: Language Socialization of Kaluli Children*, Cambridge: Cambridge University Press.

Schildkrout, E. (1978) 'Age and gender in Hausa society: socio-economic roles of children in urban Kano', in L.S. La Fontaine (ed.) *Sex and Age as Principles of Social Differentiation*, London: Academic Press, pp. 109–37.

Soffer, O. (1985) *The Upper Paleolithic of the Central Russian Plain*, Orlando: Academic Press.

Turner C.G. II. (1988) 'Comment', *Current Anthropology* 29(2): 228–9.

Ucko, P. and Rosenfeld, A. (1967) *Palaeolithic Cave Art*, New York: McGraw-Hill.

Wartofsky, M. (1983) 'The child's construction of the world and the world's construction of the child: from historical epistemology to historical psychology', in F.S. Kessel and A.W. Siegel (eds) *The Child and Other Cultural Inventions*, Houston Symposium 4 (1981) New York: Praeger, pp. 188–215.

Weiss, K.M. (1973) *Demographic Models for Anthropology*, Memoirs of the Society for American Archaeology 27.

White, R. (1986) *Dark Caves, Bright Visions: Life in Ice Age Europe*, New York: American Museum of Natural History.

White, S. (1983) 'Psychology as a moral science', in F.S. Kessel and A.W. Siegel (eds) *The Child and Other Cultural Inventions*, New York: Praeger, pp. 1–25.

Williams, H.L. (1939) *Turi of the Magic Fingers*, New York: The Viking Press.

Wobst, H.M. (1974) 'Boundary conditions for Paleolithic social systems: a simulation approach', *American Antiquity* 39(2): 147–78.

Zeller, A.C. (1987) 'A role for children in hominid evolution', *Man* 22(2): 528–57.

Chapter 4

The social status and artistic presentation of 'adolescence' in fifth century Athens

Lesley Beaumont

DEFINING ADOLESCENCE

This chapter is concerned with definitions. In particular, with the definition of the often very hazy boundaries between childhood, adolescence and adulthood. These boundaries are, of course, not immutable. They are, rather, culturally, temporally and often gender specific, and serve to contribute to the regulation of a particular social system. Here, my focus is on an examination of these boundaries as they were perceived and experienced in fifth century Athenian society.

In this context I use the term 'adolescence' advisedly and with great caution. The *Oxford English Dictionary* definition of 'adolescence' reads as follows: 'The process or condition of growing up; the growing age of human beings; the period which extends from childhood to manhood or womanhood: youth, ordinarily considered as extending from 14 to 25 in males and from 12 to 21 in females.' Significantly, this quote demonstrates that even within contemporary Western culture there are those who would variously define male and female adolescence, notably allocating a shorter duration to female than to male adolescence. Perhaps a more popular contemporary definition of adolescence would identify the adolescent phase for both male and female with the teenage years, extending from about 13 to 18. However, the very existence of two such varied contemporary definitions illustrates enduring ambiguity in the concept and perception of adolescence. We might also add that in present-day Western society, the term 'adolescence' carries with it a powerful range of associations, not all of them positive. Juvenile crime and teenage pregnancies cause our society agonies of navel-gazing in an attempt to discover the root cause and solution for these social ills (Garland 1991). Furthermore, on a more positive note, today's adolescent claims a strong social identity in the 'youth culture' and 'teen cult' created, by and large, by advertisers and the music and fashion industries who exploit the not-inconsiderable economic potential of their young audience.

However, in order to reach an understanding of youth in classical Athens we must try to put our notions of modern adolescence to one side (Kleijwegt 1991). In the ancient Greek language there is no one single word which conveys an equivalent range of meanings to that possessed by the term 'adolescence' as we use it today. Nonetheless, there did exist in ancient Greek society the concept of a transitional and liminal phase of development between childhood proper and adulthood. This, then, must be the starting point for a definition of 'adolescence' as it might be applied to fifth century Athens.

BOUNDARIES AND TRANSITIONS: THE EVIDENCE OF ICONOGRAPHY

My curiosity about the perception and experience of male and female adolescence in fifth century Athens was first aroused during the course of making an analytical study of the portrayal of childhood and youth in classical Athenian art. In seeking to establish and apply analytical criteria for the interpretation of the ages and stages of childhood and youth in classical Athenian iconography, it became clear that it was possible to identify in the artistic corpus representations of three stages of life preceding adulthood: infancy, pre-pubertal childhood, and pubertal youth (Beaumont 1994).

Characteristic Athenian examples of the artistic depiction of the infant stage, which covered approximately the first three years of life, can be found in the child figures which decorate the late fifth century *chous* (small jug), a ritual vessel used by children in their third year at the Dionysiac Anthesteria festival. On these vases the infants are often depicted in typical childlike crawling pose, and are naked except for a string of amulets (Beaumont 1998: figure 5.6). A sculptural example of the artistic representation of the infant stage is illustrated in Figure 4.1. Here, on the relief-decorated grave stele of Mnesagora and Nikochares, the little Nikochares, portrayed as a small, naked figure in semi-crawling pose, reaches out both hands towards a bird held by his sister.

Following infancy, in the years preceding puberty, the child is usually presented as a figure of markedly reduced stature, the boys often being naked and the girls frequently clothed in characteristic long or short *chiton*, or dress. An analysis of attributes and representational context further enables the sub-division of this category into a younger and an older group, particularly in the case of male children. The younger group, comprising children of approximately ages 3 to 7, can be seen at play with their toys in a domestic setting. The older group, comprising boys of approximately age 7 to the teenage years are surrounded by the paraphernalia of the school-room and usually dressed modestly in a *himation* or cloak. Figure 4.2 presents a sculptural representation of a pre-pubertal female child. Here on a funerary stele a young girl,

Figure 4.1   Attic grave stele of Mnesagora and the infant Nikochares, circa 430 BC

Source: Athens Nat. Mus. 3845. Clairmont 1993: no. 1.610. Photograph: National Archaeological Museum, Athens

wearing a sleeved *chiton* held in place by straps which cross her completely flat chest, holds a doll in one hand while her little dog jumps up to inspect the bird she clasps with the other hand. Figure 4.3 shows a well-known red-figure school scene by the early fifth century Athenian painter Douris: two young boys are concentrating on their lessons, one practising the lyre with his teacher, and the other being tested on his recitation skills.

Thanks to these well-defined iconographic types and readily identifiable pictorial contexts, infancy and the pre-pubertal life-stage can be distinguished quite easily in the Athenian artistic repertoire. The definition of the boundary between childhood proper and the stage at which the individual underwent the transition to adolescence is fairly clear for classical Athens. For both male and female this transformation was biologically determined since it occurred at the onset of puberty, gener-ally considered to take place around age 13 or 14 (Garland 1990: 167–8; Golden 1990: 28 and n. 20; Eyben 1972). However, once past this point the experience of adolescence and the stage at which the individual made the transi-tion to adulthood developed along strictly gender-differentiated lines. Further, as we shall see, the task of trying to identify adolescent figures in the iconographic record is a much more complex and difficult task, particularly for the male figure.

For adolescent females, it is sometimes possible to identify an iconographic type for the pubertal maiden phase, transitional between childhood and adulthood (Sourvinou-

Figure 4.2   Attic grave stele of a young girl, late fifth or early fourth century BC

Source: Athens Nat. Mus. 776. Clairmont 1993: no. 0.780. Photograph: National Archaeological Museum, Athens

Inwood 1988). In this case, the adolescent girl is often shown as a little shorter in stature than her adult companions, clothed, with breasts indicated under her garments and gener-ally sporting long loose or braided hair. Figure 4.4 illustrates the Athenian artistic presentation of this stage in an example drawn from the Parthenon frieze where, on the east side, a group of Athenian girls, or maidens, assists in the ritual procession by carrying sacrificial equipment. It is also worth noting that the archaic *kore* statue type, much in favour in the sixth and early fifth centuries BC, essentially presents the same iconographic type though in a different stylistic milieu. By contrast, the adult female is represented in classical Athenian art as a figure of full stature, fully clothed, with full breasts, while her hair is often pulled up on to the back of the head in a knot, and may be crowned with one of a variety of head-dresses, including the veil.

Figure 4.3   Attic red-figure cup depicting boys at school. Painted by Douris, circa 485–480 BC

Source: Berlin, Staatliche Museen F2285. *ARV2* 431.48, 1653; *Para374*; *Add2* 237. Photograph: Antikensammlung, Staatliche Museen zu Berlin – Preussischer Kulturbesitz

Figure 4.4   Athenian maidens in procession on the east side of the Parthenon frieze, 447–432 BC. They carry jugs and *phialai* (libation vessels) which will be used in the ritual sacrifices. The figure leading them and carrying a *thymiaterion* (incense burner) is apparently an older woman, whose hair is bound into a bun at the back of her head

Source: Parthenon frieze: east VIII. London, British Museum. Heads of figures in Athens, Akropolis Museum. Photograph: © The British Museum

For the adolescent, pubertal male there exists one easily recognisable iconographic type in the figure of the *ephebos*, or military cadet. The *ephebeia* in classical Athens comprised a compulsory two-year period of military training and service for all male citizen youths beginning in their eighteenth year.[1] The iconographic record reveals a distinct *ephebos* figure, easily identifiable by his uniform of *chlamys*, or short cloak, spears, and also often *petasos*, or traveller's hat. A pictorial example of such *ephebos* figures can be seen in Figure 4.5 in a scene from an Athenian red-figure vase of the mid-fifth century BC.[2] Otherwise, however, for the phase between the onset of puberty at about age 13 and the attainment of adult manhood, we are forced to rely on more general, and often less conclusive, iconographic indicators of youth. These sometimes, but not always, include reduced stature and slim, lithe physique. We are sometimes also helped in the identification of the adolescent life-stage by the appearance of downy 'fluff' on the face of an otherwise clean-shaven youthful figure or by the addition of pubic hair on an otherwise boyish figure. Although possession of the *aryballos*, or oil flask, is often relevant to the young adolescent male, being necessary equipment for his frequent trips to the *palaistra* or gymnasium, it is not limited to this group and therefore cannot, on its own, be interpreted as a definitive iconographic indicator of the adolescent life-stage.

Nonetheless, in many cases it is difficult to distinguish the adolescent male figure from that of the young adult male. Often it is only through an analysis of the pictorial context that it is sometimes possible to more closely identify the youthful figure as either adolescent or young adult. A good example of this can be drawn from the mythological pictorial corpus, though the ambivalent nature of the iconography of the adolescent figure is just as prevalent for the mortal male in genre scenes of everyday life. Figure 4.6 illustrates a scene from an Attic red-figure cup, where an older, mature man, distinguished as such by his beard,[3] is attacked by a young male figure while four further young males look on aghast. All of the young males are clean shaven, are depicted with full and well-developed physical stature, and are variously nude or partly or fully dressed. This iconographic type is widely used in classical Athenian art to depict both the adolescent and the young adult male. Here the pictorial and mythological contexts clarify matters for us: the writing tablet hanging on the wall and the lyre in the hand of the bearded man identify the action as taking place in the schoolroom between master and pupils. The mythological tradition identifies the aggressor as the schoolboy

Figure 4.5   Athenian *epheboi*, dressed in *chlamys* (short cloak) and *petasos* (traveller's hat), and carrying spears. Attic red-figure cup by the Penthesilea Painter, circa 460–450 BC

Source: Hamburg, Museum für Kunst und Gewerbe 1900.164. *ARV2* 880.4,1673; *Para* 428; *Add2* 301. Photograph: Museum für Kunst und Gewerbe Hamburg

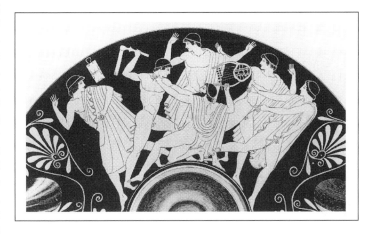

Figure 4.6   Attic red-figure cup by Douris, depicting the murder of the music teacher Linos by Herakles while his classmates look on aghast, circa 480–470 BC

Source: Munich, Antikenslg. 2646. *ARV2* 437.128, 1653; *Para* 375; *Add2* 239. Photograph: after A. Furtwängler and K. Reichhold *Griechische Vasenmalerei* II, Munich: Bruckmann, 1909, pl. 105

Herakles killing his music master Linos as his classmates look on.

While the adolescent Herakles and his classmates are represented here with the same iconographic type as that often used to denote a young adult male, it is equally true elsewhere that the adolescent male may also be represented with the iconographic type of the pre-pubertal male. Again, the most concise illustration of this may be drawn from the

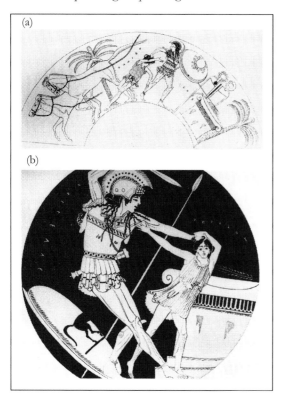

Figure 4.7   Attic red-figure cup by Onesimos. Reconstructed drawings depicting (a) the fight between Achilles and Troilos (exterior scene) and (b) the death of Troilos at the hands of Achilles (interior scene), circa 490 BC

Source: Perugia, Museo Civico 89. *ARV2* 320.8; *Para* 359; *Add2* 214. Photograph: (a) after W. Klein *Euphronios*, Vienna: Carl Gerold's Sohn, 1886, pp. 214. (b) after E. Gerhard *Auserlesene Griechische Vasenbilder III*, Berlin: Reimer, 1847, pl. CCXXVI

mythological corpus since the mythological tradition often provides us with information about the life-stage that individual personalities had reached when specific and recognisable events occurred. In the case of the Trojan prince Troilos, adolescence is clearly marked by the mythological tradition as the life-stage he had reached when killed by Achilles. Sophokles, for example, labels him as 'ανδροπαις' (andropais), literally 'man child', an identification which places him at the juncture between childhood and adulthood in late adolescence (Pearson 1917: 253–61). Amongst the representations of Troilos' death in art are two scenes on an Athenian painted cup of the early fifth century. On the exterior of the cup (Figure 4.7a) Troilos appears in the fully grown guise of a young adult male as his aggressor Achilles' equal, while on the interior (Figure 4.7b) his boyish figure contrasts markedly with that of Achilles. Both interior and exterior scenes show different moments from the same violent episode, suggesting that in these representations of the young Troilos we are presented here with the two faces of adolescence, the juvenile (cup interior) and the mature (exterior).

In fifth century Athenian art, then, the representation of adolescence is highly ambiguous and often identifiable only through an examination of the wider pictorial context, particularly in the case of the male figure. Since easily recognisable iconographic types exist for the depiction of infancy, pre-pubertal childhood, mature adulthood and also of old age, we might therefore ask why such ambivalence exists in the representation of the adolescent life-stage. Might it perhaps reflect classical Athenian awareness of adolescence as a liminal developmental stage and as a state which eluded easy definition? Or might it, conversely, be a reflection of the absence of a conscious concept of adolescence?

THE SOCIO-HISTORICAL CONTEXT

Examination of fifth century Athenian sociological realities involved in the individual's transition from childhood to adulthood suggests that there was certainly no absence of the conceptual awareness of 'adolescence' as a liminal and transitional life-stage. As such, however, particularly for the male, adolescence did indeed defy easy definition, both socially and artistically. It should be noted here that for two reasons the following discussion focuses mainly on the offspring of well-to-do Athenian citizen families. First, this is the social class about whose lives we possess most information. Second, as Garland has succinctly pointed out, 'The economically depressed and the socially downtrodden have neither the motivation, leisure nor means to dramatise life's divisions as do those who enjoy high economic and social status' (Garland 1990: 290).[4] It is therefore very likely that the children of poor, non-citizen or slave families were, through the necessity of being put out to work as soon as they were physically able, integrated into the adult world at a much earlier age than their more socially and economically favoured counterparts (Cambiano 1995).

For the female, the biological end of childhood conferred upon her a new status, that of the marriageable *parthenos*, in which 'maiden' state she was considered to be neither child nor adult woman. Her transformation from this adolescent identity to the state of adult womanhood was effected by her marriage, often around age 15 to a man commonly twice her age, and the subsequent birth of her first child. The adolescent transitional phase between childhood and adulthood was thus, for the Athenian female, a relatively short-lived and readily defined phase dependent on clear and definitive changes in her biological and social status.

The point of transition of the male from adolescence to full adult manhood was less clear cut, being variously defined according to the civic and legal, social, or biological context. Furthermore, the adolescent phase was a far lengthier and more extended life-stage for the Athenian male than for his female counterpart. The reason underlying this gender-differentiated experience of adolescence centred on the fundamentally different roles which would be assumed by male and female respectively on the attainment of adulthood. The Athenian female's life and responsibilities concentrated on the private sphere of home and family. As wife and mother she attended to the well-ordered running of the household and the raising of children and heirs. She had no part to play in the public, political and military organisation and concerns of the Athenian state. Accordingly, her youthful preparation for the assumption of her adult responsibilities took place within the private domain of the household. It involved learning from her mother and female relatives the skills and knowledge she would need on the day she was separated from her paternal home and removed to that of her husband. Many of her growing years were spent in acquiring this necessary training and her arrival at puberty confirmed her biological readiness to make the transition to womanhood. For her, the adolescent condition as a pubertal *parthenos* constituted a dangerous liminal phase when she must be protected both from external male threat and also, it was perceived, from her own instability (Garland 1990: 168–9). Thus, ideally the female adolescent life-stage should be as short-lived as possible.

By contrast, the Athenian male youth was destined for a life in the public, rather than the private sphere. His acculturation to full adult status required his complete, and therefore necessarily gradual, absorption into the civic and legal fabric of Athens, and into the network of social interrelationships that formed the basis of the many institutions which constituted the Athenian state. Like the female, the male's training for his future adult role began early in life. But, unlike the female, already around age 7 the focus of his training shifted to the world beyond the confines of the family home, when he was sent to one or more of a number of private schools where his education in reading, writing, music and athletics continued over a period of several years (Cambiano 1995). As far as we can tell, there was no set school-leaving age. A reference in Plato (*Protagoras* 326c) attests that the duration of the individual's schooling depended on the ability of his father to continue to pay for it. Furthermore, in the second half of the fifth century 'higher education' for older youths at the hands of a philosopher became an increasingly popular way in which the sons of wealthier Athenian families gained the public speaking skills essential to a successful adult life in the public sphere. Philosophical training, at its most practical, and as taught by the Sophists, consisted of lessons in rhetoric – the art of presenting a convincing argument – a talent invaluable for political life or for appearance in the law courts. In a less formal sense, the homosexual experience was sometimes also regarded as educationally valuable for Athenian boys and adolescent males. Becoming the focus of an adult male's attentions involved not only gaining a sexual education (forbidden to girls until after marriage), but could also provide the youth with a role model of the behaviour, standards and knowledge that he should aspire to. Homosexuality therefore had its part to play in the transition and development from boyhood to manhood (Golden 1990: 57–62; Buffière 1980; Dover 1978).

The gradual absorption of the young male into the public sphere, with its complex network of social interrelationships, privileges and obligations, took an early and major step forward on the occasion of the introduction of the youth into the *phratry*, or wider kinship group, to which his family belonged. This seems to have happened on two occasions, both within the ritual context of the festival of the *Apatouria*: first in infancy, and later in adolescence probably around age 16. This process required the father, in the presence of other *phratry* members, to swear an oath concerning his son's legitimacy. The adolescent youth's hair was also cut in the ritual of the *koureotis* and dedicated to Artemis, a goddess with particular responsibility for overseeing the passage of the individual from childhood to adulthood. This symbolic cutting of the hair most likely served as public confirmation that the youth had reached puberty, or adolescence, and had therefore left childhood behind him (Garland 1990: 179–80; Golden 1990: 26–9, and n.16; Cole 1984; Labarbe 1953). Though his legal position as a minor remained unchanged, the acceptance of the youth by his *phratry* nevertheless conferred on him a new status, which indicated his ripening potential soon to assume his rightful place within the Athenian citizen body.

The next recognised stage in the male youth's transition to adulthood took place in his eighteenth year and effected major changes in his civic and legal status. It involved his official enrolment in the *deme* (township) register as an Athenian citizen and conferred upon him voting rights as a member of the Athenian Assembly. Whereas his earlier admission to the *phratry* had taken place in a ritual and social context and had introduced him to broader, though passive, membership of Athenian society, his acceptance onto the *deme* register signalled civic and legal recognition of his new-found status as an active player in determining the fortunes of his city. Attaining the age of majority also meant reaching the age of legal accountability and privilege and resulted in him no longer being subject to his father's authority (Garland 1990: 180–83; Golden 1990: 38–40).

These major changes in his civic and legal position also carried with them certain obligations. One of the most important was the Athenian state's requirement that he fulfil a two-year period of military service as an *ephebe* (mentioned above). Significantly, even though he had been officially admitted to the ranks of the adult male citizen on reaching his eighteenth year, it seems that this period of military training served, at least in part, as a rite of passage overseeing his transition from adolescent youth to early manhood. The underlying reasons for this can be easily deduced. For the first time in an Athenian male's life, he was separated from his family and grouped together for an extended period of time in the company of his peers in a competitive, combative environment which measured him against those peers. This formed a model for his future adult life as an Athenian citizen, playing a full role – open only to men – in the political, civic and military life of Athens. As Vidal-Naquet (1981a, 1981b) has pointed out, the liminal status of the *ephebe* was underscored by his posting in his second year of service to the outlying districts of Attica, far from the centre of the city, to protect the borders of the state. He was also set apart from the mature fighting men of Athens by the requirement that he wear a special uniform of black *chlamys*, or short cloak. On completion of his two-year training period, he then joined the reserve ranks of the adult male *hoplite*, or citizen foot soldier, ready to be called upon in times of war to fight shoulder to shoulder for Athens alongside the other adult citizen soldiers. It is important to note that although prior to undertaking his military training he had been enrolled as an Athenian citizen, almost immediately thereafter many of his civic duties and rights were suspended until his two-year period of ephebic service was complete. Only then, it seems, had he proved himself in practice worthy to be an adult citizen member of the Athenian state.

This analysis of the Athenian male youth's development shows quite clearly that no abrupt dividing line existed between childhood and adult manhood. Although the official legal endpoint of childhood was reached in the male's eighteenth year, the years between the onset of puberty and the fulfilment of his military service – roughly between the ages of 13 or 14 and 20 – seem to have constituted an adolescent phase of ambiguous, liminal social status when the youth was considered to be neither truly child nor man.[5] By the time he attained his twentieth year, the young male was certainly in biological terms, and in many civic and legal respects, regarded as a man. Nevertheless, in certain civic aspects and in social terms, he was not deemed to have passed completely through the dangerous liminal developmental stage of youth until he was 30 (Cantarella 1990). Only then, for example, was it frequently the case that he took on the adult state and responsibilities of marriage and fatherhood. Only then did he become eligible for jury service and for membership of the Athenian *Boule*, or Council. The decade of life between ages 20 and 30 was clearly, therefore, perceived to incorporate adolescent traits within the early adult phase.

CONCLUSION

Let us, then, try to synthesise our observations on the ambiguous artistic representation of adolescence with the fifth century Athenian perception of the adolescent life-stage as it has emerged thus far through the examination of the sociological realities involved in the individual's transition from childhood to adulthood. Adolescence can perhaps best be defined as the phase of life in which tension exists between the contradictory and co-existing juvenile and mature states of being. For the Athenian female, adolescence was that short period – in some cases lasting as little as one or two years – in which biological maturity (the pubertal state) and social immaturity (the unmarried state) existed side by side. For the male, adolescence covered a much longer period, throughout the whole length of which he too was biologically mature. For him, however, adolescence did not fully come to an end until not only biological and social maturity, but also mature legal and civic status, had been attained. Therefore, from the onset of puberty around age 13 or 14 to his arrival at the age of legal majority in his eighteenth year, and even thereafter for another two years until the required period of military training had been completed, the Athenian male youth underwent an extended developmental phase intended to prepare him for his adult life in the public sphere. Furthermore, even in the early adult years represented by the third decade of life, juvenile character flaws were considered to persist. Hence, throughout this period certain social responsibilities and civic privileges were best withheld.

This contrast in the respective brief and extended nature of female and male adolescence is further underscored by a comparison of the gender specific age terminologies in use in the ancient Greek language for young people of pubertal age (Cantarella 1990; Golden 1990: 12–22, 67–72; Garland 1990: 1–6). Whereas for the male there existed nomenclature for a wide, though imprecise and often overlapping, range of age classes which denoted many various stages between puberty and the close of the third decade of life when the individual entered into his fully mature adult state, for the female who had attained puberty there existed only two named classes: *parthenos* (marriageable pubertal female) and *nymphe* (the period from betrothal to the birth of the first child) (Garland 1990: 200). From that point on, despite her tender years – usually still in her teens – the female was regarded as a fully adult woman for whom developmental age classes had no relevance. As a result, the iconography of female adolescence deals essentially with the visual characterisation of a single, well-defined life-stage. For the male, however, youth was an extended period stretching over many years and involving the gradual replacement of juvenile traits and status with maturity. Adolescence was not therefore a static state, but rather a period of flux during which the individual passed through greater to lesser degrees of juvenility.

Faced with the task of giving artistic form to this most complex of life-stages, the classical Athenian artist made little attempt to create absolute and restrictive iconographic types for the male adolescent, but rather adapted his depiction of the youthful state according to the requirements of the representational context. Returning to the two examples of the pictorial depiction of the adolescent male in Figures 4.6 and 4.7, we can see that in Figure 4.6, the murder of his music teacher by Herakles, the emphasis is laid on the biological and physical maturity of the young Herakles combining dangerously with the rash, violent, uneven temper that was believed to characterise youth (Aristotle *Rhetoric* 2.12.3–16). In this mythological context there is of course also reference to the prodigious strength that was in adulthood to become Herakles' trademark. In Figure 4.7, the fight between Achilles and Troilos, the latter is depicted in the guise of an adult fighting man as long as the battle between the combatants is relatively evenly pitched. However, at the moment of Troilos' death the artist stresses, for reasons of pathos, the youth of Troilos and the waste of a life that has barely yet reached maturity by depicting him as a boyish figure.

Though this is an extreme, though certainly not unparalleled, example of the artistic depiction of the two faces of adolescence, the juvenile and the mature, adapted to a particular representational context, it does underline the difficulties inherent for the modern-day viewer of classical Athenian art in attempting to differentiate the representation of childhood, adolescence and early manhood. Especially difficult is the recognition and distinction of early from late adolescence, and late adolescence from early manhood. That the ambiguity of the youthful experience and of its perception in classical Athens resulted in an often indeterminate and imprecise iconography should not, however, frustrate us. Instead it should add depth and caution to our 'reading' of these ancient images as we attempt to contextualise them both within their representational and socio-historical contexts.

Notes

1 There is indisputable evidence for the existence of the Athenian *ephebeia* only from the fourth century onwards. However, there was undoubtedly a fifth century equivalent (see Garland 1990: 183–7; Vidal-Naquet 1981a and b; Pélékidis 1962; Reinmuth 1971: 123–38; Roussel 1921; Brenot 1920).

2 Lissarrague (1990: 164–72, 205–210) also identifies a second iconographic type of the *ephebos* figure on a series of Athenian vases dating to around 510 BC.

3 In classical Athenian art the mature adult male is shown as a figure of full and well-developed stature who, depending on the context, may be partly or completely nude or, alternatively, clothed in one of a variety of long or short garments. If nude, he is usually endowed with a growth of pubic hair. He often has short hair and a beard.

4 The fact that social class affected the iconography, as well as the experience, of youth in ancient Athens is vividly illustrated by reference to the sculpted *kouros* figure in use between the late seventh and early fifth centuries BC. During this period the *kouros* constituted a well-defined iconographic type employed for the representation of male youth. Significantly, when used to represent mortal youth, it carried with it implications of aristocratic lineage and high social class. It is, therefore, no coincidence that the period of its popularity covers roughly the years of oligarchic and tyrannical rule at Athens. When this came to an end with the democratic reforms of Kleisthenes in the late sixth century BC, the *kouros* gradually lost its popularity and youth was robbed of this particularly distinct artistic form.

5 Since male competitors in the athletic games held as part of the Panathenaic, Nemean and Isthmian festivals were divided into three age classes, namely *paides* or children, *ageneioi* or beardless youths and *andres* or men, it would be revealing to know the age limits of these classes. Unfortunately, however, the ancient sources do not help us on this point (see Golden 1990: 67–72).

Abbreviations

Add2   Carpenter, T.H. (1989) *Beazley Addenda*, Oxford: Oxford University Press.
ARV2   Beazley, J.D. (1963) *Attic Red-Figure Vase-Painters*, 2nd edn, Oxford: Clarendon Press.
Para   Beazley, J.D. (1971) *Paralipomena*, Oxford: Clarendon Press.

References

Aristotle *Rhetoric* (1959) *The 'Art' of Rhetoric*, trans. J.H. Freese, Loeb Classical Library, London: Heinemann.

Beaumont, L.A. (1994) 'Constructing a methodology for the interpretation of childhood age in classical Athenian iconography', *Archaeological Review from Cambridge* 13(2): 81–96.

—— (1998) 'Born old or never young? Femininity, childhood and the goddesses of ancient Greece', in S. Blundell and M. Williamson (eds) *The Sacred and the Feminine in Ancient Greece*, London: Routledge, pp. 71–95.

Brenot, A. (1920) *Recherches sur l'Ephébie Attique et en Particulier sur la Date de l'Institution*, Paris: Champion.

Buffière, F. (1980) *Eros Adolescent: La Pédérastie dans la Grèce Antique*, Paris: Les Belles Lettres.

Cambiano, G. (1995) 'Becoming an adult', in J.P. Vernant (ed.) *The Greeks*, trans. C. Lambert and T. Lavender Fagan, Chicago and London: University of Chicago Press, pp. 86–119.

Cantarella, E. (1990) '"Neaniskoi". Classi di età e passaggi di "status" nel diritto Ateniese', *Mélanges d'Archéologie et d'Histoire de l'Ecole Française de Rome, Antiquité*, 102(1): 37–51.

Clairmont, C. (1993) *Classical Attic Tombstones*, Kilchberg: Akanthus.

Cole, S. G. (1984) 'The social function of rituals of maturation: the *koureion* and the *arkteia*', *Zeitschrift fur Papyrologie und Epigraphik* 55: 233–44.

Dover, K. (1978) *Greek Homosexuality*, Cambridge, Mass.: Duckworth.

Eyben, E. (1972) 'Antiquity's view of puberty', *Latomus* 31: 677–97.

Garland, R. (1990) *The Greek Way of Life*, London: Duckworth.

—— (1991) Juvenile delinquency in the Graeco-Roman world, *History Today* October 1991: 12–19.

Golden, M. (1990) *Children and Childhood in Classical Athens*, Baltimore and London: Johns Hopkins University Press.

Kleijwegt, M. (1991) *Ancient Youth: The Ambiguity of Youth and the Absence of Adolescence in Greco-Roman Society*, Amsterdam: Gieben.

Labarbe, J. (1953) 'L'âge correspondant au sacrifice du κούρειον et les données historiques di sixième discours d'Isee', *Bulletin de l'Académie Royale de Belgique: Classe des Lettres* 39: 359–94.

Lissarrague, F. (1990) *L'Autre Guerrier*, Paris–Rome: Editions La Decouverte, Ecole Française de Rome.

Oxford English Dictionary (1991) *The Compact English Dictionary*, 2nd edn, Oxford: Clarendon Press.

Pearson, A.C. (ed.) (1917) *The Fragments of Sophocles II*, Cambridge: Cambridge University Press.

Pélékidis, C. (1962) *Histoire de l'Ephébie Attique des Origines à 31 Avant J.C.*, Paris: Ecole France Athènes, Travaux et Memoires 13.

Plato *Protagoras* (1937) in *Plato IV*, trans. W.R.M. Lamb, Loeb Classical Library, London: Heinemann.

Reinmuth, O.W. (1952) 'The genesis of the Athenian ephebeia', *Transactions of the American Philological Association* 83: 34-50.

—— (1971) *The Ephebic Inscriptions of the Fourth Century* BC, *Mnemosyne* Suppl. 14, Leiden.

Roussel, P. (1921) 'Review of Brenot 1920', *Revue des Etudes Grecques* 34: 459–60.

Sourvinou-Inwood, C. (1988) *Studies in Girls' Transitions: Aspects of the Arkteia and Age Representation in Attic Iconography*, Athens: Kardamitsa.

Van Hoorn, G. (1951) *Choes and Anthesteria*, Leiden: Brill.

Vidal-Naquet, P. (1981a) 'The black hunter and the origins of the Athenian *ephebeia*', in R.L. Gordon (ed.) *Myth, Religion and Society,* Cambridge: Cambridge University Press, pp. 147–62.

—— (1981b) 'Recipes for Greek adolescence', in R.L. Gordon (ed.) *Myth, Religion and Society*, Cambridge: Cambridge University Press, pp. 163–85.

Part III

The transmission of knowledge

Chapter 5

Apprentice flintknapping

Relating material culture and social practice in the Upper Palaeolithic

Linda Grimm

INTRODUCTION

When the topic of children in the Upper Palaeolithic is discussed, it is often in terms of the most spectacular kinds of evidence, such as the elaborate (and highly atypical) Sungir burials (Bader 1978), or the preservation of a child's footprint in the clay floor of a painted cave (Garcia and Courtaud 1990). These kinds of evidence are extremely rare and their very scarcity serves to reinforce the view that knowledge about children in prehistory is inaccessible (Lillehammer 1989; Sofaer Derevenski 1994a; Moore and Scott 1997). However, this is not an accurate picture of either our present or prospective knowledge of the activities of children in late glacial prehistory. As I hope this discussion will make clear, lithic technology has a unique potential, among all the technologies employed by Upper Palaeolithic peoples, for aiding us in our efforts both to identify children and to investigate their world.

This chapter examines the case of an apprentice flintknapper from the French Upper Palaeolithic open-air site of Solvieux, Dordogne (Sackett 1988, 1999) within an analytical framework that emphasises both the technical aspects of core reduction and the social context within which such activity was pursued. The *chaîne opératoire* approach (Leroi-Gourhan 1964, 1965) provides a means for evaluating the technical details of this flintknapping episode. In turn, this analysis provides the necessary empirical foundation for exploring a social practice theory of apprentice learning, a theme developed in the second half of this chapter. This approach is consistent with the view recently articulated by Dobres and Hoffman (1994) that technology should be studied as an integral and active part of social reproduction and change (see also Lillehammer 1989; Pfaffenberger 1992; Lemonnier 1993).

APPRENTICE FLINTKNAPPERS IN THE ARCHAEOLOGICAL RECORD

Chipped stone technologies have the potential to contribute to locating children in the archaeological record in several important ways. First, stone is a fairly abundant natural resource that is often relatively easy to obtain and which, under normal circumstances, can be worked by novices without risk of serious injury. Second, the durable nature of stone, as well as the sequential and subtractive character of chipped stone technology, ensures that information relevant to knapping skill will be preserved on lithic artefactual material recovered from archaeological sites. It is widely recognised that flintknapping is a techno-logical activity which requires a great deal of practice before good results can be achieved consistently (Pelegrin 1990; Shelley 1990; Whittaker 1994). Thus, there is a general consensus that knapping practice begins early in the life cycle, that is, during childhood and adolescence (Pigeot 1990; Karlin and Julien 1994).

Given the need for a lengthy apprenticeship period, it is not surprising that a number of presumed novice knapping episodes have been identified in the archaeological record, especially by prehistorians working in late Palaeolithic contexts in Western Europe. Fischer (1989), for example, describes a case from Trollesgave, Denmark in an archaeolog-ical horizon belonging to the Bromme complex. However, the most extensive evidence for children as flintknappers comes from the Paris Basin where researchers at late Magdalenian sites such as Pincevent and Étiolles (Bodu *et al.* 1990; Bodu 1996; Karlin and Pigeot 1989; Olive 1988; Pigeot 1990) have engaged in extensive refitting studies (Cziela *et al.* 1990; Villa 1991; Hofman and Enloe 1992; Schlanger 1996). These have led to the identification of knapping events attributed to flintknappers ranging from tentative beginners to masters of the craft. Distinctions in skill level are based on detailed analyses of refitted ensembles conducted within the framework of the *chaîne opératoire*, or opera-tional chain (Pelegrin *et al.* 1988; Boëda *et al.* 1990; Karlin *et al.* 1991, 1993; Karlin and Julien 1994; Schlanger 1990, 1994). This approach seeks to reconstruct the organisation of a technological system, including all processes from the initial procurement of raw material, through tool manufacture, use, and discard. It thus provides a framework for describing the structures of specific sequences of action in material, temporal and spatial terms (Edmonds 1990).

The assumption that cores were normally shaped and worked by one person (Bodu *et al.* 1990), leads to two related notions in the 'techno-sociological' version (Karlin and Julien 1994: 159) of the *chaîne opératoire*. First, individual knappers can be identified in the archaeological record. Second, their movements can be traced across occupation surfaces on the basis of the spatial distribution of blanks produced from the cores they worked. A suite of characteristics has emerged from this research which serves to distinguish novice knappers from experienced ones: novices exhibit limited control over basic technical prin-ciples, they do not produce useful products or have access to good quality raw material, and they tend to work in locations that are peripheral with respect to adult work spaces. Each of these characteristics is discussed below.

Lack of control over basic technical principles is reflected in errors in both conception and execution in the knapping process. The reduction strategies pursued by novices are often incompletely or inadequately conceptualised. This is marked by indications of tenta-tive behaviour which result in removals which terminate prematurely in hinge or step fractures, rather than in the feather terminations that characterise the work of accom-plished knappers. Bulbs of percussion tend to be more strongly marked in the work of beginners and flakes frequently carry thick remnants of the striking platform. Both of these features suggest the use of hard hammer percussion as well as the application of excessive force. Within the framework of blade production technology, novices commonly fail to maintain either the proper platform angle or the differentiation of the striking platform and the blade production face. Commonly, novices do not attend systematically to either core maintenance during the reduction process or overall core organisation.

Non-productivity is a concept that refers to the failure of novices to produce blanks that can be put to use as tools, either directly or through additional modification. Typically, the debitage clusters of novice knappers are recovered virtually complete, a result of the debitage products having been abandoned at the knapping post (unlike the widely disseminated products of experienced knappers). This suggests that, in the apprentice case, the goal was not necessarily the production of usable tool blanks but rather gaining the experience that knapping itself provided (Pigeot 1990; Bodu *et al.* 1990). Another expression of non-productivity is seen in the tendency for apprentice knappers to abandon cores prematurely, largely because of knapping accidents and the novice's inability to conceptualise adequate solutions to problems (Bodu *et al.* 1990; Shelley 1990).

In addition, novice knapping activity can be distinguished from that of skilled workers in terms of the quality of the raw material that is associated with it. A good knapper's superior ability is reflected at every stage of the technological process beginning with the selection of raw material, which is ideally the appropriate size, shape and quality for an intended product. Apprentice knappers appear to have had limited access to good quality raw material; they either worked inferior material or reworked material that had been abandoned for one reason or another by more accomplished knappers (Pigeot 1990; Karlin *et al.* 1993).

Finally, novice knappers tended to pursue their exercises in spatial locations which were peripheral to the hearth-centred activity zones that appear to typify the open-air occupations of the Paris Basin sites (Pigeot 1990; Bodu *et al.* 1990).

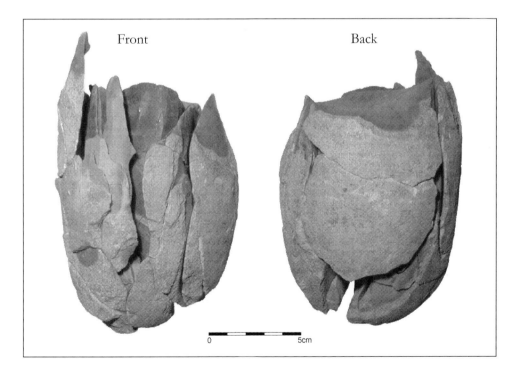

Figure 5.1   Core 5 (two views)

Source: Photograph: Linda Grimm

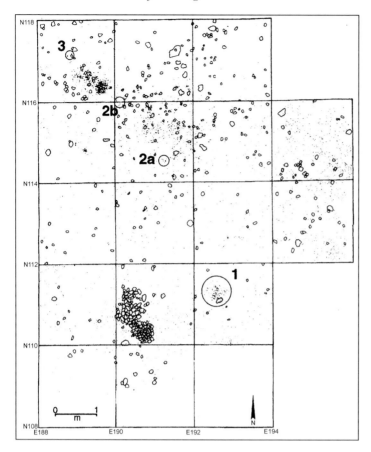

Figure 5.2   Rock plan with knapping locations

The Solvieux apprentice knapper is known from a single reduction event that is designated Core 5 (Figure 5.1). It was recovered in a Perigordian V (Raysse) occupation (Grimm and Koetje 1992), and is composed of 27 pieces recovered from three locations across the occupation (Figure 5.2). The majority of the pieces come from a well-defined concentration in the south-east corner of the exposure (Location 1), while the remaining pieces, representing the last stages of this core reduction event, derive from the north-west area of the excavation: medial and distal portions of a crested blade were recovered together at Location 2a, the last flake removal was found at Location 2b, and the spent nucleus, broken into two fragments, was found at Location 3. Core 5 shares many features with other apprentice cases reported from the Paris Basin sites.

Within the *chaîne opératoire* approach, the standard device for detailing the knapping sequence and assessing the skill of the knapper is the diacritical diagram, an interpretive drawing of a core which shows the directions of scars (the negatives of previous removals) as well as their sequence of removal (Karlin and Julien 1994; Schlanger 1994). Figure 5.3 is a diacritical diagram describing Core 5, showing three views of the refitted core as well as one of the nucleus as it appeared towards the end of the reduction process. A flake by flake analysis reveals many errors in execution typical of apprentice knapping including thick and broad removals that encroach deeply into the main body of the core. A hard hammer technique, delivered with excessive force, is reflected in strongly marked bulbs of percussion. In addition, flakes carry significant remnants of the striking platform and often end in hinge rather than feather terminations. Nonetheless, the Core 5 novice seems to have had some conception of the debitage modalities of Perigordian blade technology, which generally include a narrow core with straight-edged flanks, opposed striking platforms, and preparation of reduced striking points (Pelegrin 1990). For example, we may interpret the groups of flakes removed from each side of the core by the novice as an attempt to give proper form to the flanks (Figure 5.3 front and back views), while the other two features – preparation of both opposed platforms and striking points – remain

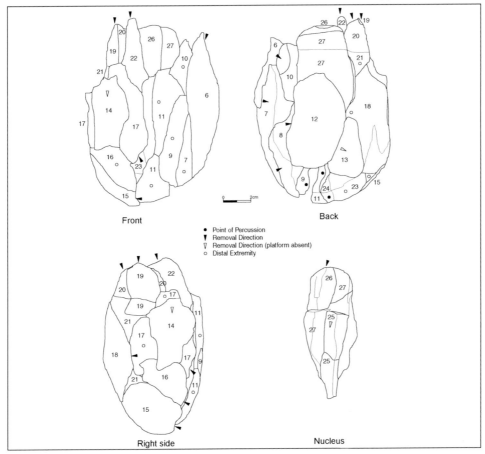

Figure 5.3 Core 5 diacritical diagram

essentially unexpressed in this knapping exercise.

As documented for other novice episodes, the Core 5 knapper appears to have had limited access to good quality raw material. Indeed, details of the reduction sequence strongly suggest that the Core 5 novice knapper adopted a core that had been worked initially by an expert knapper. This interpretation follows from a careful evaluation of five decortication flakes recovered in the Location 1 concentration which actually represent the first five removals in the reduction sequence as reconstructed through refitting. These removals, as well as the preparation of the striking plat-form, must be referred to a competent

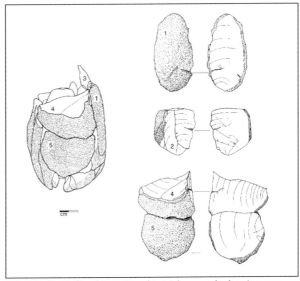

Figure 5.4 Refitted Core 5 and initial removals showing raw material flaw

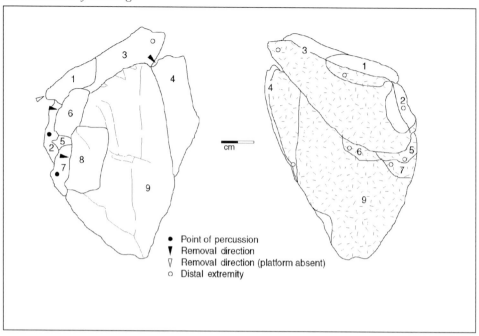

Figure 5.5   Diacritical diagram of Core 8

knapper on the basis of the substantial skill that their removal entailed. In fact, these removals appear to reflect the expert knapper's systematic exploration of a raw material flaw (Figure 5.4), which apparently was judged to be of sufficient magnitude that the nodule was abandoned. The continuing presence of the flaw would frustrate the novice's own efforts to achieve productivity from this core. Indeed, the final blow to the core, as recovered in Location 3, split it into two pieces along the flawed surface.

Two additional features that are considered to be typical of apprentice knapping activity are manifested by Core 5; most work occurred in a marginal precinct, away from a zone of heavy core reduction activity that occupied the northern half of the exposure, and the episode was largely non-productive, for the majority of knapping products were recovered within the Location 1 concentration. Thus, Core 5 nicely fits the profile of an apprentice flintknapper.

At the same time, several features set the Core 5 knapping event apart from others that have been reported in the literature. For example, while premature core abandonment may have been typical of many apprentice knapping episodes, it was not the case with Core 5. Here the reduction process was carried to the limit, for the spent core was worked to the lithic equivalent of the nubbin by the time it was abandoned at Location 3. In addition, technical details suggest that the novice knapper's movement to Location 2 may reflect the search for expert assistance in the preparation and removal of a crested blade – both expertly achieved – which would have been the next logical technical step in the creation of a blade production face on this core.

Numerous other knapping ensembles from this occupation have been restored to varying degrees through refitting; the majority of them appear to have been worked by skilled knappers and they occur primarily within the zone of heavy core reduction already

Table 5.1 Summary of core products and their spatial distribution

Location	Core 5 products	Interpretation	Core 8 products	Interpretation
Unknown	Initial removals and platform preparation (no flakes recovered)	Executed by expert knapper		
1	Decortication flakes (removals #1–5)	Exploration of flaw leads expert knapper to discard core	Platform preparation flakes (removals #1–6)	Expert knapper prepares striking platform
			Flake struck from right side of core (removal #7)	Core flank preparation
	Core preparation flakes: (removals #6–11 from right flank; removals #13–24 from left flank)	Novice attempts to establish blade production face through preparation of parallel flanks on either side of core		
	Flake struck perpendicular to long axis from core back (removal #12)	Maintenance of core back related to preparation of parallel flanks		
2a	Medial and distal portions of crested blade (removal #25)	Crest shaped and blade removed most likely by an expert knapper		
2b	Flake struck from blade production face (removal # 26)	Flake hinged off due to presence of flaw	Flake struck from left side of core (removal #8)	Expert knapper fails to rejuvenate left margin of blade production face
3	Core abandonment (#27: nucleus)	Core exhausted; flaw surface exposed when core broken in two	Core abandonment (#9: nucleus)	Expert knapper discards exhausted core

mentioned. Among these, Core 8 is noteworthy for a potential behavioural connection to the Core 5 reduction activity. While it has been possible to refit only 8 flakes to the Core 8 nucleus, the elements constituting this ensemble gain importance by virtue of their spatial locations, which coincide with those of Core 5. At Location 1 (Figure 5.2),

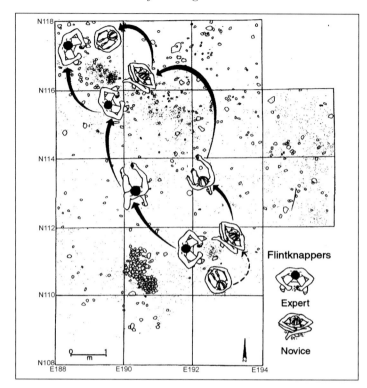

Figure 5.6   Cores 5 and 8 behavioural scenario

seven flakes related to initial core shaping and platform preparation were excavated, while a sidestruck flake, the last removal from this skillfully worked core, was found at Location 2 only centimetres away from the final flake struck from Core 5. Finally, the abandoned Core 8 nucleus was recovered at Location 3, also within a few centimetres of the fractured Core 5 one. Core 8 was a productive blade core, exhibiting all of the standard Perigordian debitage modalities, as indicated in the diacritical diagram of Figure 5.5. No blades could be refitted to it, presumably indicating that they were either modified into tools or curated for use at some future time.

BEHAVIOURAL SCENARIOS

The intriguing patterns of association between Cores 5 and 8 are summarised in Table 5.1. Within the framework of the *chaîne opératoire*, as previously described, we may ask what these patterns tell us about children as flintknapping apprentices at Solvieux. I evaluate this through the use of a heuristic device in the form of two mutually exclusive behavioural scenarios, which attempt to account for the material, temporal and spatial details that connect the two cores.

One behavioural scenario that is suggested by the Core 5 and 8 patterns is graphically depicted in Figure 5.6. Here, two knappers, one an expert, the other a novice, worked side by side at three locations. At Location 1, the novice's initial role may have been as an observer of the expert who worked Cores 5 (removals 1–5) and 8 (removals 1–7), in succession, before the expert departed with Core 8 for the knapping zone in the north-west quadrant. Upon the expert's departure, the novice became an active agent who knapped 17 flakes from the abandoned core. Uncertain of how to proceed, the novice next sought expert assistance in the preparation and removal of a crested blade at Location 2.[1] Finally, their labours complete, the two knappers sat together at Location 3 to review their work before moving on to other activities, leaving their respective waste cores side by side.

A second possibility is that the concentration at Location 1 is merely a refuse deposit of material that had been worked elsewhere in the occupation and later transported here for disposal. Such residual scatters are seen by archaeologists as the products of housekeeping practices where flaking waste is collectively discarded in secondary locations (Bodu *et*

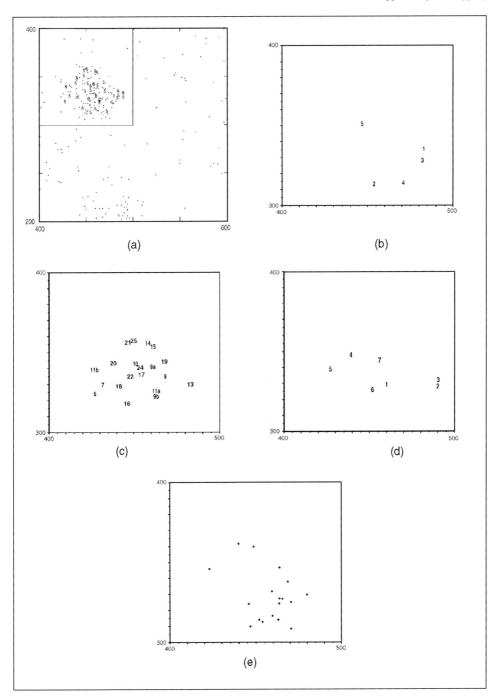

Figure 5.7   Location 1 knapping concentration: (a) whole concentration; (b) Core 5 removals 1–5; (c) Core 5 removals 6–24; (d) Core 8 removals 1–7: (e) nine refit clusters

al. 1990; Schmider and Croisset 1990). Under these circumstances, refitted groups of primary debitage such as flakes and blades may not be indicative of *in situ* knapping activity. Rather, debris that results from core faceting is considered to be more directly diagnostic of primary flaking locations (Villa 1991: 27). In this instance, however, the low frequency of small-fraction debris of the kind that results from core faceting activity may indicate a limited technique on the part of a novice knapper whose technical repertoire did not extend to the preparation of striking points on the core.

Furthermore, the refuse deposit scenario does not square very well with the details of artefact patterning in the Location 1 concentration. In fact, in some respects, it possesses significant characteristics of a standard knapping post. In terms of size (63 cm east–west by 45 cm north–south) and shape (Figure 5.7a), it equates well with archaeological and experimentally derived knapping scatters (Schmider and Croisset 1990; Newcomer and Sieveking 1980). Moreover, the distribution pattern of Core 5 products within the concentration seems to preserve some of the sequential order of a knapping event. In Figure 5.7b, the initial Core 5 removals that were earlier attributed to an expert knapper are largely localised in the south-east quadrant of the concentration. The novice knapper's work on Core 5 (Figure 5.7c), on the other hand, seems to define the shape of the concentration itself and sequential removals are found together in a non-random pattern that is more consistent with knapping than discard behaviour.

The spatial distribution of nine additional clusters of refitted primary debitage, totalling 22 items, further complicates the effort to interpret the Location 1 concentration. Included here are several groups of large decortication flakes and conjoined blade segments, platform rejuvenation flakes, and an intact crested blade which is the only piece of the 22 that conjoins with material outside the concentration. As Figure 5.7e indicates, this miscellaneous collection exhibits a distribution pattern that most closely approximates a discard pile, and it is located mainly south and east of the area occupied by the novice's work on Core 5. Finally, the Core 8 products also seem to be dispersed more or less randomly across the concentration (Figure 5.7d). We will consider these patterns again towards the end of the chapter.

APPRENTICESHIP AS SOCIAL PRACTICE

In reality, the question of what these various patterns mean in terms of human activity cannot be investigated simply by reference to the character of the debitage or its spatial patterns, for each one carries sociological implications which must be examined within the broader contexts in which technological production was situated (Edmonds 1990). Dobres and Hoffman (1994: 237) suggest that a social theory of human agency is necessary to contextualise the *chaîne opératoire* and make it anthropologically relevant (see also Johnson 1989; Edmonds 1990; Dobres 1995; Gamble 1998). In their view, practice theory (Bourdieu 1977; Giddens 1979; Ortner 1984), with its focus on micro-scale processes of daily life (such as tool manufacture, use and discard), can serve as a point of departure for archaeological studies of the sociality of technology (Dobres and Hoffman 1994; see also Lightfoot *et al.* 1998).

A social practice theory of learning recently formulated by Lave and Wenger (1991), two scholars of cognitive science, provides a basis for exploring the social dynamics of prehistoric flintknapping. Here, learning is seen as an aspect of all activities rather than as a special process that goes on in situations where explicit instruction is given. Learning and knowledge, as in other accounts of situated cognition, are viewed as relations between individuals and their social contexts. Lave and Wenger identify a particular feature of these relations as crucial for learning which they refer to as 'Legitimate Peripheral Participation' or LPP (ibid.: 34–36). Learning occurs through apprentices engaging in the real practices of experts. Through this practice, learners move from being peripheral to being fully participating members of a community. Learning occurs in a 'participation framework' among a community of participants rather than in the minds of individuals. Accordingly, the goals of research on learning should be to describe the structure of participation frameworks and to seek to discover what people learn in these frameworks (ibid.).

While a comprehensive assessment of apprentice flintknapping is beyond the scope of this chapter, I will explore two aspects of LPP with regard to communities of practice in an initial effort to achieve a more dynamic account of the social relations involved in learning the craft of flintknapping. The first concerns the structuring of resources. The second explores the role of motivation and identity in apprentice learning.

The structuring of resources

How do resources shape the process and content of learning possibilities for apprentices structured under LPP? In order to address this question, two related issues need to be considered: what is the nature of the master-apprentice relationship, and on what basis do apprentices gain access to communities of practice?

No specific master-apprentice relationship is characteristic of LPP. Under some kinds of technological production, apprentices must be sponsored by masters, thereby gaining initial access to the community of practice. However, the form in which legitimate access is secured for apprentices often depends on the characteristics of the division of labour in the social milieu in which the community of practice is located (Lave and Wenger 1991: 92). According to Goody (1989), most learning in small-scale societies occurs within the domestic group, with sons learning from fathers and daughters from mothers (see also Lorber 1994). In other words, communities of practice with respect to prehistoric technology must frequently have been structured by gender distinctions (Conkey 1991; Dobres 1995; Sofaer Derevenski 1994a, 1994b, 1997).

What are the implications of this for activities that took place in the occupation at Solvieux? As mentioned previously, intense core reduction and stone tool manufacturing activities were carried out in the northern half of the occupation. Within this zone, the north-west corner in particular was an area where expert knappers produced blades and manufactured them into lithic weapon armatures (Winterman 1975). Indeed, every stage in the production sequence of gravette points has been recovered here. Recent replicative research (Perpere 1997) supports the interpretation that these tools were in fact used as elements in missile systems. Thus, the Core 5 knapper can be characterised as an apprentice in blade production technology, which in turn is part of the technology of big game hunting (Pike-Tay and Bricker 1993). If we assume, for the purposes of argument, that large mammal hunting during the Upper Palaeolithic was primarily a male domain, the apprentice knapper may be identified as a male child or adolescent whose community of practice would have included senior kin such as father and uncles as masters, along with male siblings and cousins as fellow apprentices.

The identification of blade production technology with male activities in this instance is not intended to suggest that only males were flintknappers. Nonetheless, while Upper Palaeolithic females must have utilised stone tools frequently in their daily tasks, and equally must have been capable of producing blanks for themselves (Bodu *et al.* 1990; Gero 1991; Karlin *et al.* 1993), it is unlikely that they would have needed to become highly skilled at the technology of lithic armature production. Their flintknapping would have been pursued within a separate community of practice, which directly reflected their particular activities and economic pursuits (Conkey 1991). Several archaeologists are currently exploring variables that will help to give definition to such gendered frameworks of participation in future research (Gero 1991; Bird 1993; Gorman 1995; O'Brien 1990).

According to Lave and Wenger (1991: 93), learning is itself an improvised practice that unfolds in opportunities for engagement and is given structure by work practices. The trail of Core 5 products from Location 1 to 3 is evidence that the novice knapper had access to precincts occupied by expert knappers, just as the core itself indicates access to raw material resources that would have been controlled by these same experts. Learners may also occupy a space of benign community neglect (of which Location 1 may be an example), where they configure their own learning relations with other apprentices.

The role of motivation and identity in apprentice learning

Motivation to continue and improve is generated by participation. Similarly, participation increases a sense of identification with master practitioners. LPP is therefore an initial form of membership and acceptance, as well as interaction with acknowledged adept practitioners, which makes learning legitimate and valuable from the point of view of apprentices (Lave and Wenger 1991: 110). At the same time, movement towards full participation in practice involves an increasing sense of identity as a master practitioner (ibid.: 111).

Ethnographic case studies consulted by Lave and Wenger (1991: 111) demonstrate that distinctions between play and work are often blurred for apprentices. This notion fits well with empirically based archaeological expectations about novice knapping. Play knapping provides opportunities to practice and develop both conceptual and motor skills. In the case of lithic technology, the path to full participation is a long one. It would have involved mastery of related skills (e.g. learning to throw a spear or shoot a bow and arrow) which would also have been explored through the medium of play, undertaken in the company of other apprentices (ibid.: 93; also see Lillehammer 1989).

An important aspect of LLP theory is that apprentices are seen to participate not only in a community of practitioners, but also in productive activity (Lave and Wenger 1991: 110). This latter point contrasts with Western views where children are marginalised and rarely perceived as significant participants in productive labour (Scott 1997; Sofaer Derevenski 1997). Thus, three additional characteristics of apprentice participation need to be kept in mind when describing the structure of the participation framework for apprentice knappers: even the initial, partial contributions of apprentices are useful; tasks undertaken by apprentices tend to be positioned at the end of branches of work processes rather than in the middle of linked work segments; the engagement of apprentices is limited under peripheral participation and they are only partially responsible for the end-product of the practice (Lave and Wenger 1991: 110–11; see also DeBoer 1990).

Yet, what kinds of initial or partial contributions could apprentices make that would be considered 'useful'? How should we think about apprentices as productive members of a community of practice? In a preliminary attempt to map out the participation framework of apprentice flintknapping, following Conkey's (1991: 78) 'associational strings' approach to gender roles in the Magdalenian, a list of tasks based on a general model of the Upper Palaeolithic and incorporating details pertinent to the Late Perigordian occupation at Solvieux, can be suggested. The exact tasks performed by a particular apprentice would depend on where they were in the transition from peripheral to full participation. Thus, in addition to flintknapping, a participation framework for apprentices in flint working may have involved some or all of the following activities:

1   cleaning up and discarding lithic manufacturing debris from primary work zones (Lillehammer 1989, after Whiting and Whiting 1975);
2   gathering fuel for fire-pits/hearths, around which flintknapping was often focused in the Upper Palaeolithic (Audouze *et al.* 1988; Audouze and Enloe 1997);
3   transporting non-flint stone such as quartzite from river and stream sources to the work zones of skilled knappers, where they would have been used as hammerstones and anvils in tool manufacture, or alternatively, as construction elements in hearths (Olive and Taborin 1989; Bodu 1996),[2] which provided warmth and possibly served as ad hoc facilities for heat treating flint (Grimm 1983; Griffiths *et al.* 1987;
4   collecting and preparing adhesive materials for use in hafting projectile points to shafts (Cattelain 1997; Perpere 1997), perhaps including bitumen (Boeda *et al.* 1996), or tree and plant resins that could have been gathered around campsites. Alternatively, mastics could have been prepared by cooking animal or fish glues (Bergman and McEwan 1997);
5   processing sinew for wrapping points to shafts (ibid.: 150–1);
6   gathering shed antler for use as billets and punches by master knappers (Tixier *et al.* 1980);
7   directly assisting expert flintknappers in the production of tool blanks (e.g. by supporting a core from which blades were punched) (Bordes and Crabtree 1969; Newcomer 1975) and in the manufacture of finished tools (e.g. mounting points to shafts);
8   accompanying skilled knappers to flint quarry sites to gather raw material, or on expeditions to obtain wood for spear or arrow shafts.

A FINAL ASSESSMENT

A social practice theory of apprentice learning leads us to expect that the performance of daily routines, such as those listed above, will produce patterned accumulations of material culture that are recoverable in the archaeological record. We should be able to observe the basic organisational principles of individuals in action through examination of how tools are made and used, how residential space is laid out, and how garbage disposal is organised (Lightfoot *et al.* 1998). Earlier, a scenario was proposed which relied solely on the character of refitted debitage and its spatial patterns to account for the relations between master and apprentice knappers (Figure 5.6). However, the validity of this reconstruction was called into question by contradictory artefact patterns within the Location 1 concentration. Furthermore, the scenario has the disadvantage of being too driven in its conception by a western pedagogical model – 'let me show you how it's done' – that is strongly at odds with a theory of situated learning which grounds practice in legitimate participation. There is, in fact, no logical reason why both of these activities – knapping and refuse clean-up – should not be referred to the agency of the apprentice knapper. Indeed, one could argue that the Location 1 concentration represents precisely the kind of concatenation of lithic debris that one might well expect an apprentice with a multi-faceted agenda to have produced, containing as it does the knapped remnants of a prized chunk of raw material (reject Core 5), half a dozen groups of technologically interesting large flakes, one admirably achieved crested blade and, much less interesting but nonetheless significant for its presence, a moderate collection of miscellaneous 'clean-up' debris. Thus, although part of the perceived invisibility of children is that there is a supposed difficulty in knowing what type of deposits might result from their activities in the past (Sofaer Derevenski 1994b: 8), the Location 1 concentration provides an example of just such a deposit. Moreover, it is significant that this deposit is the only evidence for housekeeping behaviour in an occupation otherwise characterised by piles of *in situ* knapping waste.

The factor of materiality (see Dobres and Hoffman 1994), appropriately, provides a basis for definitively rejecting the behavioural scenario described in Figure 5.6 as an adequate characterisation of relations between master and apprentice. The crested blade, discussed above, is the only piece in the cluster of nine refits (Figure 5.7e) that can be tied to activity beyond the concentration, for it conjoins with two blades that were recovered together within 30 centimetres of Location 3. These locational particulars suggest that the crested blade and, by implication, all nine refits were carried to Location 1 as part of the apprentice knapper's clean-up activities. Moreover, while the presence of the novice in all three locations seems beyond dispute, the evidence of the crested blade refit suggests that his trajectory was more probably a loop that originated and ended in the northern zone, rather than the linear path proposed in the behavioural scenario of Figure 5.6. Finally, this new understanding of the apprentice's activities makes it likely that experts worked Cores 5 and 8 only in the northern zone and that the resulting eleven removals (see Table 1) were also transported as clean-up debris to Location 1 by an apprentice. This apprentice withdrew to Location 1, loaded, as it were, with 'food for thought' and flint to knap.

Though only examined here in a preliminary fashion, Lave and Wenger's (1991) concept of LPP provides a promising analytical perspective for defining participation frameworks relevant to understanding microscale social dynamics of apprentice flintknapping. Their ideas have led to a more fully contexualised and theoretically grounded account of one particular case of apprentice flintknapping. This account shows, moreover, that the problem of locating children in prehistory is not separate from the task of locating other social actors (Moore and Scott 1997). This raises an important point concerning archaeologists' narratives about the past: 'Implicitly, men have been the actors in the past' (Hastorf 1998: 127) and women and children have remained essentially invisible (Sofaer Derevenski 1994b; Scott 1997). This has been especially true in Palaeolithic studies, where lithics and hunting weapons are significant elements in material culture systems (Gero 1991; Finlay 1997). It is particularly ironic that this is so, given the tremendous potential of lithic studies for exploring issues of human agency in prehistory (Gero 1989; Dobres and Hoffman 1994: 235–9). It is telling that unit 27 M.89 at Pincevent, like the Upper Perigordian occupation at Solvieux, was interpreted as a specialised hunting camp reflecting the activities of an all male group until novice flint-knappers were recognised through refitting and technical analysis (Bodu *et al.* 1990: 156). The discovery of youthful knappers led to revision in the interpretation of local group organisation to that of nuclear families composed of men, women and children. All the current indications are that Solvieux's Upper Perigordian occupation similarly preserves routine activities of a simple family hunting camp.

The analysis presented here contributes to a growing awareness that apprenticeship is indeed a key dimension of technological variability, and one that deserves more attention from prehistorians (Dobres and Hoffman 1994). However, as Edmonds (1990: 67) asserted nearly a decade ago, 'a move beyond description is essential if the study of technology is to shed light on the broader debate regarding the nature of social reproduction and the conditions of social change'.

ACKNOWLEDGEMENTS

This project has gone through several permutations in the last couple of years. I am especially indebted to Dr Michael Stafford for both his initial encouragement and continuing interest in this research. The present effort substantially revises a paper (Grimm 1998) delivered at the Annual Meeting, Society for American Archaeology, Seattle, Washington, 25–29 March 1998. I thank the organisers for the opportunity to participate in the symposium on Learning and Craft Production in Prehistory and also for calling Lave and Wenger's (1991) work to my attention. Special thanks to RHG and VLG for many and diverse expressions of their interest and support. Timothy J. Henrich contributed significantly to this research, and I gratefully acknowledge his invaluable assistance with several aspects of the project. As an undergraduate at Oberlin College and a sometime flint-knapper, his insights contributed significantly in the task of sorting out the details of the Core 5 reduction process. More recently, he applied his skills with computer graphics to the production of the final versions of all the figures included in this chapter. I extend my appreciation and thanks to Catherine Wilber for her artistic contributions in the preparation of Figure 5.6, which was itself inspired by Bodu (1996).

NOTES

1   Although the remnants of the crested blade (Removal 25 in Figure 5.3) were found together at Location 2a, evidence points to Location 2b as the place where the blade was probably removed. The preparation of the crest seems technically beyond the knapping ability of the novice knapper (it is perched precariously, yet effectively, on the right edge of the nearly exhausted core), and the removals which formed the crest are regular and controlled. Furthermore, the proximal portion is missing; it appears to have broken off from the rest of the blade, at the flaw, at the time of manufacture, in the same manner as the final removal (Removal 26) which was recovered at Location 2b. It appears that one blade (not recovered) was successfully struck off between the crest and final removals. Finally, Location 2b is also the place where the last removal from the expertly worked Core 8 was found (Removal 8).

2   Virtually all the rocks in Figure 5.2 were introduced into the occupation by human action. More than 93 per cent are quartzite cobbles, but micaceous schist, granite,

diabase, limestone and gravel flint are also present. Many rocks show signs of thermal alteration and 36 rocks comprise a rock tool industry.

REFERENCES

Audouze, F. and Enloe, James G. (1997) 'High resolution archaeology at Verberie: limits and interpretations', *World Archaeology* 29(2): 195–207.

Audouze, F., Karlin, C., Croisset, D. de, Coudret, P., Larriere, M., Massou, P., Mauger, M., Olive, M., Pelegrin, J., Pigeot, N., Plisson, H., Schmider, B. and Taborin, Y. (1988) 'Taille du Silex et Finalité du Débitage Dans le Magdalénien du Bassin Parisien', in M. Otte (ed.) *De la Loire à l'Oder: Les civilisations du Paléolithique final dans le nord-ouest européen*, Oxford: British Archaeological Reports, International Series 444 (i), pp. 55–84.

Bader, O. (1978) *Sungir Upper Paleolithic Site*, NAUKA: Moscow.

Bergman, C.A., and McEwan, E. (1997) 'Sinew-reinforced and composite bows: technology, function, and social implications', in H. Knecht (ed.) *Projectile Technology*, New York, London: Plenum, pp. 143–64.

Bird, C.F.M. (1993) 'Woman the toolmaker: evidence for women's use and manufacture of flaked stone tools in Australia and New Guinea', in H. du Cros and L Smith (eds) *Women in Archaeology: A Feminist Critique*, Occasional Papers in Archaeology No. 23, Canberra: Department of Prehistory, RSPS, Australian National University, pp. 22–30.

Bodu, P. (1996) 'Les chausseurs Magdaléniens de Pincevent: quelques aspects de leurs comportements', simultaneously published in English as 'The Magdalenian hunters of Pincevent: aspects of their behavior', *Lithic Technology* 21(1): 48–70.

Bodu, P., Karlin, C. and Ploux, S. (1990) 'Who's who? The Magdalenian flintknappers of Pincevent, France', in E. Cziesla, S. Eickhoff, N. Arts and D. Winter (eds) *The Big Puzzle: International Symposium on Refitting Stone Artefacts*, Studies in Modern Archaeology 1, Bonn: Holos Verlag, pp. 143–63.

Boëda, E., Geneste, J.M. and Meignen, L.(1990) 'Identification de Chaînes Opératoires Lithiques du Paléolithique ancien et moyen', *Paléo* 2: 43–80.

Boëda, E., Connan, J., Dessort, D., Muhensen, S., Mercier, N., Valladas, H. and Tisnerat, N. (1996) 'Bitumen as a hafting material on Middle Paleolithic artifacts', *Nature* 380: 336–8.

Bordes, F. and Crabtree, D. (1969) 'The Corbiac blade technique and other experiments', *Tebiwa: Journal of the Idaho State University Museum* 12: 1–21.

Bourdieu, P. (1977) *Outline of a Theory of Practice*, Cambridge: Cambridge University Press.

Cattelain, P. (1997) 'Hunting during the Upper Paleolithic: bow, spearthrower, or both?', in H. Knecht (ed.) *Projectile Technology*, New York: Plenum, pp. 213–40.

Conkey, M.W. (1991) 'Contexts of action, contexts for power: material culture and gender in the Magdalenian', in J.M. Gero and M.W. Conkey (eds) *Engendering Archaeology: Women in Prehistory*, Oxford: Blackwell, pp. 57–92.

Cziesla, E., Eickhoff, S., Arts, N. and Winter, D. (eds) (1990) *The Big Puzzle: International Symposium on Refitting Stone Artefacts*, Studies in Modern Archaeology 1, Bonn: Holos.

DeBoer, W. R. (1990) 'Interaction, imitation, and communication as expressed in style: the Ucayali experience', in M. W. Conkey and C. A. Hastorf (eds) *The Uses of Style in Archaeology*, Cambridge: Cambridge University Press, pp. 82–104.

Dobres, M.-A. (1995) 'Gender and prehistoric technology', *World Archaeology* 27(1): 25–49.

Dobres, M.-A. and Hoffman C. R. (1994) 'Social agency and the dynamics of prehistoric technology', *Journal of Archaeological Method and Theory* 1(3): 211–58.

Edmonds, M. (1990) 'Description, understanding and the chaine operatoire', *Archaeological Review from Cambridge* 9(1): 55–70.

Finlay, N. (1997) 'Kid knapping: the missing children in lithic analysis', in J. Moore and E. Scott (eds) *Invisible People and Processes: Writing Gender and Childhood into European Archaeology*, London and New York: Leicester University Press, pp. 203–13.

Fischer, A. (1989) 'A late Palaeolithic "school" of flint-knapping at Trollesgave, Denmark', *Acta Archaeologica* 60: 33–49.

Gamble, C. (1998) 'Palaeolithic society and the release from proximity: a network approach to intimate relations', *World Archaeology* 29(3): 426–49.

Garcia, M.H D. and Courtaud, P. (1990) 'Les empreintes du Réseau Clastres', *Bullétin de la Société Préhistorique Ariege-Pyrénées* 45: 167–74.

Gero, J. (1989) 'Assessing social information in material objects: How well do lithics measure up?' in R. Torrence (ed.)*Time, Energy and Stone Tools*, Cambridge: Cambridge University Press, pp. 92–105.

—— (1991) 'Genderlithics: women's roles in stone tool production' in J.M. Gero and M.W. Conkey (eds) *Engendering Archaeology: Women in Prehistory*, Oxford: Blackwell, pp. 163–93.

Giddens, A. (1979) *Central Problems in Social Theory: Action, Structure and Contradiction in Social Analysis*, Berkeley: University College Press.

Goody, Esther N. (1989) 'Learning, apprenticeship and the division of labor', in M.W. Coy (ed.) *Apprenticeship: From Theory to Method and Back Again*, Albany: SUNY Press, pp. 233–94.

Gorman, A. (1995) 'Gender, labour and resources: the female knappers of the Andaman Islands', in J. Balme and W. Beck (eds) *Gendered Archaeology: The Second Australian Women in Archaeology Conference*, Research Papers in Archaeology and Natural History, Canberra: Australian National University, pp. 87–91.

Griffiths, D.R., Bergman, C.A, Clayton, C.J., Ohnuma, K., Robins G.V. and Seeley, N.J. (1987) 'Experimental investigation of the heat treatment of flint', in G. de G. Sieveking and M.H. Newcomer (eds) *The Human Uses of Flint and Chert*, Cambridge: Cambridge University Press, pp. 43–52.

Grimm, L. (1983) 'Systematic heat-treatment of flint in the Upper Perigordian at Solvieux', Paper delivered at the Society for American Archaeology annual meeting, Pittsburgh.

—— (1998) 'Apprentice knapping: relating the cognitive and social dimensions of lithic technological behavior', Paper delivered at the Society for American Archaeology Meetings, Seattle, Washington.

Grimm, L.T. and Koetje, T.A. (1992) 'Spatial patterns in the Upper Perigordian at Solvieux: implications for activity reconstruction', in J.L. Hofman and James G. Enloe (eds) *Piecing Together the Past: Applications of Refitting Studies in Archaeology*, British Archaeological Reports, International Series 578, Oxford, pp. 264–86.

Hastorf, C.A. (1998) 'Women and children first: review of invisible people and processes', *Cambridge Archaeological Journal* 8: 126–8.

Hofman, J.L. and Enloe, J.G. (eds) (1992) *Piecing Together the Past: Applications of Refitting Studies in Archaeology*, British Archaeological Reports, International Series 578, Oxford.

Johnson, M. (1989) 'Conceptions of agency in archaeological interpretation', *Journal of Anthropological Archaeology* 8: 189–211.

Karlin, C. and Julien, M. (1994) 'Prehistoric technology: a cognitive science?' in C. Renfrew and E.B.W. Zubrow (eds) *The Ancient Mind: Elements of Cognitive Archaeology*, Cambridge: Cambridge University Press, pp. 152–64.

Karlin, C. and Pigeot, N. (1989) 'Chasseurs-cueilleurs magdaleniens. L'apprentissage de la taille silex', *Le Courier du CNRS (dossiers scientifiques)* 73: 10–12.

Karlin, C., Bodu, P. Pelegrin, J. (1991) 'Processus techniques et chaînes opératoires: comment les préhistoriens s'approprient un concept élaboré par les ethnologues', in H. Balfet (ed.) *Observer l'action technique: Des chaînes opératoires, pourquoi faire?*, Paris: Editions du CNRS, pp. 101–18.

Karlin, C., Ploux, S., Bodu, P. and Pigeot, N. (1993) 'Some socio-economic aspects of the knapping process among groups of hunter-gatherers in the Paris Basin area', in A. Berthelet and J. Chavaillon (eds) *The Use of Tools by Human and Non-Human Primates*, Oxford Science Publications, Oxford and New York: Clarendon Press/Oxford University Press, pp. 319–40.

Lave, J. and Wenger, E. (1991) *Situated Learning: Legitimate Peripheral Participation*, Cambridge: Cambridge University Press.

Lemonnier, P. (1993) 'Introduction', in P. Lemonnier (ed.) *Technological Choices: Transformation in material culture since the Neolithic*, London: Routledge, pp. 1–35.

Leroi-Gourhan, A. (1964) *Le Geste et la Parole I: Technique et Langage*, Paris: A. Michel.

—— (1965) *Le Geste et la Parole II: La Mémoire et les Rythmes*, Paris: A. Michel.

Lightfoot, K.G., Martinez, A. and Schiff, A.M. (1998) 'Daily practice and material culture in pluralistic social settings: An archaeological study of culture change and persistence from Fort Ross, California', *American Antiquity* 63(2): 199–222.

Lillehammer, G. (1989) 'A child is born: the child's world in an archaeological perspective', *Norwegian Archaeological Review* 22(2): 89–105.

Lorber, J. (1994) *Paradoxes of Gender*, New Haven: Yale University Press.

Moore, J. and Scott, E. (eds) (1997) *Invisible People and Processes: Writing Gender and Childhood into European Archaeology*, London : Leicester University Press.

Newcomer, M.H. (1975) '"Punch technique" and Upper Paleolithic blades', in E. Swanson (ed.) *Lithic Technology: Making and Using Stone Tools*, The Hague: Mouton Publishers, pp. 97–102.

Newcomer, M.H. and Sieveking, G. de (1980) 'Experimental flake scatter-patterns: a new interpretive technique', *Journal of Field Archaeology* 7(3): 345–52.

O'Brien, P.J. (1990) 'Evidence for the antiquity of gender roles in the central plains tradition', in S.M. Nelson and A.B. Kehoe (eds) *Powers of Observation: Alternative Views in Archeology*, Archeological Papers of the American Anthropological Association, vol. 2, Washington, DC: American Anthropological Association, pp. 61–72.

Olive, M. (1988) 'Une forme particuliere d'économie de débitage à Étiolles', in J. Tixier, (ed.) *Journée d'Études Technologiques en Préhistoire*, Notes et Monographies Techniques 25, Paris: Editions du CNRS, pp. 27–36.

Olive, M. and Taborin, Y. (1989) *Nature et Fonction des Foyers Préhistoriques*, vol. 2, Actes du Colloque International de Némours 12–14 Mai 1987, Némours: Ilê de France.

Ortner, S. B. (1984) 'Theory in anthropology since the sixties', *Comparative Studies in Society and History* 26(1): 126–66.

Pelegrin, J. (1990) 'Prehistoric lithic technology: some aspects of research', *Archaeological Review from Cambridge* 9(1): 116–27.

Pelegrin, J., Karlin, C and Bodu, P (1988) '"Chaînes opératoires": un outil pour le préhistorien', in J. Tixier (ed.) *Journée d'Études Technologiques en Préhistoire*, Notes et Monographies Techniques 25, Paris: Editions du CNRS, pp. 55–62.

Perpere, M. (1997) 'Les Pointes de la Gravette de la Couche 5 de l'Abri Pataud: Reflexions sur les Armes de Pierre dans les Outillages Périgordiens', in *Colloques International: La Chase dans la Préhistoire, Treignes, 1990. Artefacts 8:9–15*, Études et Recherches Archéologiques de l'Université de Liège 51. Liège.

Pfaffenberger, B. (1992) 'Social Anthropology of Technology', *Annual Review of Archaeology* 22: 491–516.

Pigeot, N. (1990) 'Technical and social actors: flintknapping specialists and apprentices at Magdalenian Etiolles', *Archaeological Review from Cambridge* 9(1): 126–41.

Pike-Tay, A. and Bricker, H.M. (1993) 'Hunting in the Gravettian: an examination of evidence from southwestern France', in G.L. Peterkin, H.M. Bricker, and P. Mellars, (eds) *Hunting and Animal Exploitation in the Later Palaeolithic and Mesolithic of Eurasia*, Archaeological Papers of the American Anthropological Association 4, pp. 127–43.

Sackett, J.R. (1988) 'The Neuvic Group', in H. Dibble and A. Montet-White (eds) *Upper Pleistocene Prehistory of Western Eurasia*, Monograph 54, Philadelphia: University Museum.

—— (1999) *The Archaeology of Solvieux*, Institute of Archaeology, University of California at Los Angeles.

Schlanger, N. (1990) 'Techniques as human action: two perspectives', *Archaeological Review from Cambridge* 9(1): 18–26.

—— (1994) 'Mindful technology: unleashing the chaine operatoire for an archaeology of mind', in C. Renfrew and E.B.W. Zubrow (eds) *The Ancient Mind*, Cambridge and New York: Cambridge University Press, pp. 143–50.

—— (1996) 'Understanding Levallois', *Cambridge Archaeological Journal* 6(2): 231–54.

Schmider, B. and Croisset, E. de. (1990) 'The contribution of lithic refitting for spatial analysis of capsite H17 and D14 at Marsangy', in E.S. Cziesla, S. Eickhoff, N. Arts and D. Winter (eds) *The Big Puzzle: International Symposium on Refitting Stone Artefacts*, Studies in Modern Archaeology 1, Bonn: Holos Verlag, pp. 431–46.

Scott, E. (1997) 'Introduction: on the incompleteness of archaeological narratives', in J. Moore and E. Scott (eds) *Invisible People and Processes: Writing Gender and Childhood into European Archaeology*, London: Leicester University Press, pp. 1–12.

Shelley, P.H. (1990) 'Variation in lithic assemblages: an experiment', *Journal of Field Archaeology* 17: 187–93.

Sofaer Derevenski, J. (1994a) 'Editorial', *Archaeological Review from Cambridge* 13(2): 1–5.

—— (1994b) 'Where are the children? Accessing children in the past', *Archaeological Review from Cambridge* 13(2): 7–20.

—— (1997) 'Engendering children, engendering archaeology', in J. Moore and E. Scott (eds) *Invisible People and Processes: Writing Gender and Childhood into European Archaeology*, London: Leicester University Press, pp. 192–202.

Tixier, J., Inizan, M.-L. and Roche, H. (1980) *Préhistoire de la Pierre Taillée 1: terminologie et technologie*, Valbonne: Cercle de Recherches et d'Études Préhistoriques.

Villa, P. (1991) 'From debitage chips to social models of production: the refitting method in Old World archaeology', *The Review of Archaeology* 12(2): 24–30.

Whiting, B. and J.W.M. Whiting (1975) *Children of Six Cultures: A Psycho-Cultural Analysis*, Cambridge, Mass.: Harvard University Press.

Whittaker, J.C. (1994) *Flintknapping: Making and Understanding Stone Tools*, Austin: University of Texas Press.

Winterman, R. (1975) 'Problems in the horizontal analysis of archaeological remains from Upper Paleolithic sites', unpublished MA thesis, Archaeology Program, University of California at Los Angeles.

Chapter 6

Children, material culture and weaving
Historical change and developmental change

Patricia Greenfield

INTRODUCTION

The Soviet psychologist and semiotician, Lev Semenovich Vygotsky, pointed to the connections between cultural development and individual development (Vygotsky 1962, 1978). He suggested that as children grow, they acquire the use of tools and speech through social interaction, these cultural forms being themselves the product of historical development (Scribner 1985). The ideas of Vygotsky form the central core of a prominent theoretical strand of developmental psychology – the socio-historical approach (e.g. Rogoff and Wertsch 1984; Wertsch 1985).

Yet, despite the importance of socio-historical theory, the developmental implications of historical change have not been studied in a direct, empirical manner by comparing the development and socialisation of one generation with that of the next. Our two-decade follow-up investigation of weaving apprenticeship among the Zinacantecs, a Maya group in Chiapas, Mexico begins to fill this gap. Across a span of more than twenty years, we have studied two generations of mothers and children as their society moves from subsistence to an entrepreneurial cash economy. Because such economic changes transform human relations, Vygotsky, in the tradition of Marx and Lenin, would have expected this economic transformation to change the social processes of ontogeny (Scribner 1985). Weaving apprenticeship is just such a social process of ontogeny.

Insofar as the process of socialisation prepares the next generation to participate in society, it should change when the conditions faced by that next generation differ from the environment in which their parents grew up. Socialisation is intrinsically future oriented – it prepares children for an adulthood that has not yet arrived. It follows that changing socialisation patterns should be a key component of the psychological adaptation to social change. But does socialisation really work this way? An important question is, in conditions of change, do parents merely recreate the socialising process that they underwent as children? Or is there a capacity to develop new methods and processes as societal conditions, in this case, economic conditions, change? What, if any, are the consequences of such changes in socialisation for the development of children?

Furthermore, there is a connection between socialisation and cultural artefacts. In non-industrial societies, children are socialised to produce cultural artefacts through a process of informal education or apprenticeship; in this study the artefacts produced are woven and embroidered textiles. What is the relationship between pedagogical methods of informal education and the nature of the cultural artefacts that are produced?

Artefacts in the form of tools are also a means of socialisation and informal education. What therefore is the relationship between pedagogical methods of informal education and the cultural tools that are utilised in the apprenticeship process? Are historical changes in pedagogy reflected in changes in the tools that are used in the learning process? If we are to answer these questions in the most rigorous way possible, longitudinal, diachronic study of families across more than one generation is required. The evidence must be both behavioural *and* historical. It is precisely this sort of controlled empirical historical data that has, up to now, been lacking and it is precisely this kind of evidence that is presented in this chapter through the study of the domain of weaving apprenticeship in a Zinacantec Maya community in Chiapas, Mexico.

Vygotsky also emphasised another kind of change – developmental change – although his notion of developmental stages was less detailed than that of his contemporary, Piaget (1967). Vygotsky and Luria (1993) saw 'the ability to make use of tools' as 'indicative of psychological development' (ibid.: 174). The second part of the chapter examines the tools of weaving apprenticeship and relates them to cognitive development (integrating notions from Piaget and Vygotsky), historical development, and historical constancy in Zinacantec culture.

THE STUDY

In 1969 and 1970, I carried out a number of studies on culture, learning, and cognitive development in Nabenchauk, a hamlet of the Tzotzil-speaking agrarian Maya community of Zinacantán in Highland Chiapas. My collaborator in this research was Carla Childs (cf. Childs and Greenfield 1980; Greenfield and Childs 1977, 1991; Greenfield *et al.* 1989). The Zinacantecs had been very successful at carrying a traditional, albeit syncretic, Mayan way of life into the modern world (Vogt 1969). Corn and beans were their most usual crops, supplemented by peaches in more recent years.

Weaving was the cultural domain on which our research focused. The activity of weaving and the cloth it produced were central to the creation of both cultural and gender identity. Weaving apprenticeship was utilised as a means to investigate processes of informal education, teaching and learning in a society in which education does not traditionally take place in school. Figure 6.1 depicts a 1970 weaving learner seated in a prototypical Maya backstrap loom, which design goes back to ancient Maya times (Figure 6.2).

1970: Weaving apprenticeship, textiles and cultural conservatism

In 1970, we concluded that the goal of Zinacantec education and socialisation was the intergenerational replication of tradition (Greenfield and Lave 1982). This was in accord with broader cultural goals of maintaining the *baz'i* or 'true' way of acting; the 'true' way being the Zinacantec way (Vogt 1969). The manner in which weaving was taught in 1970 fostered this goal of cultural conservation. Our videos of weaving apprenticeship revealed the instructional process to be a highly scaffolded, relatively error-free one, in which the teacher, usually the mother, sensitively provided help, models and verbal direction in

Figure 6.1   Katal 1 seated in a backstrap loom. Nabenchauk, 1970

Source: Photograph: Sheldon Greenfield

Note: Numerals after subject names refer to codes in our database and identify subjects by family and generation

accord with the developmental level of the learner (Childs and Greenfield 1980; Greenfield 1984). The learner had little chance to make a mistake, let alone experiment and innovate.

Thus, the maintenance of tradition excluded the value of innovative creation. The relatively conservative nature of the value system and culture was manifest in the stable repertoire of woven patterns, limited to two red-and-white striped configurations, one multi-colour stripe, and one basketweave pattern.

Figure 6.2   Ancient Maya statue of a woman seated in a backstrap loom. This statue is a ceramic from Jaina, Campeche, 700–900 AD

Source: Photograph: Museo Nacional de Antropologia e Historia de Mexico

1970–1991: Economic transition from subsistence to commerce

Side by side with the emphasis on cultural tradition was a process of economic change, already in motion in 1970, from corn-based subsistence to money-based commerce (Cancian 1990, 1992). This process was accelerated when the Mexican Government made it possible for Zinacantec communities such as Nabenchauk to acquire vans and trucks. Men who were farmers went into the transport business; in essence, they became entrepreneurs, often buying and selling other people's goods. Based on the fact that commercial entrepreneurship entails an ideology of innovation, I made a series of predictions regarding changes in informal weaving apprenticeship and changes in textiles, the artefactual products of weaving.

Implications of economic change for weaving apprenticeship and woven textiles: predictions from theory

I developed a theory (Greenfield 1984; Greenfield and Lave 1982) that there is a contrast between the goals of two methods of informal education: scaffolding plus observation of models (as we found in 1970), on one hand, versus relatively independent trial-and-error learning on the other. Whereas the first is adapted to the transmission of tradition (and was what we found in 1970), the second, with its emphasis on the learner's own discovery process, is adapted to the development of skill in innovation. If innovation had entered the culture as a value orientation in response to entrepreneurship, I thought that weaving education would make a corresponding shift away from scaffolding (or developmentally sensitive guidance) to a more discovery-orientated and independent trial-and-error process.

A second related prediction was that woven artefacts would no longer be limited to a small stock of patterns. Instead, weavers would constantly innovate new patterns. Innovative pattern representation was conceived as a major change in cognitive processes associated with weaving.

Both these hypotheses were formulated on the basis of theory alone (Greenfield and Lave 1982). I had not been back to Zinacantán in twenty-one years. With Carla Childs, I returned in 1991 to test these predictions.

HYPOTHESIS 1: HISTORICAL CHANGE IN WEAVING APPRENTICESHIP

According to my theory, the old method of observation of models, in conjunction with receiving developmentally sensitive help, would change. Earlier the teacher had carefully built a scaffold of help for the learner, providing help before the learner had an opportunity to make a serious error (Childs and Greenfield 1980; Greenfield 1984; Greenfield and Childs 1991; Greenfield *et al.* 1989). In this situation the learner received very little opportunity to make a mistake, let alone explore. We therefore predicted that *methods of teaching and learning would have changed to a more independent trial-and-error approach.*

In order to test this hypothesis, we went back to study the daughters of our 1970 weaving subjects. We had fourteen in our original sample, one of whom, Katal 1, is shown in Figure 6.1. Between 1970 and 1991, Katal grew up and had five daughters of her own. Four were old enough to weave and became subjects in our historical replication twenty-one years later. In all, we succeeded in locating fourteen daughters (of seven mothers) whose mothers had been in our study of weaving apprenticeship in 1970 and who were old enough to weave for our study in 1991 or on another visit in 1993, some for the very first time. As before, we videotaped the apprenticeship process.

In addition, we expanded our sample of weaving learners to 58, so that we would be able to statistically examine the effects of various new factors, such as attending school or selling weaving, on the methods of informal education. The additional weaving learners were from the same group of extended families from which the original fourteen learners had been drawn in 1970; many were nieces or godchildren of the 1970 sample of weaving learners. This chapter focuses on well-controlled historical comparisons from the two epochs. The qualitative findings presented here have been confirmed by quantitative analysis of the entire sample (Greenfield *et al.*, in press).

Figure 6.3   Mother helping Katal 1, age 9, with her weaving. Nabenchauk, 1970

Source: Video: Patricia Greenfield

Figure 6.4   Weaving learner (Loxa 1–201, about age 9) and teacher (older sister, age 12 or 13). Loxa is the daughter of Katal 1, shown learning to weave in Figure 6.3. Nabenchauk, 1991

Source: Video: Patricia Greenfield

Apprentice weavers

The video frame of Katal learning to weave shown in Figure 6.3 symbolises weaving apprenticeship, *circa* 1970. She was nine years old at the time of the study. Her mother served as her weaving teacher and was continuously present, helping and guiding her.

Her mother was so involved that there were often four hands on the loom. This scene from Katal's weaving apprenticeship in 1970 is very different from the way Katal's daughters learned to weave in 1991. Learning to weave is a developmental process. Therefore, for comparative purposes, I observed a daughter who was about the same age as Katal had been in 1970. Figure 6.4 shows a frame of Katal's daughter, Loxa 1–201, learning to weave in 1991.

The first major difference to note is that Katal, the mother, is not even present. Katal had assigned an older daughter, Xunka', age 12 or 13, to serve as the teacher. This change from older-generation to peer-generation teachers was one of our more general findings (Greenfield *et al.* in press).

Katal, the mother, was at home, but chose not to be part of the weaving session. In point of fact, she was embroidering a blouse to sell on order. This situation illustrates a direct connection between the commercial involvement of mothers and changes in the apprenticeship process. Indeed, our quantitative analysis confirms that commercial involvement of mother and daughter is causally linked to a change in the relationship of the weaving teacher from older generation to peer generation (Greenfield *et al.*, in press).

The second, and even more important difference, is that in Figure 6.4 the older sister is not paying visual attention to her younger sister, the weaving learner, despite the fact that the younger sister is in fact a novice. Indeed, in one scene, Loxa had to call the 'teacher' twice to get her attention.

The teacher's behaviour is in sharp contrast to that of their grandmother in Figure 6.3. Figure 6.3 shows a typical scene from 1970: the teacher/mother was in constant visual contact with her daughter's weaving activity and therefore consistently anticipated her need for help. Teacher, rather than learner, took the initiative when help was required.

In sum, the 1991 weaving learner, as illustrated in the comparison of Figure 6.3 and Figure 6.4, had become much more independent. The movement from interdependence to independence (Greenfield 1994; Markus and Kitayama 1991) is also illustrated by the greater physical distance between learner and teacher in 1991 (Figure 6.4), compared with 1970 (Figure 6.3). The difference in teaching styles is all the more amazing given the fact that we generally learn how to teach from the way our mothers taught us (Childs, personal communication). In addition, compared with her sisters, Katal is temperamentally most like her mother (Loxa's grandmother), so, on the basis of both her mother's genes and her mother as model, one would have expected Katal to have followed her mother's teaching style with her own daughters. The fact that she did not is a powerful example of adapting teaching to changed conditions in the space of a single generation.

A different 1970 weaving subject presents another controlled comparison. We observed one family (No. 146) in which there were two weaving subjects in 1970 the same age as Loxa and her sister Xunka' (approximately age 9 and 13). Given this identical configuration of siblings, would the role of mother and older sister have changed in the twenty-one intervening years? One would predict from the theoretical model that mother and elder daughter would be more involved in guiding and helping the learner in 1970 than a similar pair would have been in 1991. This is precisely what we found.

Figure 6.5 shows a frame from the 1970 video of Katal 146. Note that the mother is close at hand; analysis of their action and interaction from the video showed that she was helping (e.g. making a measuring stick to be used in the weaving process) and advising the older daughter on how to help the learner. There was a hierarchy of control from eldest (mother) to next eldest (older sister) to youngest (learner). Both mother and older daughter were very attentive to the learner's needs and were constantly involved in the learner's weaving.

This is a very different scene from that shown in Figure 6.4, twenty-one years later, with the same configuration of gender, age and family relationships. In Figure 6.4, the older sister is uninvolved, physically distant from the learner, and inattentive to her needs. The 1991 mother uses the older sister as a *substitute* for herself as teacher. In contrast, the 1970 mother uses the older sister as an *adjunct* (Figure 6.5). Rather than a hierarchy of control from elder to younger, in 1991 both sisters (teacher and learner) are operating quite independently of the immediate authority of the older generation.

In 1970, the flow of authority from elder to younger was a central value in Zinacantec society (Vogt 1969). By 1991, this age-graded hierarchy was disappearing in many areas of life (Collier 1990). Indeed, it was disappearing in the basic economic system, where dependence on the land held by the older generation was being replaced by independent entrepreneurship (ibid.). The movement away from an age-graded flow of authority was particularly dramatic in weaving where older women do not even know all of the new techniques mastered by their daughters.

Figure 6.5   Katal 146, age 9, learning to weave with the aid of her mother (partly shown on right) and older sister, age 13, (left). Nabenchauk, 1970

Source: Video: Patricia Greenfield

Figure 6.6   Two Zinacantec brothers, Marian 1 (left) and Antun 1 (right) dressed in ponchos utilising the woven stripe that was standard in 1969 and 1970. Nabenchauk, 1970

Source: Photograph: Sheldon Greenfield

In sum, we found more independent learning in 1991 than in 1970, whether we compare Loxa, our 1991 learner, with the way her mother learned to weave in 1970, or we compare her with another 1970 weaver matched for the family configuration of people on the scene. These examples support our first hypothesis that between 1970 and 1991 the weaving novice became more independent, receiving less guidance and modelling from the 'master'.

HYPOTHESIS 2: HISTORICAL CHANGES IN WOVEN TEXTILES

According to the theoretical model, independent trial-and-error learning should be associated with pattern innovation. The reason for this is that if you are experimenting independently you might create or discover something new. Thus, in the domain of woven textiles I predicted that patterns would no longer be limited to a basketweave and three striped patterns. Instead, there would be an ongoing process of pattern innovation and creation.

When we returned in 1991, the extent to which this historical hypothesis was confirmed was quite astonishing. Changes in the men's poncho illustrate the growth of innovation and creativity in the domain of woven textiles.

Figure 6.6 shows the old-style male poncho, made from a uniform striped material. The two brothers in the photograph are dressed alike, as would be all other Zinacantec men and boys of the epoch. The area of innovation was in the striped narrow side borders of the poncho, where the colours and their order could vary. However, this domain of 'innovation' is so small that it is not even visible in the photograph.

When we returned in 1991, a fancy brocaded border had been added to the basic style and background stripe of the poncho, shown in Figure 6.6. No two were alike. Figure 6.7a and b shows two variants of the figurative and geometric designs that were being woven through a brocading process for poncho borders. In addition, fancy (and highly differentiated) embroidery had been added to the top of each poncho (most visible in Figure 6.7a).

Furthermore, entrepreneurship and commerce were not limited to transport; they had hit textile production as well. For example, girls began to sell a new woven and embroidered commercial item called the *servilleta* (napkin, towel), designed and made for outsiders to buy.

Figure 6.7(a) and (b)   Two variants of an infinite number of woven brocade borders and embroidered designs for the Zinacantec male poncho. Nabenchauk, 1991

Source: Photographs: Lauren Greenfield

In sum, Hypothesis 2 was also confirmed: in 1991 we found constant pattern innovation. This innovation included the creation of new motifs, the recombination of existing motifs, and the development of new tourist items.

Figure 6.8   Use of a printed pattern to create a brocaded weaving design.
Nabenchauk, 1991

Source: Photograph: Lauren Greenfield

WEAVING TOOLS, HUMAN DEVELOPMENT, AND HUMAN HISTORY

Moving on from the artefacts that are produced as a result of weaving apprenticeship to the artefacts that are used in weaving and in learning how to weave, this section begins by discussing a new tool that has facilitated the development of the brocade weavings shown in Figure 6.7(a) and (b). This tool is the printed pattern (Figure 6.8).

Paper patterns, schooling, and graphic representation

Our statistical results indicate that there is a significant relationship between schooling and the ability to use printed patterns to create textile designs (Greenfield and Maynard 1997). Schools have had a direct effect on weaving and embroidery by introducing external forms of representation (notably reading and writing) into Nabenchauk's predominantly oral culture. External representations have entered textile production by way of printed patterns. Teachers are said to have introduced printed patterns into the school. The schooling of girls itself increased dramatically from the early 1960s, when it was zero, to 1991, when the rate of exposure to at least some elementary schooling was about one-third (Greenfield and Maynard 1997).

Printed patterns were originally developed for cross-stitch embroidery; the pattern is printed on a grid of squares, and each square represents one cross-stitch (i.e. an X-shaped stitch) on a piece of embroidered fabric. Cross-stitch patterns are used in this way in Nabenchauk. However, it is much more difficult to use the patterns to weave. Unlike embroidery, weaving is not naturally organised in a grid of squares (Greenfield 1999). There are parallel warp (or frame) threads (shown in white in Figure 6.8); and there are parallel weft threads that go over and under the warp threads, at right angles to them. (In Figure 6.8, the weft are the darker threads in the woven part of the warp, to the left of the unwoven white warp threads).

It is therefore necessary to develop a representational strategy for creating hypothetical squares in order to use the printed patterns for weaving. This is exactly what Zinacantec weavers have done. One weaver told me that one square would correspond to one thread in the warp dimension and to four threads in the weft dimension (Greenfield 1999). This is a fairly complex representational code to create, especially with just a few years of formal education. Zinacantec girls have appropriated a new symbolic tool, the printed pattern, and transformed it, as part of the process of cultural appropriation (Saxe 1991).

Most of the older generation of mothers do not know how to weave with paper patterns. For them, the absence of formal schooling is a barrier to understanding the code of symbolic correspondences (Greenfield and Maynard 1997). Because of the much higher rate of using paper patterns in the younger generation, we see that innovative cognitive change is concentrated in the younger generation, a phenomenon that is very familiar in our own societies.

In a Nabenchauk school of the 1990s, external representation goes beyond reading and writing to the presence of graphic representations, such as

Figure 6.9   The girl on the left is drawing patterns to use in embroidering. The two girls have already made cut-out patterns to trace around, with internal designs to copy or transfer to fabric; these are seen to the right of the girls, on the ground. Nabenchauk, 1991

Source: Photograph: Lauren Greenfield

pictures, in the classroom. Pictures have also moved from school to home (Greenfield and Childs 1996). Graphic representation at school and home has had direct impact on the creation of textile designs by children. In Figure 6.9, one sees children drawing and cutting out paper patterns. These patterns can be transferred to fabric and used for embroidering blouses, shawls or ponchos.

Play weaving and the toy loom

Play weaving appears to have been a constant in learning to weave across the two generations of learners in our study; however, it is uncertain whether play weaving was done on a toy loom in the earlier period. In any case, the toy loom, as I discovered in 1991, illustrates another kind of change – developmental change. The developmental progression of weaving tools from the toy loom (at age 3 or 4) to the real loom and winding board (at age 6 or later) indicates a kind of implicit cultural knowledge of cognitive development built into the tools and their use.

My theme here is that *cultures have sets of artefacts and practices that respect and stimulate sensitive periods for cognitive and neural development.* A sensitive period is a developmental window, an age range, when stimulation of a skill will have maximum impact on the development of that skill. The *developmental timing* and *order* in which girls are exposed to various weaving tools shows implicit knowledge of, and respect for, cognitive development. Specifically, these tools show implicit knowledge of progression from Piaget's pre-operational stage to concrete operational stage (Piaget and Inhelder 1969) and the timing of this transition.

Vygotsky noted the degree to which cognitive history is contained in cultural artefacts; he also noted that these artefacts, in turn, function as tools for the stimulation of current

Figure 6.10   Play weaving on a toy loom. Nabenchauk, 1991

Source: Photograph: Lauren Greenfield

Figure 6.11   *Komen* or winding board. Nabenchauk, 1995

Source: Photograph: Patricia Greenfield

cognitive development (Cole 1996; Scribner 1985; Vygotsky and Luria 1993). I would like to take this line of thinking a step further: not only cognitive history but cognitive development can also be contained in cultural artefacts. Analysis of the cognitive requirements of a developmentally gradated set of weaving artefacts – the toy loom, the winding board, and the real loom – demonstrate this point (Greenfield 2000).

Play weaving on the toy loom, illustrated in Figure 6.10, is widespread in Nabenchauk. It begins at age three or four, in Piaget's pre-operational period (Piaget and Inhelder 1969). It is used several years earlier than the real loom and winding board, which are not used before age six, the beginning of the transition to the concrete operational stage (ibid.). Preparing the real loom to weave is a concrete operational task. However, because the toy loom is just slightly different in one respect from the real loom, it does not require concrete operational thinking to set it up. The difference lies in the ropes between the two end-sticks, one on each side (Figure 6.10). These ropes permit the warp or frame threads (shown in Figure 6.10) to be wound directly onto the loom.

The real loom (shown in Figure 6.1) does not have these extra supports. Note that only the white threads (warp or frame threads) hold the loom together. The warp cannot be wound directly onto the loom because, if it were not there, the loom would collapse; there is nothing to hold the loom together before the winding starts. Therefore, a real loom must have the warp pre-wound on an apparatus such as the *komen* or winding board shown in Figure 6.11.

Winding the warp on the winding board intrinsically involves concrete operational thinking, as it requires mental transformation. The form of the warp threads, where they twist around the winding frame (Figure 6.12), is quite different from the form of the threads on the final loom, where they have been straightened out (Figure 6.1).

Complex topological transformation is required to understand the connection between how you wind and how the thread ends up on the loom. Compare Figure 6.12 with Figure

6.13. Figure 6.13 shows a cross-section of the warp or frame threads after being transferred to the loom. Note the difference in the configuration of threads between Figure 6.12, where the warp threads are still twisted around the winding board and Figure 6.13 where the warp threads have been straightened out and transferred to the loom (Greenfield 2000).

The important cognitive point is that a complex series of mental transformations is required for a weaver to understand the connection between how the threads are wound on the winding board and how they end up in the configuration that you see on the loom in Figures 6.1 and 6.13 (from different angles). In terms of Piagetian stages of cognitive development, mental transformations characterise the level of concrete operations (e.g. Piaget 1963).

Such mental transformations are not required for the toy loom. The extra supporting ropes or strings on the side mean that the warp can be wound directly on the loom (see Figure 6.14). Using a toy loom, a young girl winds, making repeated figure-eights between the end sticks. This process of winding figure-eights makes the cross con-

Figure 6.12   *Komen* with a few threads wound on it. Nabenchauk, 1995

Source: Photograph: Patricia Greenfield

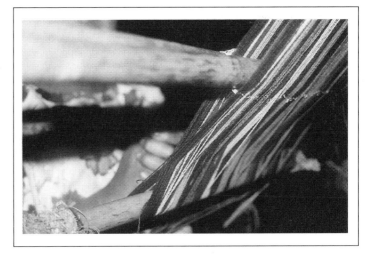

Figure 6.13   Cross-section of warp or frame threads after they have been taken off the *komen* and put on the loom. Nabenchauk, 1995

Source: Photograph: Patricia Greenfield

figuration (visible in Figure 6.14 on the play loom and Figure 6.12 on the winding board) that we saw as the final warp on the real loom in Figure 6.13. In this process, there is no mental transformation required to go from winding (Figure 6.12) to the set-up loom (Figure 6.10).

The important conclusion from this analysis is that Piagetian theory is part of the Zinacantecs' implicit ethnotheory of development. Whereas Zinacantec girls start on the toy loom from age 3, they do not set up a real loom before age 6 at the earliest, the normal beginning of concrete operations. So, most interestingly, Piagetian theory is implicitly (but not explicitly) built into the developmental progression of Zinacantec weaving tools. If we think of Piagetian stages as age-dependent sensitive periods requiring environmental stimulation, then learning how to set up a real loom can be seen as an activity that actualises the

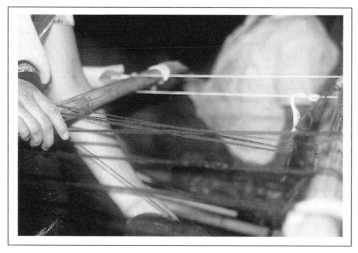

developmental stage of concrete operations in a culture-specific form (Greenfield 2000). This analysis is very much aligned with Vygotsky and Luria's notion that processes of tool acquisition are an important element in 'the cultural development of a child's mind' (Vygotsky and Luria 1993: 175).

Figure 6.14   A young girl winds the warp of her toy loom. One of the two supporting loops of string is visible in white near the top of the photo. Nabenchauk, 1995

Source: Photograph: Patricia Greenfield

CONCLUSION

The teaching of weaving turned out to be remarkably responsive to societal changes, notably the movement from agricultural subsistence to an entrepreneurial cash economy. As predicted, we found a definite shift from highly scaffolded relatively errorless learning, involving a great deal of observation of models (1970), towards a much more independent form of trial-and-error learning (1991). These conclusions were reached by following families over two generations of weaving apprenticeship.

At the same time, and also as predicted, the stock of four rather carefully defined striped and basketweave patterns grew to an infinite number of complex figurative and geometric patterns, with motifs that are constantly changing and being recombined in new ways. Independent trial-and-error learning was, indeed, associated with pattern innovation, as the theoretical model predicted.

This example of weaving instruction indicates that the process of socialisation prepares the next generation to participate in society, even under conditions of societal change. In Zinacantán, a society that in 1970 was based on respect for tradition, changing socialisation patterns are a very real component of the psychological adaptation to social change. For the first time, we have empirical and direct historical evidence on this issue in the psychology of teaching and learning.

We have found that parents do not merely recreate the socialising process that they underwent as children. There is a tremendous capacity to develop new methods of cultural apprenticeship as societal conditions, in this case, economic conditions, change. These new methods entail changes in human relations, as well as changes in cultural artefacts. Changes in the creation of cultural artefacts, such as the woven and embroidered textiles in this study, imply cognitive consequences for creativity and visual representation.

More broadly, our diachronic study of informal weaving education demonstrates the intergenerational transmission and transformation of cultural elements, important mechanisms behind the cumulative quality of human culture. Most important, however, this study of three generations of Zinacantec weavers – grandmothers, mothers and daughters – exemplifies learning and teaching as key components of the human capacity to adapt to a changing environment.

An important part of this adaptation lies in the development of new tools. The appearance, adaptation and utilisation of paper patterns is one aspect of adaptation to a new environment. This aspect of material culture, so important to young girls in their contemporary weaving and embroidery, is tied to another socialising institution – the school – an outside influence that appears to have originated the genre and has, without intending to, prepared girls cognitively to utilise this new form of external, visual representation.

Finally, the toy loom, the real loom, and the winding board, are utilised by girls of different ages and have developmental significance. Importantly, the developmental progression of Zinacantec weaving tools from the toy loom to the real loom and winding board indicates that the Zinacantecs have implicit cultural knowledge of stages of cognitive development. Each tool is therefore available to stimulate and actualise the particular cognitive stage to which it is adapted. In the domain of textile production, children's material culture is adapted both to the developmental stage of children and to the historical stage of communities.

ACKNOWLEDGEMENTS

Portions of this chapter were originally presented at two symposia in memory of Sylvia Scribner, one at the Society for Research in Child Development, New Orleans, March 1993, the other at the International Society for the Study of Behavioral Development, Recife, Brazil, July 1993. Elements of this chapter have appeared in *Mind, Culture, and Activity*.

The research on which this chapter is based was supported by: the Spencer Foundation; National Geographic Society; UCLA Latin American Center; Wenner-Gren Foundation for Anthropological Research; National Institutes of Health Fogarty International Center, Minority International Research Training Program; Colegio de la Frontera Sur; UCLA Academic Senate; Harvard Center for Cognitive Studies; the Bunting Institute of Radcliffe College; and the Milton Fund of Harvard Medical School. I thank our friends and study participants in Nabenchauk, Zinacantan.

This paper is dedicated to the memory of Sylvia Scribner. An inspiring and supportive colleague, she highlighted Vygotsky's uses of history in a path-breaking article (Scribner 1985).

REFERENCES

Cancian, F. (1990) 'The Zinacantan cargo waiting list as a reflection of social, political, and economic changes, 1952–1987', in L. Stephen and J. Dow (eds) *Class, Politics, and Popular Religion in Mexico and Central America,* Washington, DC: American Anthropological Association, pp. 63–76.

—— (1992) *The Decline of Community in Zinacantan: Economy, Public Life, and Social Stratification, 1960–1987,* Stanford, CA: Stanford University Press.

Childs, C.P. and Greenfield, P.M. (1980) 'Informal modes of learning and teaching: the case of Zinacanteco weaving', in N. Warren (ed.) *Studies in Cross-Cultural Psychology,* Vol. 2, London: Academic Press, pp. 269–316.

Cole, M. (1996) *Cultural Psychology: A Once and Future Discipline,* Cambridge, MA: Harvard University Press.

Collier, G. A. (1990) 'Seeking food and seeking money: changing productive relations in a Highland Mexican community', Discussion Paper 11, United Nations Research Institute for Social Development.

Greenfield, P.M. (1984) 'A theory of the teacher in the learning activities of everyday life', in B. Rogoff and J. Lave (eds) *Everyday Cognition: Its Development in Social Context,* Cambridge, MA: Harvard University Press, pp. 117–38.

—— (1994) 'Independence and interdependence as developmental scripts', in P.M. Greenfield and R. Cocking (eds) *Cross-Cultural Roots of Minority Child Development*, Hillsdale, NJ: Lawrence Erlbaum, pp. 1–37.

—— (1999) 'Cultural change and human development', in E. Turiel (ed.) *Development, Evolution, and Culture, New Directions in Child Psychology*, San Francisco: Jossey Bass, pp. 37–59.

—— (2000) 'Culture and universals: integrating social and cognitive development', in L. Nucci, G. Saxe, and E. Turiel (eds) *Culture, Thought, and Development*, Mahwah, NJ: Erlbaum, pp. 231-37.

Greenfield, P.M. and Childs C.P. (1977) 'Weaving, color terms, and pattern representation: cultural influences and cognitive development among the Zinacantecos of Southern Mexico', *Interamerican Journal of Psychology*, 11: 23–48.

—— (1991) 'Developmental continuity in biocultural context', in R. Cohen and A.W. Siegel (eds) *Context and Development*, Hillsdale, NJ: Lawrence Erlbaum. pp. 135–59.

—— (1996) 'Learning to weave in Zinacantan: a two-decade follow-up study of historical and cognitive change', in Isabel Zambrano and Evon Z. Vogt (chairs) *Microcosms of the Social World: Formal and Informal Education in the Maya Area of Chiapas*, San Francisco: American Anthropological Association.

Greenfield, P.M. and Lave, J. (1982) 'Cognitive aspects of informal education', in D Wagner and H. Stevenson (eds) *Cultural Perspectives on Child Development*, San Francisco: Freeman, pp. 181–207.

Greenfield, P.M. and Maynard, A.E. (1997) 'Women, girls, apprenticeship and schooling', in I. Zambrano (chair), Women's schooling in Maya Chiapas: Naming the unnamed, Symposium at the American Anthropological Association, Washington, DC.

Greenfield, P.M., Brazelton, T.B. and Childs, C.P. (1989) 'From birth to maturity in Zinacantan: ontogenesis in cultural context', in V. Bricker and G. Gossen (eds) *Ethnographic Encounters in Southern Mesoamerica: Celebratory Essays in Honor of Evon Z. Vogt*, Albany: Institute of Mesoamerican Studies, State University of New York, pp. 177–216.

Greenfield, P.M., Maynard, A.E. and Childs, C.P. (in press) 'History, culture, learning, and development' *Cross-Cultural Research*.

Markus, H.R. and Kitayama, S. (1991) 'Culture and the self: implications for cognition, emotion, and motivation', *Psychological Review* 98(2): 224–53.

Piaget, J. (1963) 'Intellectual operations and their development', reprinted in H.E. Gruber and J.J. Voneche (eds) (1977) *The Essential Piaget: An Interpretative Reference and Guide*, New York: Basic Books, pp. 342–58.

—— (1967) *Six Psychological Studies*, New York: Random House.

Piaget, J. and Inhelder, B. (1969) *The Psychology of the Child*, New York: Basic Books.

Rogoff, B. and Wertsch, J.V. (eds) (1984) *Children's Learning in the 'Zone of Proximal Development'*, San Francisco: Jossey Bass.

Saxe, G. (1991) *Culture and Cognitive Development: Studies in Mathematical Understanding*, Hillsdale, NJ: Erlbaum.

Scribner, S. (1985) 'Vygotsky's use of history', in J.V. Wertsch (ed.) *Culture, Communication, and Cognition*, Cambridge, England: Cambridge University Press, pp. 119–45.

Vogt, E.Z. (1969) *Zinacantan: A Maya Community in the Highlands of Chiapas*, Cambridge, MA: Harvard University Press.

Vygotsky, L.S. (1962) *Thought and Language*, Cambridge, MA: MIT Press.

Vygotsky, L.S. and Luria, A.R. (1993) [1930] *Studies on the History of Behavior: Ape, Primitive, and Child* (V.I. Golod and J.E. Knox (eds)), Hillsdale, NJ: Erlbaum.

—— (1978) *Mind in Society: The Development of Higher Psychological Processes*, Cambridge, MA: Harvard University Press.

—— (1993) *Studies on the History of Behavior: Ape, Primitive, and Child*, Hillsdale, NJ: Erlbaum.

Wertsch, J.V. (ed.) (1985) *Culture, Communication, and Cognition: Vygotskian Perspectives*, Cambridge, England: Cambridge University Press.

Part IV

Childhood lives

Chapter 7

Neanderthal cognitive life history and its implications for material culture

Jennie Hawcroft and Robin Dennell

INTRODUCTION

The Middle and Upper Palaeolithic periods in Europe differ widely in terms of the material culture associated with them. Each period is also associated with two distinct types of hominids: the Neanderthals, in the Middle Palaeolithic, and anatomically modern humans – people who were physiologically like ourselves – in the Upper Palaeolithic. The purpose of this chapter is to outline the degrees of difference between the stone tool material cultures of the two periods, and to explore a way of accounting for these differences through the idea that Neanderthals did not have the same pattern of childhood and development as that demonstrable in modern humans. We will discuss what is and is not known about childhood in Neanderthal societies, and propose a model of how such knowledge can be used to interpret the material culture of those societies.

WHY IS SO LITTLE KNOWN ABOUT NEANDERTHAL CHILDREN?

Palaeoanthropology has been more guilty than other sections of the archaeological community in terms of avoiding childhood studies. The recent trend towards childhood interests in archaeology has yet to penetrate very far into the work of the 'monkeys and stones' brigade, although there are, thankfully, some notable exceptions (e.g. Mann *et al.* 1987, Stringer *et al.* 1990). In palaeoanthropology, human remains are rare and precious, because the fossilisation and survival of skeletal material over a timespan of a million years or more is a very lucky and unusual event. For juvenile remains to survive this test of time is yet more miraculous: their smaller size and more fragile, uncalcified structure render them unlikely candidates for fossilisation. So, one can forgive palaeoanthropologists for not launching themselves wholeheartedly into studies of juvenile early hominids – the skeletal evidence is barely there.

This paucity of skeletal evidence is compounded by the nature of the stone tool record, which is the main archaeological evidence. Flaked stone forms virtually all of the material record prior to the appearance of anatomically modern humans. The problem with stone tools is that they do not carry any recognisable markers suggesting who made them, used them, or for what enterprise. In many cases there is wide debate over what tools were used for, or even which categories of flaked stone were waste by-products of other tools. There are well-defined stylistic groupings within assemblages (notably the Mousterian of south-western France), which may well have had enormous sociological import for their makers, owners or users. However, these are not markers that we as archaeologists can read; unlike Upper Palaeolithic rock art or the deliberate associations of artefacts and persons found in graves in later times (both of which attract debate in their own right), there are no obvious inferences to be taken from a stone tool other than those concerning the primary practical elements of how it could best be used and how it was flaked. Even the size of the stone tool itself is not much use in telling us whether it was used by a man, woman or child. Lithics that start out being used as large implements are often reduced and retouched down to thumbnail size over the course of their useful lives.

The nature of the evidence that palaeoanthropologists traditionally study does not encourage them to engage with research into childhood. This is reflected in artists' representations of early hominids and their lives in archaeological reconstructions. Children are rarely depicted and, if they are, they are usually in the background, playing or sleeping rather than engaging in any economic or materially significant behaviour (see Stringer and Gamble 1993). Nonetheless, drawing ideas from other disciplines such as child development and cognitive science, it is possible to investigate trends (rather than individual fossils or tool assemblages) in Neanderthals and their material culture.

BACKGROUND TO THE MOUSTERIAN

Probably the best-known of the non-*Homo sapiens sapiens* hominids, the Neanderthals, lived in Europe and adjacent Near Eastern and North African littoral areas between approximately 150 thousand years ago (kya) and 35 kya.[1] Their physical appearance has been reconstructed and depicted in many paintings and sculptures, with their elongated occipital, prognathous (forward-projecting) maxillo-facial region and prominent brow-ridge. In terms of posture and brain size they are no different from the modern human pattern, and postcranially they are stocky and heavy but not outside the modern human range.

One of the most intriguing aspects of Neanderthals is that they are so tantalisingly close to ourselves, yet inexplicable differences prevent them being entirely modern humans. Neanderthals are, as far as is known, the first hominids to engage in burial of their dead – a practice so familiar as a part of modern human behaviour. Yet, they apparently lack other traits considered equally innate to modern 'humanness' such as the production of art, and possibly even full symbolic language. Anatomically, they could easily pass for a robust modern human in terms of postcranial structure, but their bones exhibit a huge number of breaks, traumas and other injuries, especially upper limb injuries, compared to those of Upper Palaeolithic modern humans. Indeed, Trinkaus and Zimmerman (1982) likened the level of trauma seen in Neanderthal males to those found in modern rodeo riders. This has been taken to underline the harshness of Neanderthal life and their relatively short lifespans.

Another of these teasing differences concerns the Mousterian, the lithic industry classically associated with the Neanderthals. This is a stone tool industry which is found wherever Neanderthals occur, from the eastern extreme of Teshik-Tash, a site in Uzbekistan, to the far westerly sites in France, Spain and Gibraltar. The Mousterian is a lithic technology that is well-made, complex, efficient and technically advanced. As such, it fulfils the standards of modern human lithics users, such as those occupying Europe in the Upper Palaeolithic, and those contemporary peoples who include a lithic element in their technological repertoire. The main components of the Mousterian are the side-scraper and the small, distinctive, bifacial 'hand-axe'. The industry also incorporates the Levallois technique of flaking a prepared core, which was practised to a high art at some Neanderthal sites.

This is an industry that would be recognised as a useful and intelligently designed toolkit by a modern human familiar with lithics. Yet, there is something curious about the Mousterian which holds us back from pronouncing Neanderthals to be thoroughly modern-like in their toolkit behaviour. This is not any technical feature of the Mousterian artefacts as such – it is the temporal and spatial duration of the Mousterian industry as a whole. That is, the Mousterian is characterised by marked conservatism, while the later Upper Palaeolithic stone tool record is characterised by its diversity and speed of change and development, both over time and between different regions. The oddity of the Mousterian and of Neanderthal behaviour is that the toolkit endures with virtually no variation over enormous distances, and over a period of time (150–135 kya) which far exceeds the 35,000 years that have elapsed since the Neanderthals became extinct. As such it is atypical of the Upper Palaeolithic of Europe, wherein styles, designs and methods in stone tool traditions change and diversify frequently. The degree of conservatism seen in the Neanderthal Mousterian is unknown in the technologies of any anatomically modern human group, and as such constitutes a major behavioural difference between Neanderthals and their anatomically modern successors in Europe.

This is not intended to suggest a return to absolutist species-toolkit correlations. In the past, Neanderthals were thought to have been intellectually or physically incapable of making such 'advanced' stone tool cultures as those seen in the Upper Palaeolithic, characterised mainly by blade technologies and by the use of bone and ivory as well as stone. In tandem with this idea was the notion that no anatomically modern *H. s. sapiens* group would use an industry as flake-based as the Mousterian. Both these ideas are now known to be false: at the site of St Cesaire in western France, a late Neanderthal burial was found directly associated with the Chatelperronian, a blade-using Upper Palaeolithic-type industry previously thought to be attributable to some unspecified anatomically modern group. At the Levant sites of Skhul and Qafzeh, very early anatomically modern *H. s. sapiens* groups were found to be associated with classically Mousterian artefacts. However, the demise of assumptions linking technologies and/or intellect with specific human groups does not necessarily mean that behavioural differences between Neanderthals and anatomically modern human technologies cannot be postulated. While the anatomically moderns in the Levant at 100 kya–90 kya were using the Mousterian, later groups of the same species used different technologies. The anatomically modern pattern of change and replacement of technologies still stands despite the fact that one of their technological stages in one area was of Mousterian type. Similarly, the association of Neanderthals with the Chatelperronian in their most westerly and latest sites is no barrier to the claim that Neanderthals were extremely conservative in their stone tool manufacture. The Chatelperronian itself, moreover, looks distinctly like an imperfect attempt to copy the Upper Palaeolithic blade technologies of the anatomically moderns, and the Chatelperronian only occurs in those Neanderthal sites that are dated younger than 40 kya and are in Western Europe – a place and time where Neanderthals overlapped with anatomically moderns, and where it is conceivable that Neanderthals would have had an opportunity to observe and copy anatomically modern lithic styles. Additionally, the presence of anatomically modern human groups in territory previously occupied only by Neanderthals (in hominid terms) would have created extra competition for resources, the pressure of which may have pushed the local Neanderthal groups to do something they had never done before and attempt to improve or change their stone tool culture.

How can we research Neanderthal childhood patterns?

Having established this peculiarity of Neanderthal behaviour, how can we account for it in terms of Neanderthal childhoods? Is there something equally 'different' about Neanderthal childhoods that could feasibly provide a reason for this technological conservatism? Work on Neanderthal juvenile fossils such as those from the Devil's Tower 1 (Gibraltar) has focused on determining the age of the individual and rate of growth by examining the present dentition (Stringer *et al.* 1990). Studies on the perikymata (incremental growth ridges) on the teeth of the Devil's Tower child have suggested that Neanderthal children matured skeletally somewhat faster than modern children do. This evidence has been more recently confirmed by demographic studies suggesting that in order to keep a viable gene pool, considering group size and age of death, Neanderthals would have needed to reach reproductive age much earlier than modern humans (Aiello, personal communication).

The idea that pre-*H. s. sapiens* might have had a pattern of growth and development different from modern humans is not an unlikely one. Modern humans represent a marked extreme in the general primate pattern of extended periods of juvenile development, compared with our closest great ape relatives and all other primates. What is uncertain is when in the palaeoanthropological record this modern-type pattern of long childhoods began. Until recently, many scholars assumed that hominids generally followed the modern human developmental schedule, at least physically if not mentally. This was largely due to a lack of good fossil evidence of juvenile hominids. Since the discovery of an extremely well-preserved skeleton of a sub-adult *Homo ergaster*[2] male at Nariokotome, designated as WT 15,000 and dated to 1.6 mya (million years ago) (Brown *et al.* 1985), the situation has improved and growth studies on this individual have yielded results consistent with those of the Neanderthal studies. Specifically, work on the dentition of this specimen suggests that *H. ergaster* matured skeletally faster than expected, causing palaeoanthropologists to revise their estimation of WT 15,000's age down from 15 to 11 years (Smith 1986).

How is material culture affected by patterns of childhood?

In modern humans, childhood is the period where critical skills for adult life are acquired through learning, experimentation and practice. While adults also learn, the process differs; adults find it more difficult to absorb large amounts of information, to question received wisdom and to make inquisitive mental leaps outside what they already know about the world. Children are biologically set up for learning to the extent that some researchers (e.g. Pinker 1994) have argued for specific acquisition devices for certain skills, and these 'mental sponges' only remain open in childhood. Thus, an adult will have to learn something new by memory. The best known example of this is language, where children are astonishingly adept at learning and using new native words or a whole new language while their 'language acquisition device' remains, but an adult will struggle to remember the words and rules of a new language. Thus, it is in the juvenile period that the majority of complex learning occurs.

As the juvenile period is one which is greatly extended in ourselves in comparison to other primates and other mammals as a whole, modern humans spend a greater proportion of their lifespans in the 'apprenticeship' stage of cultural interaction. There is more real time for absorption and appreciation of material and social aspects of a child's environment. It is this luxury of time that allows modern human children the indulgence of learning their social crafts through a process of experimentation, exploration and experience. Certainly, twentieth century children are formally taught many of their skills, both at school and at home, but at least as much of the knowledge and skills that a young adult possesses has been gained by his or her own curiosity, investigations, discoveries and experiences. The extension of the juvenile period in modern humans allows their young the freedom to gain part of their adult knowledge through such non-directed instructive processes as role-playing, peer group interaction and physical play, wherein they can experiment with unknown factors in their social and physical environment with the freedom to form their own reactions.

This is not so in other primates with a less extended juvenile period. While there is an element of play and exploration in the behaviour of young chimpanzees, for example, the time spent in the pre-adult stage is proportionately shorter. This puts pressure on the sub-adult to learn all it needs to know for adulthood in this shorter time, and thus the luxury of gradually finding out for oneself is to a large extent replaced by the quicker method of learning by adult instruction. In the case of the great apes and other primates, this is an effective method of learning for the young because their adult lives will be less culturally complex than those of humans. However, in postulating the idea of a human species (such as the Neanderthals) with a pattern of juvenile life history which is shortened in comparison to modern humans, how can we reconcile their possession of a complex material (and probably social) culture with this model of instruction of the young?

In examining the archaeological record, we might consider likely differences between a material culture made by a hominid used to absorbing, and reacting to, directional instruction, as opposed to a material culture made by a hominid accustomed to learning through experimentation and questioning. Such a self-directed learning process would only be allowable in circumstances of a long juvenile period, since it would take longer than directed learning.

HOW MIGHT MOUSTERIAN CONSERVATISM BE CAUSED BY CHILDHOOD FACTORS?

If this notion of a shorter juvenile period in the Neanderthals were true, what would be the effect on the material culture of their societies? Would a decreased childhood period for Neanderthals have any tangible impact on their lithic technology when compared to anatomically modern human societies?

If we consider that the Neanderthals had less time spent as juveniles, both relatively and absolutely when compared with anatomically modern humans, this suggests that in terms of learning the prerequisite material and social skills for adult life, the Neanderthals would be under pressure to choose the model of directed instructional learning, where sub-adults take on board existing knowledge from their elders, rather than the model of exploratory, experience-based learning. With a shorter childhood, they simply would not have time for the question-based learning enjoyed by anatomically moderns with their longer childhoods. Neanderthal children would receive knowledge which was a copy of that received by their parents or carers in a previous generation, who would in turn have gained that knowledge as a copy of their own carers, and so on. Neanderthal children receiving such knowledge would be disposed against challenging the given wisdom because of the short amount of learning time available and the large amount of cultural knowledge that must be learned in that short time. Learning would thus occur by imitation rather than innovation. This notion of time pressure on child learning schedules is consistent with skeletal research suggesting both shortness of lifespan (Smith 1986) and the harshness of Neanderthal life (Trinkaus 1983; Trinkaus and Zimmerman 1982), two factors which suggest Neanderthal children would not have had the luxury of learning by innovation.

By contrast, in modern human groups, individuals whose minds have not yet acquired adult characteristics, but retain childlike learning and thinking patterns, form a large section of the population because of the greater proportion of lifespan spent in the pre-adult mode. Moreover, a large number of such individuals will be juveniles who, despite their deferral of adult status, are old, articulate and experienced enough to interact with, and influence the behaviour of, adults in the group. These adults, in turn, will be people whose behaviour has been influenced by spending a large amount of their own lives in the sub-adult stage, and as a result may be more inclined to take on board the suggestions or interests of sub-adult members of their group. It is this blurring of the roles between adult and child in the adolescent part of the juvenile period which, we feel, would result in the increased dynamism and experimentalism which appears in Palaeolithic Europe with the arrival of the anatomically moderns.

In terms of stone tools, the increased diversity of the Upper Palaeolithic can be accounted for by the extended juvenile period of anatomically modern humans in several ways. First, older juveniles would be physically large and co-ordinated enough to be taught, and to contribute to, the stone tool industry of their group. As sub-adults they would be inclined to challenge and explore what they were taught about flintknapping, and to master the skill partly through experiment and exploration. This may have led to the invention of new techniques or designs. As articulate and contributing members of the group they would then be in a position to demonstrate the benefits of the new method to adults. Second, the adults may be more disposed to assess the ideas of young toolmakers on their merits, or to copy the juvenile method by experimenting with flintknapping themselves, remembering how they may have solved a problem through this method when a juvenile.

This familiar picture of human toolmaking and interaction would be different in a society where play and reinterpretation was the preserve of toddlers and very young children. Here, the difference between adult and juvenile mentality would be much sharper. Unlike the blurred roles of adolescence seen in anatomically modern human groups, such a society would not reap the benefits of interaction between question and instruction.

HOW CAN THIS HYPOTHESIS BE TESTED?

We have already outlined the biological elements of accelerated childhood development and maturation in terms of comparison with other primates and physical studies of Neanderthal juveniles themselves. Biological ontogeny is only incompletely preserved in hominid fossils and behavioural traits cannot be extrapolated at all safely from such remains. As a result, the authors propose to construct a model of childhood effects on societal material culture as a whole, which can then be tested on modern humans and applied to Neanderthals.

The first task in constructing such a model is to gain a better understanding of the material culture producing capabilities of the young of any primate species. Perversely, the young of non-human primates seem to have been more widely studied than the young of humans in palaeoanthropological works. We set out to test a number of primary school age children on skills relevant to stone toolmaking. This produced some interesting results, which are detailed below. In terms of constructing our model, the next step is to suggest that this information would also be true of anatomically modern children in the Upper Palaeolithic and compare it with the stone tool record of that period. This will provide a model of how the accumulative learning of childhood skills affected the material culture of their society, which can be tested by application to other material records from different archaeological periods and ethnographic data. When this model is established, we will be able to identify elements in the Mousterian which do not conform to this model and suggest ways in which these non-conformities could have come about in terms of ontogeny.

EXPERIMENTS IN A SHEFFIELD PRIMARY SCHOOL
Approaching the need for practical work

Clearly, the most desirable test would be to ask children to try their hand at knapping flint for real, but this posed two problems. First, modern children are unfamiliar with the process and products of flintknapping, with the use of stone as a raw material, and with the concept of producing tools at all from raw material rather than receiving ready-manufactured goods. Neanderthals and anatomically modern Upper Palaeolithic children would have been readily familiar with stone tools, and so the skills of contemporary children would not be a reasonable reflection of those in the past. Second, and more important, flintknapping poses not inconsiderable dangers, with sharp chips flying and hammerstones coming close to small thumbs. In the light of these problems, we undertook to break down the process of stone toolmaking into its component skills, and devise safer, more representative tests for each of these skills. In this we were advised by the Child Development department at Sheffield University and informed by Piagetian theory (Piaget 1952; Piaget and Inhelder 1956). We developed four tests: one testing the strength with which a child could hit a large target with a round, handheld hammer; one testing the accuracy with which a child could hit a small target with the same hammer; a third testing the sequential design skills of the child; and a fourth testing a child's abilities to envisage and extract a given shape from a ball of solid matter. In all cases we used familiar, everyday objects such as modelling dough, clay, household utensils and sweets. The experiments were filmed on a hand-held camcorder as well as recorded on score sheets to alleviate observer bias.

Practical work

The tests we devised reflect the component skills involved in toolmaking. The strength test referred to whether the child could physically hit the target (representing a flint nodule) hard enough to have detached a flake of flint. We measured the force of the child's blow and later fitted their scores against flint hardness tests. While strength had to be controlled for, this in fact forms the least crucial part of flintknapping – a relatively light blow can detach a flake if the angle of the strike is correct. In our tests of 300 children aged five to eleven, we found that only some of the very youngest lacked the physical strength to detach a flake, and this was probably due to lack of focus rather than lack of muscular development itself.

The accuracy test tried to duplicate the need for angle and focus in flintknapping. The skill in toolmaking is to judge the right plane and striking point and then apply a blow to that specific point. To mimic this, we asked the child to strike a small target which had been fixed to an irregular object, the latter being large enough to hold. Success in this test depended largely on the speed of the blow, accuracy decreasing as velocity increased. Children were encouraged to hit the target gently in order to alleviate this, although some persisted in hitting hard. This test showed a wide variety in ability amongst different children of the same age group, but there was still a significant improvement in accuracy as age increased.

The sequential design test arose out of our recognition of the fact that when making a stone tool, although the knapper begins with a mental template of what the finished product should look like and the steps needed to reach this end, the nature of stone knapping is such that frequently a flake will detach in a slightly different way from that anticipated. The knapper must then readjust the image of the finished product and navigate his or her way around the unexpected change in design plan in order to accommodate the mistake. In order to test this, we asked the child to draw a picture of something familiar, only to interfere by making a blob on the drawing when the picture was almost finished. The child then had to finish the drawing, incorporating the unexpected blob by making it into something, either by changing the overall look of the original object being drawn (for example, in drawing a house, the child might make the blob into a round window, thus still ending up with a drawing of a house) or by developing the blob into an additional character of the picture (in the house example, by turning the blob into part of a person, a car or a flower). The way the blob was used was left completely to the child's imagination. There were few children who failed to think of anything they could do with the blob in any age group, but again, there were significantly more who failed to incorporate it in the younger age groups (5–6 years and 6–7 years) than in the older (7–11 years).

The fourth test was used to ascertain the child's abilities to work a shape out of a three-dimensional lump of solid matter, in this case modelling dough. Every child was given a ball of dough to start with and asked to make the same shape. In this test we were limited by the fact that the younger children had a more limited knowledge of shapes than the older ones. Specifically, we asked the children to make a triangle. We expected to find from this test that the younger children automatically opted for two-dimensional triangles while the older ones tended towards three-dimensional cones, pyramids or trapezoids. This is in line with Piagetian theory and more recent works suggesting that young children's modelling skills typically take a two-dimensional format even when asked to make something as solid as a person (Ecran, personal communication). However, with our request for a shape, many of the older children knew that a 'triangle' was properly a two-dimensional shape and deliberately flattened the ball of dough before cutting a triangle out of it.

Even controlling for this limiting factor, a clear pattern emerged from this test. Virtually none of the youngest children made a solid triangle by chopping three sides off the ball, something that most of the older ones did immediately. A few of the youngest made a triangle by the flattening method, but the most common pattern by far was the method of pulling bits of dough off the ball and laying them out on the table one by one to form a triangular outline. Some younger children also rolled their pulled-off bits of dough into sausages and lay three of them down in a triangular outline rather than build up the lines bit by bit. This was something that only 1 out of approximately 180 children over the age of 7 did. This pattern confirms our hypothesis that the younger children were far more comfortable interpreting our request in the two-dimensional medium than the three-dimensional. In a sense, the younger children were making a 'drawing' of a triangle, flattened and stuck to the table, whereas all of the older children bar one made a triangle that could be picked up in the hand, whether it was a flattened one, a solid pyramid, or trapezoid. We were further encouraged in this belief by the younger group's performance on the sequential design test where conventional drawing was required; most of them seemed very accomplished at regular drawing on paper but were much less accomplished with the modelling dough, often losing track of what they were doing, or making something which was not recognisable to adult eyes as a triangle, whereas they easily made a recognisable house, car or person with paper and pen.

The older groups' interpretations of 'triangle' were more diverse, with many opting for the flattening technique while others chopped three sides off the ball of dough. These were the most common techniques, but a wide range of alternatives were observed, including making a hollow pyramid out of triangular slices, making a hollow, open-bottomed cone by pushing thumbs into the ball and shaping a pointed top with the fingers, or simply hand-moulding the whole ball into a triangular shape without cutting. The over-sevens were far more confident and accomplished than the younger ones in their approach and completion of this task, but their drawings, while rather more complex and controlled than those of the younger group, did not show a proportional increase in skill equal to that witnessed in the modelling test.

It appeared from these observations that two-dimensional drawing was well within the capabilities of the youngest children (the youngest being aged 5) and that this skill was already fairly accomplished, improving only gradually as age increased. Three-dimensional modelling skills, however, were not well grasped at the level of 5 and 6 year olds, but showed a significant improvement amongst the 7 and 8 years olds, with the skill fully grasped by the 10 and 11 year old group. Performance in the accuracy test is also relevant as it combined the spatial co-ordination of eye and hand needed for drawing with the three-dimensional physicality of the modelling task.

The next steps

The results of the above tests have produced information about aspects of children's reaction to material culture and manipulation. In particular, the results of two-dimensional and three-dimensional modelling were of relevance to a discussion of stone toolmaking in the Palaeolithic, since the creation of a stone tool from a flint nodule is a process which involves reductive three-dimensional skills and sequential design. The lack of three-dimensional skills in pre-operational children contrasted with their accomplishments in two-dimensional drawing tasks, indicating that two-dimensional and three-dimensional design skills are quite separate aspects of a child's repertoire, and are achieved independently of each other. Pre-operational children would be incapable of learning to make stone tools as a result of the fact that they lack three-dimensional skills, although they might exhibit expertise in awareness of two-dimensional design factors. In terms of the Mousterian question outlined above, the results of this work show that there is a clear link between stage of development and material culture performance. This means that the limits imposed by Piagetian theory can be shown to impact on material culture, ancient examples of which make up the archaeological record. While this is not directly involved in an argument for a shorter childhood for Neanderthals, it encourages the notion that the nature of the Mousterian – indeed of any assemblage – includes the influence of development. In other words, we have shown that processes of cognitive development are not separate from the material, practical world, but have a significant impact upon it. Cognitive issues are not just the preserve of child psychologists, but can be demonstrated to produce real effects in material production. So, if the Mousterian is conservative, or the Upper Palaeolithic is dynamic, these characteristics may feasibly be reflections of the characteristics of childhood learning and development in the societies which produced them. Future work will focus on reasserting these findings in different contexts, through archaeological, primatological and ethnographical data.

CONCLUSION

It is our conclusion that the evidence for Neanderthals having a differential pattern of childhood from that seen in modern humans is significant. We further conclude that despite the need for inference and application of models in order to say anything sensible about children in the past, practical work to date suggests this line is worth pursuing, and that this hypothesis offers a more viable alternative to explanation of Neanderthal conservatism than the currently fashionable language hypothesis. Many scholars (Lieberman 1991; Gargett 1989) have argued that Neanderthals' apparent lack of symbolic behaviour such as art and experimental design in stone tools is due to their not possessing full symbolic language. While this has been cogently argued, the fact remains that there is, and can be, no concrete evidence for Neanderthals lacking language. It is our feeling that this line of study has reached a cul-de-sac situation and that learning patterns, as evidenced by the material culture and ontogenetic studies we have discussed, will yield more fruitful conclusions if pursued. Finally, in terms of our immediate concern, the study of Neanderthal childhoods, we believe we have identified an under-used resource in the campaign to discover what makes the Mousterian what it is.

NOTES

1   Proposed dates for the beginning and end of the Neanderthal period vary widely from author to author. Some recent data suggests the last Neanderthals may be as recent as 28 kya, whereas some authorities have defended the inclusion of the so-called 'pre-Neanderthals' such as Arago and Petralona in the period, which would push the beginning of the period back to approximately 230 kya. Here, we do not wish to confuse interpretation by including controversial specimens at either end of the timespan, so have chosen to use the traditional 'classic' period of Neanderthals as our chronology. Thus, the Neanderthals included in our time window are only those well established as classic Neanderthal types.

2   *Homo ergaster* is the name given to the African group, formerly included in *Homo erectus*, after it was suggested that the African hominids from this period were sufficiently different from the Asian specimens to merit creating a new species (Groves 1989; Wood 1991, 1992).

REFERENCES

Beynon, D. and Dean, M.C. (1988) 'Distinct dental development patterns in early fossil hominids', *Nature* 335: 509–13.

Brown, F., Harris, J., Leakey, R. and Walker, A. (1985) 'Early *Homo erectus* skeleton from West Lake Turkana, Kenya', *Nature* 316: 788–92.

Dean, M.C., Stringer, C.B. and Bromage, T.G. (1986) 'Age at death of the Neanderthal child from Devil's Tower, Gibraltar and the implications for studies of general growth and development in Neanderthals', *American Journal of Physical Anthropology* 70: 301–9.

Gargett, R. (1989) 'Grave shortcomings: the evidence for Neanderthal burial', *Current Anthropology* 30: 157–90.

Groves, C.P. (1989) *A Theory of Human and Primate Evolution*, Oxford: Oxford University Press.

Lieberman, P. (1991) *Uniquely Human: The Evolution of Speech, Thought and Selfless Behavior*, Harvard University Press: Cambridge and London.

Mann, A.E., Lampl, M. and Monge, J. (1987) 'Maturational patterns in early hominids', *Nature* 328: 673–4.

Piaget, J. (1952) *The Origins of Intelligence in Children*, New York: International Universities Press.

Piaget, J. and Inhelder, B. (1956) *The Child's Conception of Space*, London: Routledge and Kegan Paul.

Pinker, S. (1994) *The Language Instinct*, Penguin: London.

Smith, B.H. (1986) 'Dental development in Australopithecus and early Homo', *Nature* 323: 326–30.

Stringer, C.B. and Gamble, C. (1993) *In Search of the Neanderthals*, London: Thames & Hudson.

Stringer, C.B., Dean, M.C. and Martin, R.D. (1990) 'A comparative study of cranial and dental development in a recent British sample and among Neanderthals', in C. Jean DeRousseau (ed.) *Primate Life History and Evolution*, New York: Wiley-Liss. pp 115–52.

Trinkaus, E. (1983) *The Shanidar Neanderthals*, New York: Academic Press.

Trinkaus, E. and Zimmerman, M.R. (1982) 'Trauma among the Shanidar Neanderthals', *American Journal of Physical Anthropology* 57: 61–76.

Wood, B.A. (1991) *Koobi Fora Research Project IV: Hominid Cranial Remains from Koobi Fora*, Oxford: Oxford University Press.

—— (1992) 'Origin and evolution of the genus *Homo*', *Nature* 355: 783–90.

Chapter 8

Not merely child's play

Creating a historical archaeology of children and childhood

Laurie Wilkie

INTRODUCTION

In a grudging and minimal manner, historical archaeologists have acknowledged that children peopled the past. However, the presence of children in this sub-discipline arises not from any superior or enlightened interpretative or theoretical frameworks, but rather as an artefact of the material culture that historical archaeologists study. The material culture of the recent past, particularly since the mid-nineteenth century, includes a wide range of materials that were designed, manufactured and sold with children in mind as the users. It is the presence of these mass-produced, easily recognisable artefacts that has compelled historical archaeologists to at least admit that children once peopled the past (e.g. di Zerga Wall 1994; Farnsworth and Wilkie-Farnsworth 1990; Larsen 1994; McKillop 1995; Praetzellis and Praetzellis 1990; Pritchett and Pastron 1980; Reinhart 1984; Wilkie 1994a).

However, within historical archaeology, children's intentions and experiences, as reflected by their material culture, are not discussed. Children's artefacts are discussed as by-products of parents' attempts to instil values into their children, not as statements made by children (e.g. Larsen 1994; Praetzellis and Praetzellis 1990). The ethnocentric biases that lead twentieth century archaeologists to underestimate the economic and social roles of children in the deep past (see Moore and Scott 1997; Sillar 1994; Sofaer Derevenski 1997, 1994a, 1994b), are even more prevalent within American historical archaeology, where, in many instances, we could be studying the archaeology of our grandparents' or great grandparents' lives. How can we seriously study the social and economic role of children, who, as adults, may have told us they walked to and from school in the snow? In many cases, the artefacts of childhood may be familiar to us from our own childhoods, leading us again to assume that we already know the experiences of the users.

Unfortunately, beyond being cited as the users and disposers of certain artefacts, children are not considered as actors engaged in social dialogues, nor are they considered by historical archaeologists as active participants in shaping the archaeological record. Just as importantly, children are not seen as the users and consumers of non-children's artefacts. Children, however, were undeniably actors in the past, and childhood was a stage of life that all adults once occupied (Lillehammer 1989; Scott 1997; Sofaer Derevenski 1994a). Children were more than smaller versions of adults, and maintained their own sense of identity, world-view, priorities and social networks.

Historical archaeology, with its wealth of documentary and oral historical sources to draw upon, has the greatest potential of any of the archaeological sub-disciplines to identify children in the past. In my own research, tight dating of archaeological deposits, combined with oral historical and documentary data, has often allowed me to identify not only the occupants living within a particular house at a particular time, but the ages of occupants at the time of material deposition. The ability to identify age, ethnic and gender composition of families associated with particular artefacts, while not possible for every site, is possible in enough cases to allow controlled studies of family dynamics, which, hopefully, can eventually inform prehistoric studies.

In this chapter, I would like to introduce some of the children whom I have encountered archaeologically and some of the ways that I have approached integrating documentary and archaeological resources in an attempt to understand these children as social actors among their peers, in their families and in their communities. Some of these children I have come to know quite intimately and can discuss their experiences as individuals; others, I have been able to know only collectively as a group within their community. My intent is not to produce a formula or methodology for the historical archaeological study of children, but merely to explore how a consideration of children and childhood can enrich our archaeological interpretations of the past. In other words, if we assume that children were active participants in the creation of the historical archaeological record, what new insights does that assumption engender?

TOYS: DIALOGUES OF CONTROL AND RESISTANCE

While many of the prehistoric archaeologists studying childhood have justifiably avoided the subject of toys as 'an attempt to avoid stereotypes and to stimulate exploration of a variety of approaches to children in the archaeological record' (Sofaer Derevenski 1994a: 4) and escape the Euro-American association between children and toys (Sofaer Derevenski 1994b: 10), within historical archaeology, toys and children-specific artefacts are a constant and recognisable component of the material record. In addition, many of the cultures that we study are either culturally European/European-American, or represent ethnic groups within a European/European-American society. Therefore, we must ensure that we see these artefacts as more than play things (Sillar 1994).

Toys and children-specific artefacts (such as cups, clothing, mugs, medicines, school paraphernalia, etc.), when purchased or made for children, represent attempts, made by adults, to suggest and enforce certain norms of behaviour for children based upon their gender, age, socio-economic class and even socio-cultural ideals of beauty.

The male/female gender stereotypes of childhood found in European-America were well established in the nineteenth century as part of the larger division of domestic and commercial realms that were visible in society (di Zerga Wall 1994). As women became increasingly associated with the 'domestic' sphere, and men with the 'commercial' sphere, the ways in which children were raised and socialised also had to change.

By the early nineteenth century, popular publications (see Child 1989, 1992, 1996) informed mothers of the most appropriate games, activities and intellectual pursuits for their sons and daughters. These books were most likely to have been consulted by upper-class and aspiring middle-class families. Diane di Zerga Wall summarised mid-nineteenth century attitudes towards childhood as follows:

> By the mid-nineteenth century, the definition of childhood had changed. It was now looked on as encompassing a series of distinct phases of life. Throughout each phase, children were seen as requiring the physical and emotional nurturing that could best be supplied by their mothers at home. Home life was no longer viewed as a microcosm of society, however, and children could learn only the values and tasks that were integral to woman's sphere at home.
>
> (di Zerga Wall 1994: 6–7)

Institutions that existed outside of the home, such as schools, or the employment of in-house tutors, became means of educating male children. It is during this time that explicitly 'male' versus 'female' children's toys and artefacts were first produced in abundance.

By the early nineteenth century, dolls portraying adults were marketed to the female children of wealthy families to instil a sense of style, fashion and etiquette (Pritchett and Pastron 1980; Goodfellow 1993). Dolls portraying children and babies were intended to impart mothering and childcare values and skills. Other commonly found toys, ceramic tea sets, also became popular among the upper classes in the early nineteenth century, and were quickly copied by the middle classes. Again, these toys were intended to reinforce a sense of female identity which was tied to the domestic sphere.

In obtaining or giving certain toys to children, adults were selling a larger ideological package. Working-class parents buying expensive dolls for their daughters may have been expressing dreams of upward mobility. The purchase of school-related artefacts may have reflected, again, hopes for mobility based upon educational status, or expectations that a child, based on their current status, would achieve a certain level of education.

While adults were promoting certain cultural agendas to their children through the purchase and production of certain toys, children were by no means passive in this process. As many parents in our own society can attest, children actively pursue toys which have status within their own circles, and can obtain toys, or objects their parents may object to, through barter with other children, theft, outright purchase, or through pleading with other indulgent relatives or adults. In such ways children can actively shape their own material cultural assemblages. Likewise, children redesign toys through the ways that they are used, ignore toys that do not suit them, and create toys from non-toy objects. Children can also destroy or lose those objects that contradict their image of themselves or the expectations of their peer group. Archaeologically, it is the act of discard, loss and destruction of child-specific artefacts that we are most likely to encounter.

Highly valued toys and childhood objects can be curated well into adulthood and passed on to subsequent generations of children; therefore, artefacts found in the archaeological record may not adequately reflect the full range of material culture used and cherished by the users. For instance, marbles are commonly found artefacts in historical archaeological settings. However, the overwhelming majority of marbles recovered are small and simply designed, usually of plain clay, porcelain or glass. These marbles could be purchased in large numbers inexpensively and, if accidentally dropped, were not always retrieved. Large ornate marbles, used as 'shooters', which were often competed for among children in shooting matches, are seldom recovered archaeologically, but, due to their high incidence of curation by children, are commonly found in antique sales and are coveted by collectors (Randall 1971; Whitton 1984).

Porcelain dolls are objects, which when beloved by their owner, are carefully cared for by children. However, in the event of breakage of arms, legs, and even heads, parts may be carefully replaced. Sears, Roebuck and Company (Adams 1986; Mirkin 1970) and

Montgomery Ward (Montgomery Ward and Co. 1924) advertised many spare parts for dolls to replace damaged ones. When a cherished doll was broken beyond repair, simple relegation to the trash pit was not an inevitable conclusion. Although I have not found published accounts of this practice, I have heard, from both oral informants and from other archaeologists, that doll 'burials' were common occurrences during the late nineteenth and early twentieth centuries. Dolls and other toys can become real animate objects to children, much as comic strip character 'Hobbes', the stuffed tiger, became real to his child sidekick Calvin. The 'death' of such a beloved toy can be traumatic and upsetting for a child. However, I would like to begin my discussion of archaeological case studies with an example of a child who did not seem to be cherishing her dolls.

Toys and status-change anxiety: the case of Irene Cordes

When analysing materials from a 1920–2 garbage pit associated with a single four-person family in Santa Monica, California, I reconstructed a minimum of two porcelain and three bisque doll heads (Wilkie 1988; Farnsworth and Wilkie-Farnsworth 1990). No limbs were recovered, suggesting that the headless dolls may have been re-capitated. When I first analysed this material in 1988, I did not further consider the pattern of breakage or think about the relative high number of dolls broken over a relatively short period of around two years. However, in reconsidering the materials, I asked myself, do these toys say something more about the experiences of the child who used and broke them?

The most likely culprit for this high doll mortality rate was Irene Cordes, the eldest daughter of Ernest and Katie Cordes. Irene was born in 1916 or 1917, and would have been between ages 5 and 7 years during the period when the garbage pit was in use (Wilkie 1988). Although recovered from a sealed context where many of the other artefacts (mainly glass and ceramics) were completely reconstructable, the doll heads were highly fragmented, as if the heads had been brutally and intentionally smashed. The lack of limbs in the deposit further suggests that intentional violence was directed at these dolls' heads, rather than random breakages associated with rough handling, which would presumably cause injury to limbs as well as heads. The high numbers of dolls deposited over a short time suggested to me that perhaps Irene Cordes was making a strong statement to her parents through the destruction of what were, in the case of the bisque dolls, very expensive toys of her time. Other toys, such as marbles and tea sets, are also present, but not in abundance. Based on densities of similar artefacts recovered from other contemporary sites from similar family sizes (see, for example, Miller 1997; Praetzellis and Praetzellis 1990; Reinhart 1984; Wheaton and Reed 1990; Wilkie 1994), I would argue that dolls are over-represented within this assemblage when compared to others.

If dolls were the target, what statement was Irene making through their destruction? An adult feminist interpretation may be that Irene was rebelling against constraining gender stereotypes of her time. However, such a simple interpretation would devalue Irene's experiences and fail to acknowledge stresses that she encountered as an individual child. I would argue that Irene's stress arose from changes in status that she was encountering, unwillingly, in her family life.

A review of the historical record reveals that Margaret Cordes, Irene's younger sister, was born in 1921 (Wilkie 1988). Irene's status in the family would have shifted, from only child to older sibling, from centre of parental attention to sharing that attention. Being an older sibling meant that new responsibilities and restraints may have entered her life. Irene's dolls may have been given to her in preparation for this event, or may have been used to instruct her on how to relate to a new sibling. Or, even without parental suggestion/interference, the dolls, and the way they were to be treated, may have come to represent to Irene the unwanted intrusion of another into her family.

As a child, in the cultural sense, Irene would not have been involved in the decision of her parents to have another child, nor would she be able to affect the outcome of such a decision. Further, given her cultural status as a child, Irene would have had limited means to protest or express her frustration in ways that would draw a response from her parents. Was the response of Ernest and Katie Cordes to replace the heads of these dolls an attempt to mollify their daughter or to symbolically enforce the status change? We cannot know. However, this case study does suggest that toys can be means of social dialogue, not just objects of play. Irene Cordes' archaeologically inferred behaviour underscores that children did undergo changes in status, both willingly and unwillingly, and could use material culture to assert both their opinions and sense of individuality.

Finally, that the addition of a sibling to a family could cause such stress for a child is also culturally informative. Diane di Zerga Wall (1994) discusses how changes in the perceived roles of children from the colonial period to the nineteenth century had impacts on family size. Middle-class parents shifted from having large families, where children were important economic contributors, to having smaller families in which greater resources were allocated to each child. In large families with short birth-spacing, the addition of a sibling or siblings would occur before the eldest child was conscious of a status change. In situations where smaller families were more common, and the birth-spacing between children was larger, the eldest child would have had greater opportunity to establish themselves and their identity as an 'only' child. Having reached the age of 5 or 6 before her sister was born, Irene Cordes may have fully expected that she would always be an only child. Irene's stress and anxiety was in part a by-product of her culture's attitudes towards family size and birth-spacing.

Toys as symbols of race and class identity: an example from African America

Toys could also be used in dialogues on race and social class, not just between parents and children, but between different communities. In her autobiography, *I Know Why the Caged Bird Sings*, Maya Angelou recounts receiving a Christmas gift from her long-absent mother. 'My gift from Mother was a tea set – a teapot, four cups and saucers and tiny spoons – and a doll with blue eyes and rosy cheeks and yellow hair painted on her head' (1969: 43). Angelou and her brother later destroyed the doll as an act of retaliation against their mother, who had left her children to be raised in rural Arkansas while pursuing better opportunities as a fair-skinned black woman in the North. While Angelou does not comment explicitly on how she reacted to the white features of the dolls, other African-American writers, such as Toni Morrison (1970) and Alice Walker (1973, 1982), have written of the anguish felt by African-American children who felt that society valued only fair, pale-skinned beauty.

A review of late nineteenth to early twentieth century mail-order catalogues, such as Sears, Roebuck and Co. and Montgomery Ward, quickly confirm that toys were marketed primarily to white consumers until 1930, when 'coloured' versions of baby dolls were first advertised (Adams 1986: 93). Even these dolls, however, were merely brown-coloured versions of the white dolls, which sported three braids typical of 'pickaninie' characters popular among white populations of the time.

Toys not only mirrored societal ideals that emphasised Aryan features (blond, blue-eyed, fair-skinned), but also reflected racial stereotypes. In 1927, the Sears, Roebuck and Co. catalogue advertised a toy which portrayed a black man stealing a chicken. The text advertising the toy read, 'One of our most novel toys. When the strong spring motor is wound up the scared looking negro shuffles along with a chicken dangling in his hand and a dog hanging on the seat of his pants. Very funny action toy which will delight the kiddies' (Mirkin 1970: 594).

While the majority of toys and children's items were manufactured with middle- to upper-class European-American children in mind, how should we interpret these items when recovered from non-European contexts? I have been attempting to deal with this issue in the American South on late nineteenth to early twentieth century African-American house sites (Wilkie 1994a).

The material I will discuss here has been drawn from two plantation sites, that of Riverlake Plantation in Pointe Coupe Parish, Louisiana, and from Oakley Plantation, West Feliciana Parish, Louisiana. These two parishes are located in the south-eastern portion of Louisiana – the former bordering the Mississippi River on the west, the latter, on the east. The two parishes are located across the river from one another.

Riverlake was a sugar plantation, founded in the 1790s and occupied by a sizeable African-American population until the early 1990s. Archaeological materials from this plantation were drawn from four house sites dating primarily from the 1880s to 1920s, and correspond to the occupation of African-American sharecropping families at the plantation. Oakley Plantation was a cotton plantation. The evidence from this plantation was primarily drawn from one household, which was occupied by a house servant, Silvia Freeman, and her five children from around 1880 to 1915, and then by her daughters, Eliza and Delphine Freeman, and their two daughters, from around 1915 to 1930.

As sharecroppers, the children of Riverlake Plantation would have had greatly different experiences from the Freeman children due to differences in socio-economic circumstances. Sharecropping was a brutal and exploitive economic system in which plantation managers sought to keep families in a continual cycle of debt from year to year. Sharecroppers lived on credit throughout the year, rarely having access to cash. Oral histories from men and women who were raised on Riverlake demonstrate that children helped their families by farming, hunting and fishing. In contrast, a position as a domestic servant offered the greatest financial opportunity for African-American families, for pay was distributed in cash wages. The greater financial security that Silvia Freeman's position afforded her, however, did not spare her children from labour. Three of the Freeman children were employed by the same planter family by the time they reached 12 years old (Wilkie 1994b).

While children at Riverlake and Oakley were employed in economic pursuits, they also had spare time in which to pursue their own activities. Toys were recovered from both sites. However, the material culture of childhood from the Freeman house is very different from that of Riverlake. The Freeman children lived in close proximity to, and in nearly daily contact with, their employers, the Matthews sisters, a pair of childless spinsters. It is clear from the documentary record that the Matthews considered Silvia Freeman herself as a sort of child, referring to her by the nickname 'Silvie' and making gifts of second-hand ceramics, glassware and clothing to her. Such a 'paternalistic' relationship between white employers and black employees was based in the period of enslavement, and stems, in part, from racist notions regarding the maturity and intelligence of African-Americans (Tucker 1988).

In addition to outfitting Silvia Freeman's household with loans of kitchen goods and gifts of tableware, jewellery and clothing, the Matthews also made gifts of toys to the Freeman children. Tea sets and dolls recovered from the Freeman house date at least twenty years earlier than the rest of the materials, and match items left in the planter residence by the Matthew sisters upon their deaths. The gold-rimmed toy tea sets and Caucasian-featured dolls recovered from the Freeman house contrast sharply with the large numbers of marbles that dominated the Riverlake assemblages. Marbles, certainly popular at Riverlake, in part due to their inexpensive nature, are non-gendered objects which stress communal over individual play. The sharecropping community of Riverlake, by accounts of informants, was tightly-knit and dependent upon one another for economic, spiritual and social support. Children at Riverlake played in large groups, making their own toys, playing communal imagination and organised games.

The Freeman children, in contrast, were spatially isolated from the children of the Oakley quarters, which were located over a mile away from their residence. The toys recovered from their house reflect individual play. In addition, the toys provided to them by the planters promoted play that was very close to their work. While a middle- or upper-class white child might play with a toy tea set in imitation of their mother's social activities, the social tea was not an established social facet of African-American plantation life. Maya Angelou's mother may have sent her a gift of a tea set and doll as a reflection of her middle-class, upwardly mobile aspirations for her daughter; but what was the intent of a white planter giving these work-related toys to young black house servants? Do these gifts represent an opportunity to play like middle-class white children, or to promote play that would provide the children with an opportunity to practice skills that they would need at work? It seems unlikely that the intention of the planters, given the strict racial caste system of the Jim Crow South, was to encourage African-American children's social aspirations.

In addition to the planters' intentions in providing these toys, we must also consider how the Freeman children may have responded to these toys. The answer may be available from the archaeological record. The two doll heads recovered from the site were broken. Doll limbs were recovered whole, suggesting that no attempt was made to replace heads, but, instead, the bodies were discarded upon loss of the heads. A minimum of six toy tea set vessels were recovered from the deposit immediately around and under the cabin (the Freeman house was on raised piers, with household debris brushed underneath). Four of the tea set pieces had been discarded or lost intact. It seems unlikely that prized possessions would be discarded, unbroken, among the garbage. Through the destruction and loss of these toys, the Freeman children may have been expressing their opinions of the materials.

While toys are the artefacts most stereotypically associated with children's activities, they are greatly under-used in historical archaeological interpretative frameworks. Toys in nineteenth and twentieth century American society represent a medium for symbolic communication between adults and children, and among children as they negotiate status and identity within their peer-groups. As one of the few mediums of social expression allowed to children during this time period, we should listen carefully to the ways that children spoke to adults and one another through the attainment, maintenance, use of and discard of toys.

CHILDREN AS SOCIAL MEDIATORS FOR ADULTS

While nineteenth and twentieth century children are often conceptualised as individuals who inhabit the domestic realm, children did act outside of their home as social agents, and created social networks and obligations independent of their parents and family. School, children's religious training classes, errands to the store for others, and children's play areas, all provided opportunities for children to meet other children and form social ties. The social ties of children could be used by adults to expand their own social and communal networks.

Silvia Freeman appears to have depended upon her children to create, at least initially, ties to other members of Oakley's African-American community. As mentioned previously, the Freemans' house was spatially isolated from the cabins of the sharecroppers. Silvia Freeman worked as the cook for the Matthews sisters. While her position earned her a four dollar a month salary, it also required that she work in the planter's kitchen from the early hours of the morning until after the preparation of the evening meal. A letter from one of the Matthews' sisters to a friend stated that Freeman worked full days except Sunday, when she prepared the evening meal early so that she could attend church (Wilkie 1994b). The church outings represented Silvia Freeman's weekly opportunity to interact with other members of the plantation community.

Freeman's interactions with the broader African-American community were very important. Within the Jim Crow South, African-Americans were politically and economically disenfranchised, and socially segregated from the European-American community. As such, all opportunities for social, economic and political advancement came from within the African-American community. Silvia Freeman may have been more financially stable than many of the sharecropping families, but she remained black in a white-dominated world. Archaeological and documentary evidence indicates that one of the ways that Silvia Freeman reinforced her bond with the African-American community was through bartering tobacco and store-bought goods for home-grown produce. Sharecroppers were cash-poor, and the purchase of items such as tobacco, dry goods and cloth would have required them to increase their annual debt to the planter (Wilkie 1994b). Silvia Freeman may have met some of the individuals with whom she traded through church; however, another medium for creating social networks was through her children.

Given her limited opportunities for socialising with other members of Oakley's community, Silvia Freeman's children were her greatest social asset. While church met just once a week, the school run by the church met every day, six months a year. While several of Freeman's children were employed at a time by the Matthews' family, at least one of her children was enrolled in school at all times. Archaeologically, broken school slates, pencils and a pen nib corroborate the documentary evidence (Wilkie 1994b). None of Silvia's individual children, however, seem to have remained in school for longer than one or two years. Perhaps the Freeman children were in school not only to learn, but also to create a social network for their family. Parents can come to know one another through the friendships of their children. Likewise, children meeting regularly at school can become the means of transporting goods between families, either in the form of barter or less formalised mutual reciprocity.

Children, then, should be considered as individual social actors, capable of creating extended social networks through friendships. The friendships of children do not exist separate and apart from the social networks of adults, but are intimately entwined. Parents can befriend one another through their children, just as children can befriend one another through their parents' contacts.

CHILDREN AS ECONOMIC PRODUCERS

Within historical contexts, children have always been contributors to household labour, and, either directly or indirectly, to household economies. While pinpointing archaeologically the contributions of any member to the overall household can be difficult, if children are not considered as part of the equation, we will continue to miss the dynamics of relationships and roles of individuals within households.

Clifton Plantation, a British Loyalist Plantation on New Providence Island, Bahamas, has provided a unique opportunity to study the economic and subsistence strategies of enslaved families who were encouraged to work for themselves by their owner. The plantations of the Bahamas, granted by the British Crown in the late eighteenth century to repay colonists who had remained loyal to the Crown during the American Revolution, were initially lucrative, and then quickly depleted. The poor soil of the Bahamas islands could not long support any intensive agriculture. Planters had accumulated large slave populations for whom they were required to provide minimum daily rations (Farnsworth 1996).

William Wylly, the owner of Clifton, fancied himself a reformer of enslaved life. To minimise his economic costs, and to create a European peasant-class lifestyle for his enslaved people, he provided the enslaved people with two days a week in which to work on their own provisioning grounds; in exchange, he would eliminate their weekly allotment of corn (Wilkie 1997). He allowed the enslaved population to raise subsistence crops, and pigs and fowl. He agreed to pay market prices for the hogs and provided transportation to the Nassau market to his enslaved people so that they could sell their surplus produce. In addition, at the rate of one shilling per yard, he paid enslaved men to build walls. Plantation ledgers clearly demonstrate that the enslaved population of Clifton raised corn, beans, squash, root crops, hens and pigs. Most of the adult men and their young sons earned additional money by building walls. Wylly stipulated to his driver, in regard to the provisioning grounds, 'each man and his wife must plant two acres of provisions: (which the wife alone will be able to attend)' (Bahamas Department of Archives 1817).

Initial archaeological excavations at Clifton Plantation (Wilkie 1997; Wilkie and Farnsworth 1997) have demonstrated that the enslaved families used their access to the market to acquire European-produced goods which conformed with African religious and aesthetic traditions. These goods account for as much as 50 per cent of their material assemblages. Such a dependence upon market goods meant that families, as an economic unit, needed to maximise the goods they had for trade as well as their access to currency.

In 1818, Wylly described himself as owning between sixty and seventy slaves, twenty of whom he considered to be 'children', and therefore, requiring their legally mandated ration of corn because they could not work (Bahamas Department of Archives 1817). Children represent nearly one-third of the enslaved population, and had no demands from the planter on their time. Although the children were not required by the planter to work, these individuals represented a potential labour source to their families. In evaluating the archaeology of Clifton Plantation, it became important to consider the potential economic activities of children.

While the documentary record suggests that Wylly intended his slaves to raise animals for their own consumption, the archaeological record suggests a very different scenario. A preliminary analysis of faunal remains from the site indicates that pork and chicken bones are almost exclusively found at the planter's residence. The main sources of protein in the slave quarters were shellfish and fish. None of the historical documents discuss either of these protein sources or by whom they may have been acquired. A closer analysis of the shellfish, however, led me to consider children as the collectors of these resources.

Within the Bahamas, both past and present, Queen Conch (*Strombus gigas*) is by far the most important shellfish resource. A full-grown individual mollusc can easily provide one pound of usable meat. Even today, with the booming market for conch, an individual diving without a tank can easily collect four or five per dive. The animals prefer the grassy beds between the reefs, however, and a boat is typically needed to reach their habitat.

Clifton Plantation is situated on the coast, and Wylly owned a long strip of beach containing both rocky outcrops and sandy dunes. With a boat, one can access conch-bearing grass fields off Clifton's shores. While conch is one of the most important marine resources available in the Bahamas, and has been found in abundance at other plantations, in Clifton's slave quarters, vast numbers of conch were recovered only from the driver's cabin. Instead, at the other six cabins, a greater abundance of smaller species, such as West Indian Top Shell (*Cittarium pica*), Tiger Lucines (*Codakia orbicularis*), and Fuzzy Chiton (*Acanthoplegia granulata*) were recovered.

West Indian Top Shell, locally known as 'Whelk', is a large snail, with shell diameters reaching as large as 6 cm, and is still harvested on the islands. It occurs in rocky shoreline areas where it can be easily pulled from exposed reefs. Fuzzy Chiton are also indigenous to rocky shores. A knife or similar object is required to remove them. Both of these species often lurk in the small crevices of exposed shoreline reefs, where they can best avoid the attention of birds. Tiger Lucines are clam-like creatures, which typically grow to be 4 to 6 cm across. They can be found burrowing in sandy shores.

None of these species require access to a boat, or specialised skill to harvest. The chiton and top shells, given their preference for burrowing into the nooks and crannies of exposed reefs, are most easily collected by individuals with small hands. Does the emphasis on these shoreline species, rather than the otherwise ubiquitous conch, reflect the children of Clifton's contribution to their families' diet? There is, of course, no way to confirm or refute this possibility: a shellfish harvested by a child looks archaeologically just like any other shellfish. However, within the plantation community, children who the planter perceived to be 'too young to work' would have the greatest opportunity to walk the half mile to the shore to harvest shellfish. Women were encouraged by the planter and driver to tend to the family provisioning grounds (where they undoubtedly were also aided by their children), while men's and older boys' time would be best served employed in the building of walls for sterling.

The harvesting of shellfish, while not requiring skilled labour, provided an important protein source for the family which did not need to be purchased, and which the planter does not seem to have been purchasing. The labour of children, who represented a sizeable proportion of the enslaved community, in a very real way may have contributed to the community's ability to maintain a sense of African identity within the context of enslavement. Children were not just the passive recipients of their African cultural heritage, but through their efforts actively helped to maintain and preserve that heritage.

While children may not have been legally employed outside of the home, they still made important contributions to their households, be it through the completion of assigned chores, assisting with the tending of livestock, or through the hunting and collecting of wild resources. Many of the sites that historical archaeologists study were situated in rural areas, where the labour of children was vital to the economic survival of families. The potential contributions of children must be acknowledged if we are to understand households as economic and social units.

THE SECRET LANDSCAPES OF CHILDHOOD

In addition to building their own social networks and liaisons, children created social spaces and landscapes that were distinctive to their communities. The desire for privacy is not unique to adults. In her vernacular architectural study of California Eichler homes, Adams (1995) demonstrated that, while the design of these suburban homes was intended to provide parents with an open view of children's backyard play areas, children commonly favoured the smaller but secluded side yards as play areas, thus maximising privacy from their parents. While archaeologists have successfully studied engendered spaces (e.g. Gilchrist 1994), we must also be sure to consider how children created and maintained spaces distinct from those occupied by adults.

Children's spaces can occur both within and beyond architectural structures. Recently, a secret children's play area was found in the attic space of a Victorian-period officer's house at the San Francisco Presidio (Barker, personal communication). The space could only be accessed through a very small, child-sized hole in a lower attic ceiling. The creator of the space used it as a retreat, leaving it filled with snacks, such as fruit pits, reading materials, and even a still-wrapped cigar, perhaps a trophy of resistance to parental rules.

At Riverlake Plantation, children living in the quarters during the late nineteenth to early twentieth centuries, inhabited a community that was slowly decreasing in size. Previously occupied houses were abandoned, the usable lumber and bricks from the tops of the chimneys were scavenged, and the yards were left to become overgrown with shrubs. The only evidence that remained of many of these abandoned houses were the ground-level brick platforms that had once supported the chimneys. These areas, while abandoned by adults, became centres of play for children (Wilkie 1994a). During the excavation of these abandoned cabins, large numbers of marbles were found wedged in cracks between the bricks. The majority of marbles from the site were recovered from these areas associated with chimneys.

Marbles was a game that was played between several different individuals at a time, sometimes with an audience. Informants from Riverlake remembered playing marbles competitively against one another in hope of winning more marbles (Wilkie 1994a). Marbles, and the possession of marbles, was tied to status and achieved skill. One boy from the plantation was reported to have buried a bucket of marbles as buried treasure when playing 'pirates', perhaps reflecting the status attributed to these artefacts.

The flat surfaces of the former chimneys would have made an adequate playing area for marbles. In addition, their location would have ensured that children could have played with little fear of being observed by adults. Riverlake's African-American community was filled with staunch Baptists, who may not have been pleased to see their children involved in a game that was essentially a form of gambling. The choice of location may have also allowed older children privacy from younger children who were under the supervision of adults in the house yards.

CONCLUSION

Children peopled the past, not just as passive recipients of their communities' and families' standards, but as individual social actors who negotiated opportunities and identities for themselves within their cultures. Children are not, and were not, just smaller versions of adults. Their age and status provided them with distinctive concerns, needs and social networks. The archaeological case studies discussed above begin to demonstrate the breadth of children's experiences as potentially explored archaeologically.

Irene Cordes, the child, may have had very different feelings and reactions to her sibling as an adult, or, as an adult, may have responded to stress and anxiety brought on by status changes in very different ways. Children were not isolated from the broader social, economic and political concerns of their times. African-American children in the American South dealt with institutionalised racism as part of their daily existence, just as adults did. However, the means of protesting and expressing frustration with racism were different from those available to adults. During Bahamian enslavement, children served as important economic contributors within their households. While children are often perceived as passive recipients of their culture, learning their heritage through enculturation, the economic activities of Clifton Plantation's children allowed them to be active participants in the creation and maintenance of an African-Bahamian identity.

While the lack of a historical archaeology of childhood is frustrating in itself, historical archaeologists are generally reluctant to consider intergenerational dynamics within any household setting, leaving the past peopled by ageless blobs similar to Tringham's now famous unengendered 'faceless blobs' (Tringham 1991: 94). Perhaps, by beginning to understand the relationships and roles of children and adults, we can also begin the process of learning how to conceptualise and understand the experiences of many different age – gender classes in the past.

In this sense, I see the archaeological recognition of children as independent social actors and as members of a distinct social class not as an end in itself, but as a means of approaching the problem of individuality, gender and stages of life within archaeology. Just as we have come to accept that gender is an important construct within human societies, we must come to understand age and stage of life as important constructs too. Although the archaeology of childhood has grown from the study of gender, it is important that we do not become entrapped in a 'women and children' mentality, which links children inevitably with the activities of women. Not only does this coupling rely too much on biological rather than cultural associations, it also conjures the distressing image of a sinking ship.

REFERENCES

Adams, A. (1995) 'The Eichler home: intention and experience in postwar suburbia', in V.E. Cromley and C. Hudgins (eds) *Gender, Class, and Shelter: Perspectives in Vernacular Architecture*, Knoxville: University of Tennessee Press, pp.164–78.

Adams, M. (ed.) (1986) *Collectible Dolls and Accessories of the Twenties and Thirties from Sears, Roebuck and Co. Catalogues*, New York: Dover Publications.

Angelou, M. (1969) *I Know Why the Caged Bird Sings*, New York: Bantam.

Bahamas Department of Archives (1817) Letter from William Wylly to Colonial Office, Colonial Office Records Microfilm 23/67/150–151.

Child, L.M. (1989) [1831] *The Mother's Book*, Cambridge, Mass.: Appleton Books.

—— (1992) [1834] *The Girl's Own Book*, Cambridge, Mass.: Appleton Books.

—— (1996) [1829] *The Boy's Own Book*, Bedford, Mass.: Appleton Books.

di Zerga Wall, D. (1994) *The Archaeology of Gender*, New York: Plenum Press.

Farnsworth, P. (1996) 'The influence of trade on Bahamian slave culture', *Historical Archaeology* 30(4): 1–23.

Farnsworth, P. and Wilkie-Farnsworth, L. (1990) 'Family life in 20th century Santa Monica: the Spencer House site', *Proceedings of the Society for California Archaeology* 3: 109–33.

Gilchrist, R. (1994) *Gender and Material Culture: The Archaeology of Religious Women*, London: Routledge.

Goodfellow, C. (1993) *The Ultimate Doll Book*, London: Dorling Kindersley.

Larsen, E. (1994) 'A boardinghouse madonna: beyond the aesthetic of a portrait created through medicine bottles', *Historical Archaeology* 28(4): 68–79.

Lillehammer, G. (1989) 'A child is born: the child's world in an archaeological perspective', *Norwegian Archaeological Review* 22(2): 89–105.

McKillop, H. (1995) 'Recognizing children's graves in nineteenth-century cemeteries: excavations in St Thomas Anglican churchyard, Belleville, Ontario, Canada', *Historical Archaeology* 29(2): 77–99.

Miller, L. (1997) 'The archaeology of an early 20th century Berkeley family', unpublished paper, on file: Historical Archaeology Laboratory, Department of Anthropology, University of Berkeley, California.

Mirkin, A. (ed.) (1970) *The 1927 Edition of the Sears, Roebuck Catalogue*, New York: Crown Publishers.

Montgomery Ward and Co. (1924) *Montgomery Ward and Co. Catalogue, Fall–Winter 1924–1925, No. 101*, Oakland: Montgomery Ward and Co.

Moore, J. and Scott, E. (eds) (1997) *Invisible People and Processes: Writing Gender and Childhood into European Archaeology*, London: Leicester University Press.

Morrison, T. (1970) *The Bluest Eyes*, New York: Washington Square Press.

Praetzellis, M. and Praetzellis, A. (1990) *For a Good Boy: Victorians on Sacramento's J. Street*, Rohnert Park, California: Cultural Resources Facility, Sonoma State University.

Pritchett, J. and Pastron, A.(1980) 'Ceramic dolls as chronological indicators: implications from a San Francisco dump site', in A. Ward (ed.) *Contributions to Anthropological Studies No. 3*, Albuquerque: University of New Mexico.

Randall, M. (1971) 'Early marbles', *Historical Archaeology* 5: 102–5.

Reinhart, T. (1984) *The Archaeology of Shirley Plantation*, Charlottesville: University of Virginia Press.

Sillar, B. (1994) 'Playing with God: cultural perceptions of children, play and miniatures in the Andes', *Archaeological Review from Cambridge* 13(2): 47–63.

Scott, E. (1997) 'Introduction: on the incompleteness of archaeological narratives' in J. Moore and E. Scott (eds) *Invisible People and Processes: Writing Gender and Childhood into European Archaeology*, London: Leicester University Press, pp.1–12.

Sofaer Derevenski, J. (ed.) (1994a) 'Perspectives on children and childhood', *Archaeological Review from Cambridge* 13(2).

—— (1994b) 'Where are the children? Accessing children in the past', *Archaeological Review from Cambridge* 13(2): 7–20.

—— (1997) 'Engendering children, engendering archaeology', in J. Moore and E. Scott (eds) *Invisible People and Processes: Writing Gender and Childhood into European Archaeology*, London: Leicester University Press, pp. 192–202.

Tringham, R. (1991) 'Households with faces: the challenge of gender in prehistoric architectural remains', in J. Gero and M. Conkey, (eds) *Engendering Archaeology: Women and Prehistory*, London: Blackwell, pp. 93–131.

Tucker, S. (1988) *Telling Memories Among Southern Women: Domestic Workers and their Employers in the Segregated South*, New York: Schocken Books.

Walker, A. (1973) *In Love and Trouble; Stories of Black Women*, New York: Harcourt Brace Jovanovich.

—— (1982) *The Color Purple*, New York: Washington Square Press.

Wheaton, T. and Reed, M.B. (1990) 'James City, North Carolina: archaeological and historical study of an African-American urban village', *New South Associates Technical Report 6*, Atlanta: New South Associates.

Whitton, B. (1984) *Toys*, New York: Alfred A. Knopf.

Wilkie, L. (1988) 'A police man's lot: family life in early 20th century Santa Monica, California', Report on file, Archaeological Facility, Fowler Museum of Cultural History, University of California, Los Angeles.

—— (1994a) 'Childhood in the quarters: playtime at Oakley and Riverlake plantations', *Louisiana Folklife* 18: 13–20.

—— (1994b) *'Never Leave me Alone': an Archaeological Study of African-American Ethnicity, Race Relations and Community at Oakley Plantation*, Ann Arbor: University Microfilms International.

—— (1999) 'Evidence of African continuities in the material culture of Clifton Plantation, Bahamas', in J. Haviser (ed.) *African Sites Archaeology in the Caribbean*, Princeton: Marcus Weiner Press, pp. 264–76.

Wilkie, L. and Farnsworth, P. (1996) 'Preliminary results of the 1996 excavations at Clifton Plantation', *Journal of the Bahamas Historical Society* 18: 50.

—— (1997) 'Daily life on a loyalist plantation: results of the 1996 excavations at Clifton Plantation', *Journal of the Bahamas Historical Society* 19: 2–18.

Part V

Children and relationships

The construction of the individual among North European fisher-gatherer-hunters in the Early and Mid-Holocene

Liliana Janik

INTRODUCTION

This chapter argues that the construction of the individual is linked to the cultural categorisation of social relations. Focusing on fisher-gatherer-hunter communities in the south-east Baltic and Scandinavia, it is argued that social relations within groups can differ despite sharing the same mode of production. In this I diverge from others who see the social construction of the individual as being more closely related to the mode of production (Zvelebil and Rowley-Conwy 1984; Hodder 1990).

Non-adults can be regarded as important participants in the construction of social relations in fisher-gatherer-hunter communities. The physical and social construction of culture is transmitted to non-adults in order to ensure the successful continuation of the community. In turn, the construction of the community and how particular individuals take their place in that social structure may be reflected in the way that non-adults are treated. In particular, burial practices can be seen as social acts, claims made on behalf of the individual being buried, revealing members of the community as either dependent or independent selves. The study of non-adults can therefore act as the medium for a wider interpretation of social relations. As an independent category in the construction of social relations, age, rather than the more frequently examined variable of sex (Albrethsen and Petersen 1976; Larsson 1993; O'Shea and Zvelebil 1984), can be regarded as the major element when interpreting and exploring differences within the social relations of prehistoric fisher-gatherer-hunters in northern Europe.

SOCIAL RELATIONS AND CULTURAL CATEGORISATIONS

The role of the individual in constructing social relations has been widely discussed in archaeological literature over the last decade (Gero and Conkey 1991; Gilchrist 1994; Engelstad 1991: 502–14, Nelson 1997). However, these discussions frequently concentrate on the relationship between sex and gender as the primary focus of interest in understanding social relations, reflecting our Western understanding of male and female. Age is often identified as influenced by these two categories rather than seen as an independent research issue. In the Western tradition, concepts of what it is to be female and what it is to be male are very strongly implicated in the foundations of archaeological interpretation: 'Sex, then as we understand it within the terms of Western discourse, is something which differentiates between bodies, while gender is a set of variable social constructions placed upon those differentiated bodies' (Moore 1994: 14). In this manner, the way we address the question of gender and social relations does not leave us with any other possibility than a straightforward relationship between biological sex and social gender. However, categories of social gender can be seen as fluid and flexible when we look at other cultures (MacCormack and Strathern 1980; Strathern 1988): 'Our own concepts provide a structure so persuasive that when we come across other cultures linking, say, a male–female contrast to oppositions between the domestic and wild or society and the individual, we imagine they are part of the same whole. Nature and culture do not exist in the Hagen as categories of the order, for example, of the clearly conceptualised distinctions between prestige and rubbishness, social goals and individual autonomy, or mind, body and spirit' (Strathern 1980: 216).

Nonetheless, although discussions concerning social relations have often focused on rather rigid, structured notions of sex and gender, the insights gained from these discussions may still prove useful to an archaeological study based on age. The cultural categorisation of gender can be determined by material culture when material culture plays an active role in defining the particular individual within the gender and social relationships of the community. Material culture is thus a focal point in this chapter in defining the individual as an autonomous member of the group. Considered in terms of the 'Gender of the Gift' (Strathern 1988), in other words through the relationship between artefact and the human body, material culture can be used to explore the role of age in the categorisation of the individual. It should be stressed that here I employ the 'Gender of the Gift' as a more broadly applicable concept than a relationship solely between material culture and gender. Namely, the role of objects in defining the place of the individual in the construction of social relations. This approach suggests that artefacts can play an active role in determining the role of group members in social interpretation. Simple examples of this approach include questions such as: Does a flint blade in a grave indicate a male burial, or does a row of pendants found alongside the deceased imply a female grave? Are adults given more artefacts than children? Applied to age, rather than sex alone, this way of looking at the role of artefacts allows us to examine the relationship between different age groups as one of the elements in establishing the role of the individual.

In addition to using the 'Gender of the Gift' as a conceptual approach to the study of age in foraging communities, feminist theory is useful in questioning the Western cultural categorisation of social relations. It problematises the accepted status quo within Western culture and exposes the mechanisms of such understanding (Moore 1994; Strathern 1980, 1987, 1988; Tong 1993; del Valle 1993). Feminist theory also encourages the creation of different understandings of the past through the use of critical dialogue in the present.

One of the major contributions to the discussion of social relations inspired by feminist approaches concerns not only gender, but also stresses the categorisation of the individual in other ways including class, ethnicity and age. Children have recently been invoked in archaeology as part of the wider discussion of gender in prehistory (Claassen 1992; Moore and Scott 1997; Sofaer Derevenski 1994), representing a welcome broadening of the discussion of gender within the discipline. In archaeology however, this discussion, although feminist inspired, is not feminist in itself as it continues to revolve around the Western tradition of gender as male or female. This dichotomy has been used to create tangible categories, or what Boyd proposes as 'useful categories of analyses' (Boyd 1997:

26). They do not go beyond the Western perspective by discussing categories outside those set as representing our own society. The potential therefore remains for archaeologists to relate to the feminist contribution in very general heuristic terms through questioning the present status quo by looking at the past.

THE 'GENDER OF THE GIFT' IN NORTH EUROPEAN FISHER-GATHERER-HUNTER CEMETERIES

There is nothing new in the idea of looking at the link between material culture and the individual in North European cemeteries. Previous interpretations have however been located firmly within the Western tradition of associations between sex and the role of the adult individual (Albrethsen and Petersen 1976; Larsson 1993; O'Shea and Zvelebil 1984). Perhaps because it is difficult to sex skeletally immature individuals, consideration of age as an element in the cultural construction of social relations has been implicitly restricted to relationships between anthropologically sexed adults. The question of children as non-adult categories in the construction of social relations has not been addressed.

O'Shea and Zvelebil (1984) discuss adult social relations based on sex, age and role of the individual from the Oleneostravsky cemetery in Karelia. They argue that there is a relationship between the sex and age of particular adult individuals and the grave goods with which they are associated (ibid.). Based on their analysis of three categories of grave goods from this cemetery (bear tusks, elk or beaver incisors, lack of tooth pendants), they go on to suggest the greater importance of male community members over female (ibid.). However, approaching the distribution of grave goods from a viewpoint that allows for other means of the construction and expression of social relations, rather than those based on a simple assumption of the sex-role of the individual, it may be possible to formulate a different interpretation.

Looking at O'Shea and Zvelebil's (1984) published data, there is considerable difference between male and female burials in the age-related deposition of these same three categories of grave goods. The categories of grave goods found in male graves vary according to the age of the interred; most bear tusks are found with adults, most elk or beaver incisors with mature individuals, and the negative category 'lack of tooth pendants' is most frequent in the graves of the old (Figure 9.1a). By contrast, in female graves, all object categories show similar distributions with age. The key difference here is not type of object, but the frequency of artefact deposition with age; all categories of grave good are found most frequently in the graves of mature females (Figure 9.1b). A greater overall proportion of male than female graves have associated artefacts, however the number of graves considered to represent high status burials is the same for both sexes. Thus, while there is therefore clear differentiation between male and female, this is based on age and does not indicate greater importance of male over female.

The interpretation of the deposition of grave goods in the Vedbæk-Bøgebakken cemetery has also been related to a dichotomy in the distribution of material culture between male and female (Albrethsen and Petersen 1976): 'There three male graves and the single female one confirm the distinction between male and female grave goods observed at Bøgebakken, where ornaments made of red deer teeth were reserved for women whereas the men were equipped with blade tools and other tools' (Albrethsen and Petersen 1976: 24). These adult-based categorisations are carried further and extrapolated to non-adults with the suggestion that particular grave goods indicate the biological sex of children,

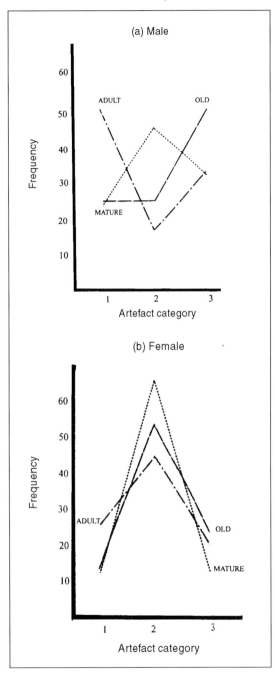

Figure 9.1   Age distribution of grave goods in (a) male graves and (b) female graves in the Oleneostravsky cemetery

Source: After O'Shea and Zvelebil 1984

Note: 1– bear tusks; 2 – elk and beaver incisors; 3 – lack of tooth pendants

even if this was not determinable from the human remains: for example, grave 8, from which was recovered a 'truncated blade, which suggests that it is a boy child' (Albrethsen and Petersen 1976: 9). It should be noted, however, that the relationship between different categories of individuals and artefacts can be more complex than a simple direct correlation between various classes of grave goods and sex. Grave number 19C contained teeth (human, red deer, wild pig, auroch) and beads, while a small blade-knife was also found below the lower jaw of the individual. On the basis of these artefacts this individual was determined as female, although once again biological sex could not be determined through analysis of the human remains. Given that the small blade-knife in grave 8 had previously been interpreted as a male artefact, and consequently the burial understood as that of a male, one might question the logic surrounding the assumptions involved in the interpretation of grave 19C.

In Albrethsen and Petersen's (1976) interpretation, certain objects arbitrarily appear to be given primacy in the interpretation of particular graves. In the case of grave 19C, the beads and teeth seem to have been more heavily emphasised as female and given interpretive priority over the blade-knife. Albrethsen and Petersen also imposed the perceived relationship between adults and material culture onto non-adults without considering particular artefacts as potentially independent interpretive categories for adult and non-adult groups.

Similar assumptions of a dichotomy in the distribution of material culture between male and female were made by Larsson (1993) in his interpretation of material from the Skateholm cemetery: 'Tools, such as knives and axes, are typically found with men, while women have ornaments like belt decorations made of animal teeth. Tooth beads are also occasionally found in male graves' (Larsson 1993: 48–9). Neither Albrethsen and Petersen (1976) nor Larsson (1993) seem to consider that the arrangement of particular artefacts and way that they are placed on the body may be seen as significant, rather than just the types of artefacts them-selves. For example, a blade-knife may represent a male when placed around the pelvis, but when located near the neck, indicates a young female. Not only may the type of arte-fact present in the grave indicate the sex of the corpse, but its placement should also be taken into account in understanding the identity of the deceased.

In all the examples of North European fisher-gatherer-hunter communities presented above, understandings of the 'Gender of the Gift' or the placement of particular artefacts alongside the deceased are linked with the Western tradition of defining gender in terms of sex. Archaeologists appropriate this categorisation by looking at the particular relation-ship between the buried individual and the material culture attributed to the deceased by the community members in the act of burial. However, in accepting the traditional Western perspective implicit in such categorisation, archaeologists unquestionably repeat the concerns of the present without exploring other possibilities for the construction of social relations in the past. They find a homogeneous history and fail to take account of age by imposing relationships between material culture and buried individuals implicitly regarded as adult. Taking age as its central focus, closer analysis of the deposition of grave goods in the cemeteries of fisher-gatherer-hunter communities in the south-east Baltic and Scandinavia suggests important differences between these communities in terms of the categorisation of individuals and the way in which social relations were constructed and signified. These differences relate particularly to patterns in the burial of non-adults and whether they were interred together with adults, or alone.

DIFFERENT COMMUNITIES: AGE, ADULTS AND NON-ADULTS IN THE SOUTH-EAST BALTIC AND SCANDINAVIA
The south-east Baltic: Zvejnieki

Zvejnieki is the largest fisher-gatherer-hunter cemetery in northern Europe (Zagorskis 1987). Situated in Latvia, it is located on a hill on the side of Lake Burtnieku overlooking the river Ruja. It was used by fisher-gatherer-hunter communities from the Middle Mesolithic (*c.* 5500 BC) to the beginning of the Early Bronze Age (*c.* 1600 BC). Food procuring was the predominant mode of production in all phases of the use of the Zvejnieki cemetery. The 316 graves, of which 172 have been dated, contained the remains of individuals of both sexes and of a wide age range. The individuals have been categorised by biological anthropologists and archaeologists researching the cemetery into adult (male, female) and non-adult (child, juvenile or child + juvenile in cases where the distinction was difficult to make).[1] Overall, adults form 37 per cent of the total number of interred individuals, and non-adults 63 per cent (Table 9.1). Of those graves categorised as non-adult, interments of children and child + juvenile are most common (Table 9.2). This suggests that younger individuals, who have not yet achieved full economic or reproduc-tive maturity, may hold greater significance than those of juveniles. The child + juvenile group can be regarded as particularly significant since it highlights the difficulty of defining the distinction between child and juvenile and foregrounds younger individuals moving towards adulthood.

Table 9.1 Number of dated and undated graves at Zvejnieki (percentage in brackets)

Category	Dated	Undated	Total
Adult	84 (49)	33 (23)	117 (37)
Non-adult	88 (51)	111 (77)	199 (63)
Total number	172	144	316

Table 9.2 Number of dated and undated non-adult graves at Zvejnieki with defined category of individual (percentage in brackets)

	Child	Juvenile	Child+juvenile	Total non-adult
Dated	35 (39)	11 (69)	42 (46)	88 (44)
Undated	56 (62)	5 (31)	50 (54)	111 (56)
Total number	91	16	92	199

The dating of particular graves is linked with the assessment of the grave goods according to style. Thus all of the dated graves contain grave goods. Of the dated graves, there is almost no significant difference in the number of burials of adults and non-adults when the whole sample is taken together. However, important differences can be detected from period to period in terms of who was buried within a particular phase (Table 9.3), indicating that social relations and the categorisation of individuals among prehistoric fisher-gatherer-hunters were based on factors other than just the mode of production. The period with the highest proportion of non-adult graves is the Late Mesolithic (71 per cent). Adult graves are proportionately most frequent in the period between the Late Mesolithic and Early Neolithic (63 per cent).

Table 9.3 Number of adult and non-adult graves in archaeological periods at Zvejnieki (percentage in brackets)

Category	MM	LM	LM /EN	MN+ LN	LN/ EB	Total
Adult	0	18 (29)	25 (63)	38 (62)	3 (38)	84 (49)
Non-adult	1 (100)	44 (71)	15 (38)	23 (38)	5 (63)	88 (51)
Total number	1	62	40	61	8	172

Note: MM – Middle Mesolithic; LM – Late Mesolithic; LM/EN – Late Mesolithic to Early Neolithic; MN+LN – Middle Neolithic and Late Neolithic; LN/EB – Late Neolithic to Early Bronze Age

Non-adults may be buried either alone or alongside adults. In Zvejnieki, both these categories of non-adult graves are furnished with grave goods.

Scandinavia: Vedbæk-Bøgebakken and Skateholm

The best known fisher-gatherer-hunter cemeteries in northern Europe are in Scandinavia. Of these, two cemeteries are discussed here: the Mesolithic cemeteries at Vedbæk-Bøgebakken (hereafter referred to as Vedbæk) and Skateholm (Albrethsen and Petersen 1976; Larsson 1983, 1984). These cemeteries are smaller than those from the south-east Baltic. At Vedbæk, 17 graves containing a total of 22 individuals were dated to the Late Mesolithic (*c.* 4100 BC) (Table 9.4). The Skateholm cemetery combines two fisher-gatherer-hunter burial locations, Skateholm I and Skateholm II, which were located on two islands divided by a waterway flowing into the Baltic Sea (Alexandersen 1984; Larsson 1983, 1984a, 1984b: 166). Skateholm I is dated to the Late Mesolithic (*c.* 5000 BC) and consists of 61 individuals, while Skateholm II is slightly older (*c.* 5300 BC) and smaller containing 22 individuals (Table 9.4).

Table 9.4   Number of graves at Vedbæk and Skateholm I and II (percentage in brackets)

Category	Vedbæk	Skateholm I and II
Adult	16 (73)	59 (71)
Non-adult	5 (23)	21 (25)
Unknown	1 (4)	3 (4)
Total number	22	83

The proportion of non-adults buried at Vedbæk and Skateholm is much lower than that from the Late Mesolithic period at Zvejnieki. At Vedbæk they form 23 per cent of burials and at Skateholm, 25 percent (Table 9.4) (Larsson 1983, 1984a, 1984b). Larsson suggests that a possible explanation for the small proportion of non-adults at Skateholm 'may be found in the many instances of *vacant* pits witnessed in junction with graves *per se*. It is not unreasonable to assume that at least some of these at one time contained the skeletal remains of young children' (Larsson 1983: 18). It is impossible to know whether this explanation is correct. Nonetheless, it does imply the degree of absence of young members of the community in the cemetery. As at Zvejnieki, non-adults at Vedbæk and Skateholm are buried either alone or alongside adults. Crucially, however, in the Scandinavian cemeteries the deposition of grave goods with non-adults was restricted to those non-adult burials associated with adults.

Differences in the proportion of non-adults found in Mesolithic fisher-gatherer-hunter cemeteries in the south-east Baltic and Scandinavia may reflect either different categories of people being buried within cemeteries, or different survival rates among different categories of individual in the two regions. While biological factors should not be dismissed, I would suggest that the significant role of burial practices is more likely to be linked with the cultural categorisation of individual. Differences between the two regions concern not only the proportion of interred non-adults, but also the way in which those non-adults were perceived through contrasting patterns in the deposition of grave goods. At Zvejnieki non-adults could receive grave goods when buried alone, whereas at Vedbæk and Skateholm they could only acquire them by association with others. Contrasts in the relative proportions of adult and non-adult burials

in the two regions can be linked to the separate ways particular communities conceptualised the self-identity of individuals.

THE CATEGORISATION OF AN INDIVIDUAL
Categorisation at Zvejnieki

The contrasting patterns of deposition of artefacts with non-adults and the differences in
the number of non-adults buried in the south-east Baltic and Scandinavian cemeteries
suggest two ways in which Mesolithic individuals were signified: either as autonomous
selves, or in relation to another. At Zvejnieki, the fact that grave goods often accompanied
non-adult group members buried in single, independent graves, as well as those buried
with adults, suggests that non-adults were largely regarded as independent individuals.
Signification was not only accorded to adults or linked to an adult presence, but also available to non-adults in their own right.

Indeed, the placement of a variety of artefacts at Zvejnieki suggests that Late
Mesolithic non-adults were signified as much, if not more, than adults of the community.
Bone fishing and hunting tools, other antler and bone tools, and flint knives/blades are
among the items deposited in both adult and non-adult graves. The proportion of adult
and non-adult graves containing bone tools for fishing and hunting is in line with the
proportion of adult and non-adult graves found to date from this period, suggesting that
they were given equally to both groups (Table 9.5). However, a disproportionate number
of other bone and antler tools, and to a lesser extent flint knives/blades, are found in non-
adult graves, emphasising younger individuals (Table 9.5). Grave goods associated with
particular activities were not therefore restricted to the graves of those who could have
physically performed the activity.

In addition to these implements, bone pendants are also found in both adult and non-
adult graves. Like bone tools for fishing and hunting, the proportion of adult and
non-adult graves containing bone pendants follows the demography of the Mesolithic

Table 9.5   Number of Late Mesolithic graves at Zvejnieki containing artefacts (percentage in
brackets)

Category	Bone tools for fishing and hunting	Other bone and antler tools	Flint knife/blade	Bone pendants
Adult	3 (38)	0 (0)	2 (25)	11 (34)
Non-adult	5 (63)	11 (100)	6 (75)	21 (66)
Total number	8	11	8	32

cemetery (Table 9.5). Bone pendants are often interpreted as hunting trophies that were
given by male hunters to other members of the group (Mithen 1990) in communities
where hunting has often been assumed to be the most important subsistence activity. This
assumption, prevalent in recent theoretical approaches to the Mesolithic and Neolithic in
northern Europe, has given rise to the view that as men were the major participants in

hunting, they also had the greatest influence in community life. They had power over other members of the community who did not hunt and so did not have access to wealth and prestige (Hodder 1990; Mithen 1990; O'Shea and Zvelebil 1984; Tilley 1991). Given that non-adults are often invisible in these theoretical narratives and interpretations, we have to ask why bone pendants are given to non-adults in equal proportion to adults at Zvejnieki. Did these non-adults participate in hunting, perhaps in some passive capacity that did not involve the co-ordination and skill that they had not yet fully developed? Perhaps these pendants had a symbolic meaning related to cultural values other than the activity of hunting itself.

The placement of objects in the grave indicates the importance and meaning assigned to particular group members by other group members. The distribution of grave goods at Zvejnieki signifies individuals whose participation created a successful community. Some of the implements in the graves at Zvejnieki are directly linked with economic activities. While these tools were placed in the graves of those who could physically participate in the activities they represent, indicating explicit involvement in such activities, they were also placed in the graves of people who would have only passively participated, indicating implicit involvement through the symbolic signification of group members. Each category of individual was signified by placement of grave goods with the body. All activities were equally important and the execution of multiple strategies required the participation of all members of the group. The evidence of fishing and hunting tools placed in graves provides us with a window into the internal dynamics of the community, vital to the cultural phenomenon of the successful execution of choices in a constantly fluctuating ecosystem. Just as fishing, gathering and hunting complement each other as subsistence activities, all the members of the group, whatever activity they undertook, complemented each other. Thus, rather than only recognising the importance of hunting, the importance of participants in all activities was recognised through the distribution of grave goods. The participation of children and juveniles in subsistence activities and their co-operation with adults was vital. Their participation did not need to be as 'active' as adults, but through their involvement the knowledge needed to successfully perform these activities, as well as about the cultural norms governing their performance, was passed on to the next generation. In this way non-adults were recognised as constituting part of the group, whose co-operation was recognised as being vital to the successful continuity of the community. In Zvejnieki, the construction of the individual as an independent self took place at an early age.

However, social relations at Zvejnieki were not static. Thousands of years of use of the cemetery by fisher-gatherer-hunter communities of the south-east Baltic provides the opportunity to examine temporal variation in the distribution patterns of grave goods within the same economy. Such variation is particularly visible among the non-adult graves at Zvejnieki which were signified by implements used in economic activities not only in the Mesolithic, but also throughout the use of the cemetery. There is noticeable variation in the deposition of these artefacts both within the non-adult category itself and between periods (Tables 9.6–9.8). These variations are a reflection of the internal dynamic within the group, which chose to highlight different categories of non-adult individual in different periods of the cemetery. This suggests changes in the importance of categories of individual in different periods, while the lack of consistency in categorisation indicates flexibility in signification.

Table 9.6   Number of graves in each archaeological period at Zvejnieki with bone tools for fishing and hunting (percentage in brackets)

Category	MM	LM	LM/EN	MN+LN	LN/EB	Total all periods
child	1 (100)	2 (40)	1 (100)	1 (50)	0 (0)	5 (50)
juvenile	0 (0)	1 (20)	0 (0)	1 (50)	0 (0)	2 (20)
child+ juvenile	0 (0)	2 (40)	0 (0)	0 (0)	1 (100)	3 (30)
Total number	1	5	1	2	1	10

Notes: MM – Middle Mesolithic; LM – Late Mesolithic; LM/EN – Late Mesolithic to Early Neolithic; MN+LN – Middle Neolithic and Late Neolithic; LN/EB – Late Neolithic to Early Bronze Age

Table 9.7   Number of graves in each archaeological period at Zvejnieki with other bone and antler tools (percentage in brackets)

Category	MM	LM	LM/EN	MN+LN	LN/EB	Total all periods
child	0 (0)	8 (73)	0 (0)	1 (25)	1 (33)	10 (56)
juvenile	0 (0)	0 (0)	0 (0)	2 (50)	0 (0)	2 (11)
child+ juvenile	0 (0)	3 (27)	0 (0)	1 (25)	2 (67)	6 (33)
Total number	0	11	0	4	3	18

Notes: MM – Middle Mesolithic; LM – Late Mesolithic; LM/EN – Late Mesolithic to Early Neolithic; MN+LN– Middle Neolithic and Late Neolithic; LN/EB – Late Neolithic to Early Bronze Age

Table 9.8   Number of graves in each archaeological period at Zvejnieki with flint knives/blades (percentage in brackets)

Category	MM	LM	LM/EN	MN+LN	LN/EB	Total all periods
child	0 (0)	1 (17)	0 (0)	1 (50)	1 (50)	3 (30)
juvenile	0 (0)	2 (33)	0 (0)	1 (50)	0 (0)	3 (30)
child+ juvenile	0 (0)	3 (50)	0 (0)	0 (0)	1 (50)	4 (40)
Total number	0	6	0	2	2	10

Notes: MM – Middle Mesolithic; LM – Late Mesolithic; LM/EN – Late Mesolithic to Early Neolithic; MN+LN – Middle Neolithic and Late Neolithic; LN/EB – Late Neolithic to Early Bronze Age

The flexible tradition of depositing tools can be seen as a dynamic process of negotiation between cultural norms and the action of individuals. Similarly, the frequency and proportion of non-adult graves with bone pendants also varies from period to period (Table 9.9), in this case declining over time from the Late Mesolithic. Members of the fisher-gatherer-hunter community modified the cultural norm of burial with bone pendants.

Table 9.9 Number of graves in each archaeological period at Zvejnieki with bone pendants (percentage in brackets)

Category	*MM*	*LM*	*LM/ EN*	*MN+ LN*	*LN/ EB*	*Total all periods*
child	0 (0)	1 (5)	4 (67)	1 (33)	1 (50)	7 (22)
juvenile	0 (0)	3 (14)	0 (0)	1 (33)	0 (0)	4 (12)
child+ juvenile	0 (0)	17 (81)	2 (33)	1 (33)	1 (50)	21 (66)
Total number	0	21	6	3	2	32

Notes: MM – Middle Mesolithic; LM – Late Mesolithic; LM/EN – Late Mesolithic to Early Neolithic; MN+LN – Middle Neolithic and Late Neolithic; LN/EB – Late Neolithic to Early Bronze Age

This modification expressed tensions within categories of individuals, which differed from period to period, emphasising difference between, as well as within, categories.

Categorisation at Vedbæk and Skateholm

The Scandinavian cemeteries present a different picture to that at Zvejnieki. Here, the potential to identify young individuals as independent selves did not exist within the mortuary context. In Vedbæk and Skateholm, non-adults are signified only when adults are present with them in the grave.

Two of the most interesting examples of such signification are grave 8 from Vedbæk (Albrethsen and Petersen 1976: 8–9, 14) and grave 41 from Skateholm (Larsson 1984: 22). Grave 8 from Vedbæk contained the remains of a woman about 18 years old and a new-born baby. The grave contained a large pile of pendants made of red deer and wild pig teeth, a clump of snail shells under the deceased adult's head, and rows of snail shells and a row of pendants (made not only from red deer and pig but also elk and seal) below her pelvis. The baby lay on a swan's wing with a truncated blade placed on the baby's pelvis. At Skateholm, grave 41 'contained an adult and a child. The adult, probably male, was placed in the hocker position with the arms fore-front. The child, also in the hocker position, lay below these, turned toward the adult. Grave goods in the form of two perforated eye teeth of bear were found on the child's chest and under these were four pieces of amber, all with extant perforation. A short bone point and flint knife lay adjacent to the child's right. Red ochre was strewn over the child' (Larsson 1984: 22). However, not all non-adults buried in conjunction with adults had grave goods, exposing tensions within the non-adult category. Grave 19 at Vedbæk contained the remains of three individuals: two adults with a child lying between them. One of the adult skeletons had grave goods (tooth beads, half of the lower jaw of a pine marten and a small blade-knife), while the other adult and child did not (Albrethsen and Petersen 1976: 14).

Single burials of non-adults, nonetheless, remain a distinct category of burial since they never contain grave goods, although ochre is sometimes present. Grave 21 at Vedbæk is a typical example: 'Undisturbed grave containing the intact skeleton of six month old child. The skeleton rests in a typical baby position on its back with its legs much bent. No grave goods or ochre were found in the grave' (Albrethsen and Petersen 1976: 15). There is a tangible difference in the examples presented above between the presence and absence of material culture within the non-adult graves in the Scandinavian cemeteries.

In Scandinavian cemeteries, the 'Gender of the Gift' is thus defined in terms of age; non-adults buried alone do not have grave goods, whereas non-adults buried with adults may receive them. This pattern defines those who were buried as much as those who buried them. It highlights the relationship between 'non-adult' and 'adult' as one of reliance upon elders. There is no positive group-specific recognition of non-adults as members of the community, although attributes of adult signification may be used to signify the non-adult. The co-dependence between categories seen at Zvejnieki does not seem to apply in Scandinavia where the physical loss of individual non-adults from the community was not enough to merit signification. Instead, the purely relational nature of the signification of non-adults in Scandinavia suggests a period of time in which the dependence of the biologically and socially immature non-adult was implicitly recognised within the patterning of material culture. One might interpret this as the material recognition of a period of childhood.

CONCLUSION

In the two regions of northern Europe represented by Vedbæk, Skateholm and Zvejnieki, material culture took an active role in the cultural categorisation of social relations. Patterning in the deposition of grave goods in non-adult graves allows the interpretation of social relations based on age rather than sex. The act of depositing this material culture was carried out by members of the community and implicit in this practice was the way in which the community categorised non-adults. The 'Gender of the Gift' became a significant aspect of the role of material culture in the cultural construction of social relations.

Two different systems of categorisation have been presented. In the case of the southeast Baltic there are indications of strong signification of non-adult members of the community through the deposition of a variety of artefacts in their graves, whether the burials are individual or multiple. In this area, young community members were defined as independent selves in their own right. In Scandinavia on the other hand, non-adult members of the community were buried with artefacts only when associated with adults. In this area, non-adults were not recognised as independent selves within the community.

These two systems of categorisation indicate that different modes of the cultural construction of social relations existed among North European fisher-gatherer-hunters. In the south-east Baltic, fishing, gathering and hunting communities were based on social relations between linked, co-dependent categories of non-adult and adult, where one category was not a reflection of the other. In Scandinavia, relations between non-adults and adults were much more restricted and unidirectional. Non-adults played an active role in the construction of social relations only when they were defined in relation to an adult community member. In addition, the case of Zvejnieki illustrates that the 'Gender of the Gift' differed through time among non-adults, indicating flexibility within the cultural categorisation of individuals, as well as between them.

Within the same economy of fishing, gathering and hunting, there was significant spatial and temporal variation in the cultural categorisation of social relations. Exploring the role of age as a major factor in the construction of social relations exposes this variation, lending new insights into North European food procuring communities.

ACKNOWLEDGEMENTS

I would like to thank Simon Kaner and Hanna Zawadzka for their help and support.

NOTES

1 Such categorisations reflect our understanding of individuals as members of a biological category, rather than an explicit understanding of the way those categories were understood in the past. Use of biological categorisation allows us to relate past individuals to other graves by preserving the same paradigm of contemporary biology.

REFERENCES

Albrethsen, S.E. and Petersen, E.B. (1976) 'Excavation of a Mesolithic cemetery at Vedbæk, Denmark', *Acta Archaeologica* 47: 3–28.

Alexandersen, V. (1984) 'Description of the human dentitions from the late Mesolithic grave-fields at Skateholm, southern Sweden', in L. Larsson (ed.) *The Skateholm Project: A Late Mesolithic Settlement and Cemetery Complex at a Southern Sweden Bay*, Meddelanden fran Lunds Universitets Historiska Museum 1983–1984, pp. 106–63.

Boyd, B. (1997) 'The power of gender archaeology', in Moore, J. and Scott, E. (eds) *Invisible People and Processes: Writing Gender and Childhood into European Archaeology*, London: Leicester University Press, pp. 25–31.

Claassen, C. (1992) 'Question of gender: an introduction', in C. Claassen, (ed.) *Exploring Gender Through Archaeology. Selected papers from the 1991 Boone Conference*, Monographs in World Archaeology 11, Madison, Wisconsin: Prehistory Press, pp. 1–9.

Engelstad, E. (1991) 'Images of power and contradiction: feminist theory and post-processual archaeology', *Antiquity* 65: 502–14.

Gero, J.M. and Conkey, M.W. (eds) (1991) *Engendering Archaeology: Women in Prehistory*, Oxford: Blackwell.

Gilchrist, R. (1994) *Gender and Material Culture: The Archaeology of Religious Women*, London: Routledge.

Hodder, I. (1990) *The Domestication of Europe*, Oxford: Blackwell.

Larsson, L. (1983) 'Ageröd V: An Atlantic bog site in central Scania', *Acta Archaeologica Lundensia* 8:12.

—— (1984a) 'The Skateholm Project: a late Mesolithic settlement and cemetery complex at a southern Sweden Bay', in L. Larsson (ed.) *The Skateholm Project: A Late Mesolithic Settlement and Cemetery Complex at a Southern Sweden Bay*, Meddelanden fran Lunds Universitets Historiska Museum 1983–1984, pp. 5–38.

—— (1984b) 'The significance of Skateholm I and II to the Mesolithic of Western Europe', in L. Larsson (ed.) *The Skateholm Project: a Late Mesolithic Settlement and Cemetery Complex at a Southern Sweden Bay*, Meddelanden fran Lunds Universitets Historiska Museum 1983–1984, pp. 164–175.

—— (1993) 'The Skateholm Project: Late Mesolithic Coastal Settlement in Southern Sweden', in P. Bogucki (ed.) *Case Studies in European Prehistory*, London: CRC Press, pp. 31–62.

MacCormack, C. and Strathern, M. (eds) (1980) *Nature, Culture and Gender*, Cambridge: Cambridge University Press.

Mithen, S. (1990) *Thoughtful Foragers*, Cambridge: Cambridge University Press.

Moore, H. (1994) *A Passion for Difference*, Cambridge: Polity Press.

Moore, J. and Scott E. (eds) (1997) *Invisible People and Processes: Writing Gender and Childhood into European Archaeology*, London: Leicester University Press.

Nelson, S.M. (1997) *Gender in Archaeology*, Walnut Creek: Alta Mira Press.

O'Shea, J. and Zvelebil, M. (1984) 'Oleneostrovki mogilnik: reconstructing the social and economic organisation of prehistoric foragers in northern Russia', *Journal of Anthropological Archaeology* 3: 1–40.

Sofaer Derevenski, J. (1994) 'Where are the children? Accessing children in the past', *Archaeological Review from Cambridge* 13(2): 7–20.

Strathern, M. (1980) 'No nature, no culture: the Hagen case', in C. MacCormack and M. Strathern (eds) *Nature, Culture and Gender*, Cambridge: Cambridge University Press, pp. 174–222.

—— (ed.) (1987) *Dealing with Inequality*, Cambridge: Cambridge University Press.

—— (1988) *The Gender of the Gift*, Berkeley CA: University of California Press.

Tilley, C. (1991) *Material Culture and Text*, London: Routledge.

Tong, R. (1993) *Feminist Thought*, London: Routledge.

del Valle, T. (ed.) (1993) *Gendered Anthropology*, London: Routledge.

Zagorskis, F. (1987) *Zvejnieku Akmens Laikmeta Kapulauks*, Riga: Zinatne.

Zvelebil, M. and Rowley-Conwy, P. (1984) 'Transition to farming in Northern Europe: a hunter–gatherer perspective', *Norwegian Archaeological Review* 17(2): 104–28.

Chapter 10

Children, gender and the material culture of domestic abandonment in the late twentieth century

Victor Buchli and Gavin Lucas

CHILDHOOD AND MODERNITY

Only in recent years have archaeologists begun to view childhood as an important aspect of social organisation, along with gender, class and ethnicity. However, while the material culture of children is a severely underdeveloped area of study (Sofaer Derevenski 1994) and the ethnographic study of contemporary childhood has only just attracted the attention of sociologists (Jenks 1996; Ribbens 1994), historians have studied children for several decades. Ariès was one of the first historians to critically examine childhood as a subject of investigation (Ariès 1962). His observations regarding the radically contingent nature of our understandings of what a child is and whether or not the concepts 'child' and 'child-hood' exist in any recognisable form in comparison to our own, are critical to any discussion. Jenks (1996) uses the term 'biologically immature people' as distinct from the culturally loaded term 'children'. Like the relationship between sex and gender, the distinction between biological and social age is fraught with problems (Sofaer Derevenski 1994).

Of course, this is not to deny that there are biologically immature human beings distinguished (by the inability to reproduce) from biologically mature humans, but these distinctions tell us next to nothing about how they are further constituted into recognisable identities of 'children' and 'adults'. For example, as with the male–female distinction, one might identify a nature–culture dichotomy traversing the child–adult division; the concept of childhood served, much like that of the 'noble savage', as the constitutive Other of Western society (i.e. Nature–non-Culture), with the 'child' and 'savage' sharing many similar traits. From here we can recognise the origins of what Jenks (1996) describes as the Dionysian and Apollonian concepts of childhood, vacillating between ideas of original purity (Apollonian) and violent disruption (Dionysian) and concomitantly, the notion of culture as either corrupting nature or improving upon it. Such debates lie at the centre of modernity, and childhood joins questions of gender and ethnicity as prime foci for such debates.

Ariès (1962) stated that prior to the seventeenth century in Western Europe, there was effectively no such thing as a 'child'. Children were biologically immature humans who, when born into the world, were not fully and socially human. Only several years later did they enter the world of humans – that is, adults – occupying adult spaces, using adult artefacts, wearing adult clothing and engaging in adult labour as best they could. Categories are only meaningful in relation to other categories, and thus before the seventeenth century the concept of 'adult' also lacked meaning. As a result of changes in theological understandings and attitudes towards education effected by religious orders in the later stages of the Middle Ages, there was a slow shift away from seeing young individuals as 'unformed humans', towards what we would today understand as 'children'. This notion of 'children' emphasised their constitution as potential souls to be guarded and developed in expectation of their maturity. 'The family ceased to be simply an institution for the transmission of a name and estate – it assumed a moral and spiritual function, it moulded bodies and souls' (Ariès 1962: 412). Such perceptions of children culminated in the eighteenth century with the recognisable institution of the family supporting a 'childhood' (ibid: 412).

Present-day children have increasingly become the object of social scrutiny, rationalisation and discipline, resulting in the highly structured social sphere of childhood, with its sciences of paediatrics, child psychology, developmental psychology, social work and 'new' child-related pathologies such as child 'abuse' and paedophilia (Ariès 1962; Jenks 1996; Hendrick 1997). The most recent critical discourse on the child closely follows the rise of feminist scholarship in seeking to re-evaluate the institutions of the family and women's roles. The development of a separate domestic sphere forced women into segregated roles outside of fully adult public life. This, together with the apparent 'infantilisation' characteristic of ideal feminine qualities, was mutually constitutive of ideals of children and maternity. The dyad of woman with child became even more elaborate as these segregated inhabitants of the domestic sphere were increasingly withdrawn from the public male realm of a developing industrialised society. Traditional Western notions of gender, public and private spheres, and children were intertwined within a social trajectory increasingly criticised by the women's movement and analysed by feminist-inspired scholarship.

As the 'feminine' and female subjectivity have been subject to ever-increasing scrutiny and social discipline, so has the child in relation to woman's roles, the domestic realm, and in constitutive opposition to the public predominantly male adult realms of social life. The constitution of the 'child' in the intertwined dyad of mother and child assumes a highly conflicted and ambivalent role in relation to the constitution and reiteration of women's identities and futures as mediated through children (see Ribbens 1994). This confusion is symptomatic of the contested and increasingly pluralistic understanding of childhood which, in the late twentieth century, is overwhelmed by variability in the construction of childhood inflected by class, gender and ethnicity (Ribbens 1994). Thus, when speaking of the way in which we constitute our offspring, we are speaking of something which is arguably one of the most important elements structuring social life (Jenks 1996; Hendrick 1997; Ariès 1962; Sofaer Derevenski 1994).

In the broadest sense, children are invariably implicated in the reproduction of society. Their constitution represents the collective future of a given society, a future that in a Western context is intimately wrapped up in Western utopian dreams and aspirations along with dystopian fears. To abandon the concept of 'child' is to abandon the concept of 'adult', one of the last remaining categories invoking a common certainty in modern experience. As Jenks has stated, to no longer be able to fix a concept of child 'is to erase our final point of stability and attachment to the social bond. In a historical era during which issues of identity and integration are, perhaps, both more unstable and more fragile than at any previous time, such a loss would impact upon the everyday experience of societal members with disorienting consequences' (Jenks 1996: 136).

At the end of the millennium, the 'child' and 'childhood' are as over-determined as they were under-determined at the beginning (Ariès 1962). Children are fully recognised as distinct identities almost upon birth, if not already in the womb. Medical technologies have developed to such a degree that the 'child' is considered socially viable even before 'natural' birth. The 'child' has been so utterly contested, articulated, commodified and disciplined from the inception of that process of differentiation in the seventeenth century as to emerge almost as infinitely distanced from adulthood as those 'unformed humans' at the beginning of the millennium. This very distance enables the concept of the 'child' to act as a refuge and hope for the future. Yet, at the same time, when it fails it becomes a threat, a fact amply illustrated in the recent public panic over child murderers (Jenks 1996: 118–20, 125–36). These constitutive disciplinary forces do not always work. They fail to produce what was intended, or produce other incipient subjectivities with unexpected consequences that are often at odds. At once coercive and enabling, the social and ontological effects of these disciplines often result in what Butler has referred to as failures of 'reiteration': the inability to adequately reiterate the disciplinary requirements for the successful realisation of a specific subjectivity, with the result that new subjectivities previously unimaginable become possible (Butler 1997: 147). With this in mind, it is useful to examine the particular and mutually constitutive circumstances of the 'child' and 'mother' in a late twentieth century British context. In this chapter we examine the material culture of the remains of one attempt to realise the subjectivities of 'woman' and 'child' which we came across through our investigations in the abandoned council house of a single mother and her two children.

THE CASE STUDY

As part of a project to investigate the material culture of alienation in a late twentieth century context, in 1997 a local British council authority gave us the opportunity to examine an abandoned council property before its clearance by council workers. In material terms, we wanted to understand the process by which individuals could become 'abject', disappear from the view of a community and state agencies, and thereby fail to be 'social', the object of care and discipline. As the forsaken status of these individuals, by definition, excluded the possibility of an informant-based ethnographic study, we could only approach this subject through the experimental modification of traditional archaeological methods.

From information gained during the investigation and subsequent enquiries with the housing authority, we discovered that the house had been occupied by a single 25 year-old mother of two children, a boy aged 4 and a girl aged 6. The woman moved into the house just after giving birth to her first child and was on full income support and housing benefit. The fact that the unit was suddenly abandoned caught the housing authority by surprise since it was not in arrears. There was nothing to indicate that there might be any trouble that would result in abandonment and the creation of what the authority called a 'void property'. Having abandoned the site without notice and according to her own free will, the woman who lived there with her two children had relinquished her right to any further housing assistance by the local authority. With increasing demands on a severely diminished stock of council housing, the authority was eager to reclaim a wilfully abandoned property in order to re-house another family. As we documented the site, it became very clear that the woman and her two children had not only left without notice, but were suddenly interrupted, hastening their abandonment and leaving many packing boxes half full. A large number of items had been left behind which had clearly been brought out and arranged to be packed and taken away.

Of the artefacts catalogued, we could clearly identify a significant proportion related to children. Of ageable finds, children's items (22.8 per cent) constituted almost the same proportion as adult objects (21.3 per cent). In other words, in terms of the number of personal objects, the material culture of the two children was quantitatively similar to the mother and mostly absent father. The children's clothing also seemed to be of a higher quality, composed of more expensive natural fibres and leather-soled shoes. Even if the children's clothing was purchased second-hand, there was a preference for better quality materials for the children as opposed to the more inferior quality of the mother's own clothing (whether bought new or second-hand). A sacrifice of resources, through which to elaborate a materially better 'childhood' (indeed perhaps better than the mother's own), was clearly apparent. Following Miller's thesis of 'shopping as sacrifice' (Miller 1998), resources were regularly being bought (sacrificed) in devotional anticipation of a better future for her children than for herself. The purchase of these items was an offering of transcendence such that the children should literally overcome the mother's decidedly precarious adult circumstances, symbolised by the mother's consumption of better quality for the children and worse quality for herself (Miller 1998: 102–3). This belief contradicts the more utilitarian argument that the children would rapidly outgrow such better quality clothes thereby rendering the items 'useless'.

The importance of the child in the home is apparent not only through the sheer quantity and quality of material culture *vis-à-vis* adults, but also through its spatial distribution. The inception of the institutions of the 'child' and 'childhood' in the seventeenth century coincided with a time when the domestic floor plan to which we are accustomed began to predominate, with its emphasis on discrete, segregated rooms opening onto corridors rather than into each other as they did earlier (Ariès 1962). Such a floor plan made possible privacy and what we understand as 'domestic comfort' (ibid. 1962: 398–9). The floor plan of the council house we examined is a direct descendant of these enlightenment era innovations. The house as it was realised as a 'home' and the use of material culture within it was productive and reiterative of this enlightenment era conception of the family. Within the particular family unit who lived in the house, the segmentation and generation of a separate child's realm with its utopian vision of an idealised childhood and family is readily apparent.

The segregation of a children's sphere is confirmed, in practice, from the distribution of child-associated artefacts in the different rooms. One room was unquestionably dominated by children's artefacts, with almost no adult-associated artefacts present (the children's room). However, in every other room child-associated artefacts were found in significant numbers, along with those associated with adults, suggesting that children may be associated with all other rooms as well. The presence of children's artefacts in other rooms is further informative if we look at what kind of artefacts these are; the two most common finds associated with children were clothing and toys. Although these appeared in near equal proportions throughout most of the house, toys were nine times more frequent than clothing in the living room. Furthermore, these items were not, for the most part, items packed up ready to go, but objects scattered on the floor, behind chairs and sofas – the debris of *in situ* play. This reinforces the idea of the ubiquity of child space, which crosses the exclusivity of the children's room. It perhaps demonstrates the not necessarily undesirable tension between childhood as a contained and classified separate sphere (utopia), and childhood as out of control and potentially dangerous (dystopia).

The exclusivity of children's material culture in the children's room does not suggest, however, that adults were never present or never used the room. Nonetheless, it was clearly a place where the artefacts that sustained adult activities did not intrude and was deliberately maintained by the adult mother as a distinct child's sphere. She also quite intentionally (and typically) differentiated the walls of this room from the other rooms of the house by the use of wallpaper representing scenes and characters from the children's cartoon 'The Flintstones' (Figure 10.1) along with blue stencilled figures of little bears, presumably done by

Figure 10.1   In situ wallpaper fragment

Source: Photograph: Victor Buchli and Gavin Lucas

herself, to further elaborate the theme of a distinct children's realm – a 'neverland' which is never truly a child's own realm but a purely adult phantasm (Jenks 1996: 108). The central image in the wallpaper design is the familial portrait of Fred Flintstone, the father, surrounded by his wife Wilma, daughter Pebbles and their pet dinosaur Dino. The archetypal nuclear family that can only claim a history of two hundred years or so in Western Europe is projected into deep prehistory as the original and eternal social unit. It is also the ideal future towards which the resources of the household are sacrificed, and is ultimately the reason for which the housing itself, though a scarce resource, is provided by the housing authority to prevent 'risk'. The mother of the household clearly attempted to produce this segregated and highly differentiated 'other' realm ('neverland') in devotional anticipation of a familial ideal (ironically embodied by a prehistoric fantasy), whose reiteration was flawed in a crucial way – the lack of a viable opposite sex partner, the father (who would be the phantasmagorical Fred Flintstone). If this ideal were indeed successfully reiterable she would have obtained, according to British housing policy, preferential access to care, protection and support as a 'wife' or co-habiting partner, in addition to being a mother.

In the kitchen we found an alternative family portrait (Figure 10.2), clearly drawn by one of the two children and probably by the four year old judging by the 'tadpole' style of the drawing (Cox 1993: 24–5). The interpretation of children's drawings is notoriously problematic (ibid.). Ultimately, however (bearing in mind the limitations of the child's cognitive abilities to plan the drawing and fit the images on the paper),

Figure 10.2   Child's drawing: family portrait

Source: Photograph: Victor Buchli and Gavin Lucas

the 'tadpole' style and its spatial hierarchy seems to correspond compellingly with what we already know of the household from other more reliable documentary sources found at the site. Here we see at the centre a figure who (going by the size of her head and proximity to the two smaller figures) is apparently the mother herself regarding her two small children. They, in turn, seem to look to her. To the left, however, is the image of another adult, who we suggest is the father; according to clinical experience with children's drawings the father is often the most distant individual (ibid.). Documents found in the house suggest that he was not married to the mother, but was the biological and social father of the two children who had his surname. He never lived at the house, but seems to have visited frequently. In the drawing he is clearly separate from the mother/child group and apparently looks at them while they seem to disregard him and look at each other.

From the artefacts and documentation found at the site, the child's understanding of the domestic situation and our guarded interpretation of the child's portrait seem to be accurate. We know that the father lived in another part of town. Direct references to him were found amidst abandoned documents and inscribed books, as well as a limited number of male-associated artefacts such as clothing and toiletries indicating a regular male visitor. We also know that his presence was sufficiently regular that his prescription for methadone was also there. The troubled image of the father, peripheral yet nonetheless within the sphere of the family unit of the mother and two children, seems correct. It is evident that despite the regular presence of the father and the separately constituted realm of the child, the familial ideal was strained. Heroin addiction and an idealised segregated and 'innocent' child's sphere suggest a troubled and conflicted setting, where the disruptive problems associated with drug addiction were an unsettling contradiction (and even threat) to the 'innocent' and utopian vision of a segregated child's environment.

The mother looms large at the centre of the household, both according to the housing authority who provided her with support as well as in the eyes of the child who drew the family portrait. Thus, she was strongly identified as head of the household, a woman constituted as 'mother' and worthy of state aid, as the regularly employed bread winner and as the gendered adult female considered most suitable to perform sacrifices towards the realisation of the familial ideal (Jenks 1996: 100; Miller 1998). However, she found that the central position she held in terms of these various and conflicting roles (supportive partner to a troubled father, single mother of two, and her own private and unarticulated ambitions suggested by the escapist novels found in her abandoned library) was not working out. Her worthiness and her social subjectivity were realised only through her reiterative ability to 'make' and rear a child. De Beauvoir claimed that the imperative to realise a woman's self through her child is the product of a social constraint where no other means towards subjectivity are possible: 'The woman cannot actually be forced to bear children, all one can do is enclose her in situations where maternity is the only way out' (de Beauvoir in Zerilli 1992: 115). Since the Housing Act of 1985, British housing policy criteria have singled out women as worthy subjects of care and housing assistance in terms of their status as married hetero-sexual mothers. In Britain, women frequently fall through the support system provided by local housing authorities because of 'relationship breakdown', trying to escape from a trou-bled relationship with a partner. Housing authorities have been notoriously indifferent to these issues, forcing women into unmanageable situations that result in their loss of housing benefit.

According to existing parliamentary legislation and housing policy, the woman of this abandoned household made herself 'intentionally homeless'. She is not therefore eligible for further aid even if she were to ask to be rehoused, which she has not. She has entirely lost her local housing benefit and support from social services. She is very much on her own with two children, when previously she was clearly in need, with access to full bene-fits and housing support. Nothing indicates that she found alternative means towards independent living. What we found strongly suggests the abandoned household of a single mother in the wake of some form of relationship breakdown. The reasons for breakdown are unknowable. However, we know she left very suddenly. Her relationship with the father of her two children was tenuous. He lived on the other side of town and visited regularly, keeping a supply of toiletries, clothes and methadone to help him overcome his heroin addiction. His methadone supply was due to be renewed just over a month before the house was reported abandoned by a neighbour, suggesting that this guarded, but ostensibly caring relationship, was still being maintained up to a few weeks before the woman decided to leave everything taking her two children with her.

Coming upon the abandoned traces of this household, it would seem to us that the pressure of maintaining the relationship with the father of their two children and the strained and tenuous family they attempted to create while coping with heroin addiction was too much to bear. Being legally single, young, able-bodied, resourceful, but poor, like many women who are compelled to flee their homes as a consequence of relationship breakdown, she would probably have known that there were no state resources to help her. Taking her chances, whilst still packing, she suddenly got up and left, leaving behind the father and what was evidently an unbearable and unmanageable household. In doing so, she also left behind dreams of an idealised nuclear family founded on the basis of a segre-gated, protected and utopian child's sphere, which both she and the local housing authority had been keen to structure and maintain.

'The child is the source of the last remaining, irrevocable, unexchangable primary rela-tionship. Partners come and go. The child stays' (Beck in Jenks 1996: 107). Considering her earlier investment in the creation of a 'sacred' and distinct realm of transcendent futu-rity through the constitution of her children, their objects and spaces, the mother left behind certain objects either wilfully or out of haste. Many of these objects would appear to be key towards this construction, calling the process into question. Besides leaving chil-dren's clothing, which her children may already have outgrown, she left behind other items, such as Christmas decorations (the ultimate celebration of idyllic familiality) and a number of photographs, notably those of the younger boy. She also left his commemorative baby book documenting the first few months of his life, including a copy of his birth certificate, his hospital bracelet and documentation of the first word he spoke ('dad').

We know that she left these things behind, or was not able to collect them in time as she was compelled to stop collecting her things. She left very suddenly without saying where she was going either to neighbours or the housing authority on which she had been so dependent for support. Having left personal objects behind, she would have to find other means by which to realise the sacral quality of her children's beginnings; these arte-facts will no longer be used as tools towards the constitution of original childlike innocence and pure futurity. Other means will have to be used to establish these vital myths, if she so chooses in future. Her circumstances were no longer viable according to the terms by which she could be considered worthy of state support and care; they were no longer reiterable and she could not trust the housing authorities to be of any further help or use. Having been so enclosed by the limited and unworkable options available, she had to find a way out. Taking matters into her own hands and scrupulously avoiding arrears, she left with her two children, along with what she could collect in time, to start again without the disciplining care of a local housing authority. Unable to continue 'the melan-cholic reiteration of a language [she] never chose' (Butler 1993: 242), she has had to rethink anew who she is, what her family is, and what her two children are outside the structures she was so intimately subject to earlier.

REFERENCES

Ariès, P. (1962) *Centuries of Childhood*, London: Jonathan Cape.

Butler, J. (1993) *Bodies that Matter*, London: Routledge.

—— (1997) *Excitable Speech*, London: Routledge.

Cox, M. (1993) *Children's Drawings of the Human Figure*, Hove (UK): Lawrence Erlbaum.

Hendrick, H. (1997) *Children, Childhood and English Society, 1880–1990*, Cambridge: Cambridge University Press.

Jenks, C. (1996) *Childhood*, London: Routledge.

Miller, D. (1998) *A Theory of Shopping*, Oxford: Polity Press.

Ribbens, J. (1994) *Mothers and their Children: A Feminist Sociology of Childrearing*, London: Sage.

Sofaer Derevenski, J. (1994) 'Where are the children? Accessing children in the past', *Archaeological Review from Cambridge* 13(2): 7–20.

Zerilli, L.M.G. (1992) 'A Process without a subject: Simone de Beauvoir and Julia Kristeva on maternity', *Signs*, vol. 18, no. 1: 111–135.

Part VI

Geographies of children

Chapter 11

The child as a node of past, present and future

Koji Mizoguchi

INTRODUCTION

Talking about children in the milieu of archaeological discourse is currently as contentious as talking about gender used to be. This is predominantly because children are often deemed to be invisible or difficult to recognise archaeologically (Sofaer Derevenski 1994). However, it is simply not accurate to state that children cannot be seen in archaeological material. Children are actually quite visible, particularly in mortuary contexts. The nature of this perceived invisibility may therefore stem from difficulties in identifying material traces of the *acts* of children rather than children themselves. This inability to distinguish child action within the archaeological record both reinforces, and is reinforced by, the modern idea that children cannot make any significant contribution to social life. Since children are unable to negotiate their position in society without help from parents or other adults, they are regarded as irrelevant to archaeological enquiry.

Children are 'half beings' since they have to be looked after by adults and are not fully socially autonomous. However, children soon become adults. Without them there can be no future for their society. In this sense children are also 'plural beings'. They need and demand continual care in the present, but their existence also embodies predictions and expectations for the future. These predictions and expectations are constituted with reference to the social norms and previous experiences of adults. The way in which children are raised is drawn from a repository of experiential knowledge accumulated over time. Furthermore, the position of a particular child within a group hierarchy may be constituted by reference to that of their parents and ancestors. Children therefore also embody the past.

In late modernity, the consequences of almost every social action are monitored and reflexively fed back to further actions. Adults feel continually compelled to consider the impact of their actions upon their children. They expect that what they do to their children and the way in which they relate to them will substantially affect the shape of their children's future. Parents worried about caring for their children in the 'right way' read tracts on how children should best be raised. The ever increasing number of 'how to' books and their competing theses form a distinct field of social communication in which a vast range of childcare choices are reduced to a narrow, socially acceptable range through the production of images of ideal social beings. By choosing one of a number of possible methods for raising children, adults implicitly identify themselves with one of these competing ideal images. Parents thus create themselves as adults in contrast to the child through the process of raising that child, and by mediating between their child and the ideal.

In late modernity, repositories of knowledge for raising children derived through close inter-generational and intra-communal ties have been lost. The possible range of individual life choices has widened dramatically and, accordingly, the pressure placed on parents in deciding how to raise their children has become increasingly severe. Nonetheless, the core of the parent–child relationship remains constant: children in past and present are constructed, and indeed construct themselves, through their situation in a web of social relations set up by their parents and other adults in the community. Children see, feel, and internalise the objective world in different ways according to their developmental stage. However, the way in which they do so is affected by their interaction with surrounding adults. Thus, while children need and demand care by adults, the manner of caring and the stage at which a particular form of care is terminated vary from culture to culture and period to period.

Relationships between children and adults are always mutual since neither is completely free from, or entirely constrained by, the other. In this sense, the notions of both 'child' and 'adult' as meaningful social categories constitute fields of social communication through which interaction is conducted. Both child and adult reflexively acquire their self-identity in reference to the other by communicating within and through these fields.

WHEN CHILDREN DIE

Given the way in which notions of child and adult are mutually imbricated, the death of a child inevitably problematises the self-identity of the parent and other adult carers. Not only is the child lost as a living, breathing individual, but all that the child represents is suddenly removed from society. Since children embody past, present and future, the treatment of a dead child may implicate concern for the past, present and future of the surviving parents, as well as the wider community.

One way of expressing these concerns may be by mobilising the child's body as a symbolic focus in mortuary practice. The funeral may act as an occasion for the mobilisation of this symbol in which an ontological understanding of the child, and his or her relationship with parents and the community, is recreated and reproduced. The investigation of the expression of these concerns through a study of child burial may therefore be a fruitful way in which to understand the particular ontological status of children in past societies. Reconstruction of the bodily movements of participants in funerals for children and the way that the child's body was carried and then deposited may permit exploration of how the dead child was mobilised as a symbol and the concerns of the living expressed and communicated. Inevitably, this form of analysis and interpretation involves the reconstruction of a specific technology with which the community reproduced itself by utilising the child as a node of its past, present and future.

The cemetery is a locale for a particular form of social communication. Relations between the participants of the funeral ceremony, between the mourners and the deceased individual, and between the recently deceased and those already buried (the ancestors) may be signified, confirmed and reproduced by allocating individual participants and their acts distinct time–space components and by depositing the deceased in a specific location within the cemetery. This location is determined by reference to the locations of other previous burials (Barrett 1988; Mizoguchi 1992). Therefore, parental and community concern with past, present and future might also be represented materially through the deposition of the dead child in a location determined with reference to burials of the ancestors. This form of deposition locates the newly deceased child in multiple levels of the constellation of living, as well as dead, individuals.

THE CASE STUDIES

An approach which seeks to reconstruct the acts of mourners in the deposition of a deceased child and examine the locations of child burials in relation to those of adults requires detailed chronological and spatial information. This chapter takes as examples two well-recorded cemetery sites from Fukuoka Prefecture in the northern Kyushu region of Japan: Nagaoka and Kuriyama. Both are dated to the middle Yayoi period (third to first century BC) although the site of Nagaoka (late early Yayoi to the end of the early middle Yayoi) slightly predates that at Kuriyama (late middle Yayoi). The Yayoi period witnessed the introduction of rice agriculture and its related techno-complex and is generally under-stood as a period in which social complexity and population increased dramatically (Barnes 1993). These sites represent two fundamentally different forms of spatial organisation of a cemetery and therefore permit a diachronic comparison of the mortuary treatment of infants (3 to 4 years of age and below) and children (between 3 to 4 years of age and 12 to 15 years of age) during the middle Yayoi period.

Nagaoka

In the Nagaoka cemetery, pit burials, wooden coffin burials and jar burials form a linear alignment consisting of two parallel rows (Hamada and Shinbara 1977; Mukaida 1990) (Figure 11.1 shows the northern half of the cemetery). This type of spatial organisation is characteristic of cemeteries in the northern Kyushu region during the late early Yayoi to the end of the early middle Yayoi period.

Several interpretations of this linear arrangement have been proposed. One of the most popular is that the formation of the cemetery followed a predetermined design, which reflected the form and structure of the community of the living. Hence, the two parallel rows of burials reflect a duality of structure within society (Harunari 1984). However, the apparent inevitability this interpretation accords cemetery development neglects the acts and experiences of the human agents who created and transformed the spatial organisation of the cemetery over time. In order to reconstruct the acts and bodily movements of mourners, and thereby understand how the child was mobilised as a symbol, a different understanding of cemetery formation is necessary.

Plotting the typo-chronological distribution of jar burials permits reconstruction of the horizontal stratigraphy of Nagaoka (Mizoguchi 1995a). This exercise suggests that, rather than a predetermined design deciding cemetery spatial organisation, the existence of a path in this locality determined its spatial structure; burials were placed at irregular inter-vals along the length of the path throughout the period of use of the cemetery. The cemetery did not grow in a systematic manner from one end to the other. The existence of a path lined with burials on either side makes people naturally form a procession when

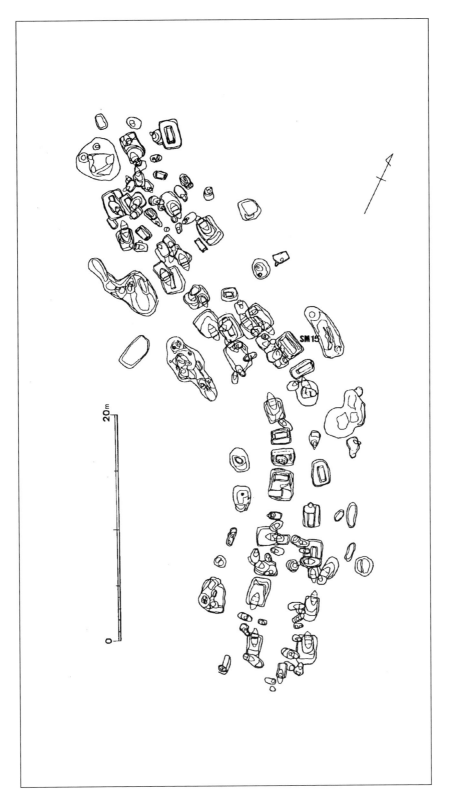

Figure 11.1   The northern half of the Nagaoka cemetery; the smaller jars are those of children
Note: Burial SM15 is shown in Figure 11.3.

moving inside the cemetery. Barrett (1993) argues that a significant feature of processional activity is that it creates leaders of the procession and those who follow. Yet, processional activity is also highly co-operative. Thus the spatial organisation of the cemetery would have functioned as a sophisticated device for simultaneously creating leadership and generating a sense of community among the funeral participants.

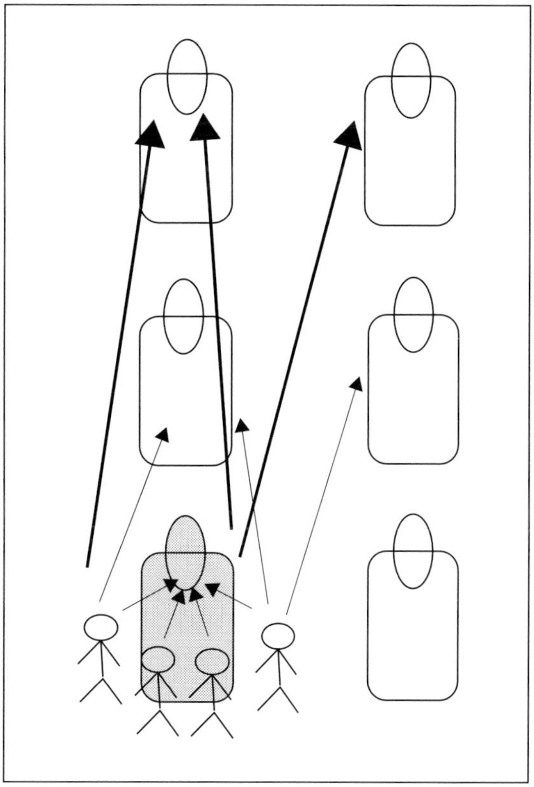

As the formation process of the cemetery progressed, the direction to which jar burials were lowered and inserted into their pits became unified. The jar was placed in the south side of the pit with its long axis running from south to north. Furthermore, towards the end of the formation of the cemetery, the majority of burials became increasingly situated in the southern half of the cemetery. Given that the mourners would have stood at the south side of the pit in order to lower the jar into the grave, this would have controlled the gaze of mourners at all such ceremonies in terms of their view across the cemetery. The unified line of sight would have maximised the number of small mounds covering pre-existing burials visible to the funeral participant (Figure 11.2). Thus the vista seen at the time at which an individual was buried would have acted to further promote the sense of community among the living and link them to their past by viewing the graves of their ancestors.

The frequency of infants and children suggests that no selection was carried out in

Figure 11.2 Schematised diagram of how the gaze of the mourners was controlled in the Nagaoka cemetery. A large number of pre-existing burials would have been visible when the mourners stood at the edge of the pit into which a jar burial was deposited in the middle and final stage of the formation of the cemetery

terms of who was accorded burial within the cemetery. The majority of child burials in the Nagaoka cemetery are jar burials inserted into the pits of pre-existing adult interments (Figure 11.3). In some cases, more than four or five infant burials are inserted into that of a single adult. Given the depositional sequence of insertion into an adult burial, it can be concluded that the deaths of the infants occurred at the same time, or shortly after, that of the adult. It therefore seems unlikely that the relationship between the deceased was that of parent and children. It might be safer to postulate a wider kin group revolving around grandparents and grandchildren or uncles and aunts, nephews and nieces. Unfortunately, however, biological evidence that might support this interpretation is not currently available.

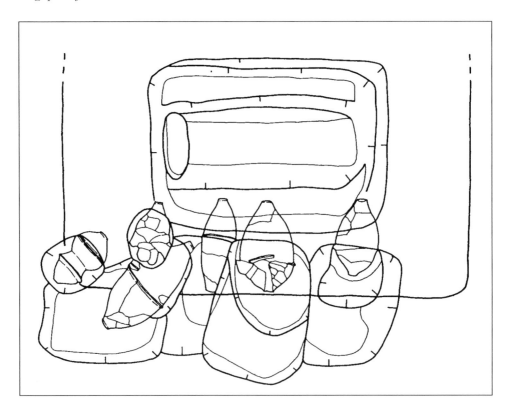

Figure 11.3   Nagaoka burial SM15: wooden coffin burial of an adult with six child jar burials inserted into the grave

Source: Mizoguchi 1995a

Kuriyama

In the late middle Yayoi period the spatial organisation of cemeteries changed dramatically. At Kuriyama, as in other cemeteries of this period, jar burials were agglomerated in clusters (Sasaki 1982) (Figure 11.4). The principle of linear alignment was abandoned. Children and infants were no longer inserted into adult burials but were treated in the same manner as adult jar burials. Explanations for the cause of this change centre round assumptions of a major change in social organisation (Harunari 1984). The clusters of burials are interpreted as disposal areas for household units, reflecting the increasing independence of the household as the basic unit of production and ownership from the larger communal unit such as clan or lineage (ibid.).

However, detailed examination of the spatial sequence of cluster C at Kuriyama suggests a rather different story. Once again, the typo-chronological distribution of jar burials permits reconstruction of the horizontal stratigraphy (Mizoguchi 1995b). This shows seven spatially discrete series of burials within the cluster. Each series was formed through the deliberate deposition of a new burial immediately adjacent to the previous interment. Each burial within the series, including those of infants and children, was aligned with a similar axis of deposition. In terms of the positioning of the mourners

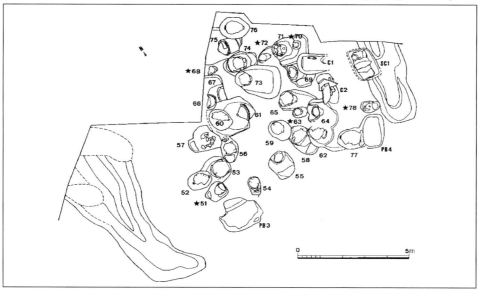

Figure 11.4 Burial cluster C at the Kuriyama cemetery; infant burials are starred

during the mortuary ritual, their gaze would have been particularly drawn to the last burial (Figure 11.5). This suggests that the specific image of the individual deposited in the preceding burial was intentionally recalled and utilised during the funeral. This technology of control over visual orientation is radically different to that adopted at Nagaoka. At Kuriyama it was the image of the individual, as opposed to the collective, which formed the focus of attention. Furthermore, by locating a new burial next to the previous interment the burial sequence becomes similar to beads on a string, giving a sense of linear continuity. This was signified, recognised and confirmed by the directed gaze of the mourners during the funerary ritual. In contrast to the cemetery at Nagaoka, at Kuriyama only one or two infants or children were deposited next to an adult, indicating a degree of selection. Consequently, the number of infants and children buried in the cemetery is far fewer. At Nagaoka, ninety-six out of 183 interments (52.5 per cent) are children, mostly infants, whereas at Kuriyama only six out of thirty-three interments (18.2 per cent) are infants and children.

UNDERSTANDING THE CHANGES IN CEMETERY ORGANISATION AND CHILD BURIAL

How can we account for this change in cemetery organisation and for the distinctive ways that children are treated in the two cemeteries? In order to do this it is necessary to explore the changes in social and economic life that occurred during the Yayoi period.

The late early Yayoi to early middle Yayoi saw a rapid increase in population. Many small settlements budded off from core settlements to the outskirts of flood plains (Hashiguchi 1987). In this unstable and fluid social environment, the acquisition of land for paddy field agriculture was of great importance. Evidence for small scale inter-communal fighting is found on skeletons who appear to have been mortally wounded (ibid.). The creation of strong leadership would have been necessary in order to lead this aggression. Furthermore, in order to maintain an advantageous position in such conflicts,

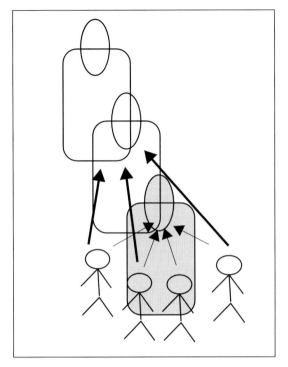

Figure 11.5 Schematised diagram of how the gaze of the mourners was controlled in the Kuriyama cemetery. The last burial in the sequence would have been visible when the mourners stood at the edge of the pit into which a jar burial was deposited

it would have been crucial to sustain the growth of the community by bolstering the labour force and securing marriage partners. In this sense, the survival of infants and children would have been vital. Thus, the well-being of children would have been a communal concern. In this situation it is likely that the child as a social category would have held significant symbolic meaning derived from communal aspirations. The promotion of communal ties would have been essential for the well-being of the community and this may have been advanced through the symbolic potential of children.

The linear, processional organisation of the Nagaoka cemetery reflects the importance of leadership and communal corporation, while the mortuary practices reflect the attitude to children in late early Yayoi to early middle Yayoi society. Given the similar treatment of child interments and that all children appear to have been buried in the cemetery, this implies a common, collective concern with children. Care for children, who represented the future of the community, was expressed and confirmed in death as well as in life and was of communal importance. Were those dead children inserted into the graves of their ancestors to have been cared for by the ancestors in the afterlife? Viewing the ancestors during burial linked both the deceased individual and the living to the past. The burial of a child by adult members of the community mobilised the child as a symbol of communal well-being and mutual concern in past, present and future.

The late middle Yayoi saw another dramatic shift in settlement systems. Small settlements on the edge of the flood plain, founded in the previous period by splitting off from core settlements, were abandoned. Concomitantly, the size of the core settlements increased (Hashiguchi 1987). Since these movements do not seem to result from a sudden drop in population, these shifts may be related to innovations in agricultural technology, which permitted more intensive rice agriculture. Agricultural tools, irrigation facilities and paddy fields indicate that the intensity and extent of agriculture reached a new height in this period (ibid.).

These archaeologically observable changes in settlement systems and subsistence technology would inevitably have altered the way in which social categories and relations were structured. It is therefore possible that the transformation in the way that children were treated in mortuary contexts was related to these changes. Social concerns shifted from the promotion and enhancement of communality to the signification of individual identity and a sense of linear continuity.

Those infants and children selected for burial within the Kuriyama cemetery, and their deposition in the same manner as adults, can be thought of as successors to group leadership. Had they survived they would have assumed that leadership. Adults whom a child had predeceased buried the child in the same manner as their predecessors in order to mark the child's unrealised social status. In doing so, the living would have recognised and confirmed the character of their own social existence by materially mapping the lineage of the corporate group leader. They identified themselves as part of a continuous line from past to present. The dead child became incorporated into the creation of a spatio-temporally mapped genealogy in which the child was treated as a marker of an unfulfilled future.

CONCLUSION

In both the Nagaoka and Kuriyama cemeteries the body of the child was mobilised for the signification of a specific social message. Although the nature of this message changed between the two cemeteries as it was transformed over time, in both cases perceptions of 'child' as a social category determined the way in which infants and children were treated in the funerary ceremony.

The terminated life of children and the unrealised potential, unfulfilled predictions and expectations of parents and other adult members of the community made the dead child a uniquely powerful symbol. The mobilisation of the child as a symbol was enhanced by the sense of individual and communal loss and the way in which the death of a child problematised the self-identity of the parent and other adult carers in a manner which life-course transitions of the living did not. Adults acquired their own self-identity with reference to children and by acknowledging the existence of children within society. The death of a child therefore required the resolution of adult identity through the situation of the dead child and the living adult within the community or the lineage.

Adults expect children to outlive them and, to some extent, for the lives of children to mirror their own experiences. A void is created when this does not happen. The child is, and was, a node of past, present and future. By caring for children in life and death, adults map themselves in a mesh of imagined life-courses, genealogies, self-identities and social expectations from which they reconstitute themselves.

REFERENCES

Barnes, G.L. (1993) *China, Korea and Japan: The Rise of Civilisation in East Asia*, London: Thames & Hudson.

Barrett, J.C. (1988) 'The living, the dead and the ancestors: Neolithic and early Bronze Age mortuary practices', in J.C. Barrett and I.A. Kinnes (eds) *The Archaeology of Context in the Neolithic and Bronze Age: Recent Trends*, Sheffield: John R. Collis, pp. 30–41.

—— (1993) *Fragments from Antiquity: An Archaeology of Social Life in Britain, 2900–1200*, Oxford: Blackwell.

Hamada, S. and Shinbara, M. (eds) (1977) *Fukuoka minami baipasu kankei maizoubunkazi chosa hokoku, 5, Chikushino-shi shozai Nagaoka kamekan iseki (A report on the excavation of the jar burial site of Nagaoka, Chikushino City, Fukuoka Prefecture)*, Fukuoka: Fukuoka Prefectural Board of Education.

Harunari, H. (1984) 'Rules of residence in Kyushu district during the Yayoi period', *Bulletin of the National Museum of Japanese History* 3: 1–40.

Hashiguchi, T. (1987) 'Shuraku richi to tochi kaihatsu' (Settlement location and land exploitation in the Yayoi period), *Higashi Ajia no koko to rekishi (Studies in East Asian Archaeology and History)*, Kyoto: Dohosya, pp. 703–54.

Mizoguchi, K. (1992) 'A historiography of a linear barrow cemetery: a structurationist's point of view', *Archaeological Review from Cambridge* 11(1): 39–49.

Mizoguchi, K. (1995a) ' Fukuoka Ken Chikushino Shi Nagaoska iseki no kenkyu: iwayuru niretsu maiso bochi no ichirei no shakai kokogaku teki saikento' (A study of the Yayoi period jar burial cemetery of Nagaoka: a social archaeology of a linear-aligned cemetery with two rows of burials), *Kobunka danso (Journal of the society of Kyushu prehistoric and ancient cultural studies)* 34: 159–92.

—— (1995b) 'Fukuoka Ken Amagi Shi Kuriyama iseki C gun boiki no kenkyu: Hokubu Kyushu Yayoi jidai chuki kohan bochi no ichirei no shakai kokogaku teki kennto' (A study of burial cluster C at the cemetery site of Kuriyama, Amagi City, Fukuoka Prefecture, Japan: The social archaeology of a jar burial site of the middle Yayoi period in northern Kyushu), *Nihon Kokogaku (Journal of the Japanese Archaeological Association)* 2: 69–94.

Mukaida, M. (ed.) (1990) *Nagaoka iseki II (A report on the second and third excavation of the jar burial site of Nagaoka)*, Chikushino: Chikushino Municipal Board of Education.

Sasaki, T. (ed.) (1982) *Kuriyama iseki (A report on the excavation of the jar burial site of Kuriyama, Amagi City, Fukuoka Prefecture)*, Amagi: Amagi Municipal Board of Education.

Sofaer Derevenski, J. (1994) 'Where are the children? Accessing children in the past', *Archaeological Review from Cambridge* 13(2): 7–20.

Chapter 12

Child burials in ancient Athens

Sanne Houby-Nielsen

INTRODUCTION

It is something of a paradox that despite the silence regarding child mortality and childhood in early Greek art and literature, infants and small children were among the most carefully buried individuals in ancient Athens. Cemeteries devoted primarily to infants and small children extended over large areas at the most important and prestigious city gates. No less paradoxical is the fact that ancient Greek vocabulary is comparatively unconcerned with the growing child, although the age group to which a child belonged was often well defined in burial. The absence of detailed descriptions of childhood has often led scholars to conclude that Greek society took no interest in the small child until the fourth century and the Hellenistic period, when iconographic and textual references become plentiful and refined (Garland 1990: 106–11, 160–2; Golden 1990: 12–22). Debate on infancy and early childhood has frequently centred on the extent to which exposure of newborn children took place, adding to an impression of parental indifference towards young children in ancient Greece.

This chapter explores attitudes to small children in ancient Athens through almost 2,000 child burials dating from 1100 to 0 BC.[1] During this long and turbulent period in her history, the scattered communities in the area of present-day central Athens developed into one of the most prosperous, culturally developed and powerful city-states in Greece with a unique political system, the democracy. Towards the end of the fourth century, Athens was overthrown by the Macedonian kingdom and, later still, subject to the Roman Empire. The development of definitions of age through burial practice demonstrates remarkable continuity throughout the first millennium BC. Yet, the emphasis placed on formal child burial varied over time, particularly between the period covering the formation and peak of the Athenian city-state (720–400 BC) (hereafter referred to as the 'city-state period' even though one cannot speak of a proper state before the sixth century BC), and the centuries before and after (1100–720 BC and 400 to 0 BC).

The emphasis on child burial was particularly strong during the period of the city-state with distinct categorisations applied to infants and small children. Furthermore, the city plan of Athens was fundamentally affected by changing geographies of formal child burial, a feature that has not so far been addressed in studies of children. Far from being individuals in whom Athenians showed no official interest, infants and small children held special significance in burial customs at the height of Athens' powers.

MODES OF BURIAL AND GRAVE GOODS FOR CHILDREN

When studying the infant and child burials of ancient Athens, one is immediately struck by the care characterising the arrangement of grave goods and the disposal of the small body. No less striking is the way in which the age of the deceased child significantly influenced the choice of burial type and grave goods. From 1100–400 BC, those who buried children found it natural and necessary to express through burial customs the fact that a child (as opposed to an adult) had died.

It is likely that female relatives of a deceased child were responsible for his or her burial (Houby-Nielsen 1997, in press). A rich body of evidence points to women, mainly close kin, as the main caretakers of the corpse and as mourners and performers of laments, just as they are in modern, rural Greece (Alexiou 1974; Pomeroy 1975; Danforth and Tsiaras 1982; Garland 1985; Caraveli 1986; Siurla-Theodoridou 1989; Just 1991; Shapiro 1991; Seremetakis 1991; Holst-Warhaft 1995). Archaic and Classical vase paintings depict women paying visits to tombs (Kurtz and Boardman 1971; Kurtz 1988; Rehm 1994; Lissarrague 1992; Garland 1985; Stears 1995). Women often buried their children in such a way that it is possible to distinguish up to three age groups: the infant (0–1 year old), the small child (1–3 to 4 years old) and the older child (3–4 to 8–10 years old). Over time, these age groups were increasingly formalised through choice of burial type and the nature of accompanying grave goods. In addition, children may also be identified through skeletal analysis or the length of the grave, pit or coffin. The categorisation of infants, small children and, to a lesser extent, older children culminated during the city-state period, becoming particularly prescribed with regard to burial type and choice of grave goods. However, at no time were adolescents (skeletally immature individuals older than 8–10 years) distinguished from adults in burial rites.

Temporal development in modes of burial

The Submycenaean period (1100–1050 BC) saw the first attempts to distinguish infants as an age group. In contrast to older children and adults inhumed in cist tombs, infants were often buried in a pit or grave built of small stones. Examples are four Submycenaean infant graves on the Acropolis termed 'Säugling' by the excavator (Cavvadias and Kawerau 1896: 38, pl. Z: 72). However, this was not an exclusive division. A diminutive cist grave in Th. Renti Street 8 is likely to have housed an infant or small child, indicating that a lack of interest in expressing a notion of childhood sometimes prevailed (*Archaeologikon Deltion* 34 B, 1979 (1987): 16–17, t. V).

The Protogeometric period (1050–900 BC) saw a radical shift in the burial of adults, with the vast majority being cremated. This tradition lasted until the sixth century, and remained active even in the fifth and fourth centuries. However, the category 'infant' remained unique since infants and small children continued to be inhumed. In this period we first meet the custom of inhuming infants in medium-sized storage jars, a custom that was to last throughout the remaining part of Athens' ancient history (*Archaeologikon Deltion* 34 B 1979 (1987): 16, Robertou Galli and Karytidon Street). These infant burial urns were often closed carefully with a stone, a large potsherd or a vase, and the grave pits into which they were inserted likewise covered with slabs. Carbonised remains of food attest to the need to provide the child with nourishment. Thus, in this period not only were younger individuals distinguished from older ones, but distinct categories of 'child' started to develop. Nonetheless, the division between adults and older children remained indistinct. The cremation burials of two older children (aged 5–10 years and 11–16 years) were found with those of two youths (a man aged 18 years and a woman aged 17 years) in a burial plot south of the Acropolis (Brouskari 1980: graves G, Z and I). At Drakou Street, a Protogeometric pyxis buried in a small pit covered by a stone slab contained the burned bones of a child (*Archaeologikon Deltion* 32 B 1977 (1984): 19, Drakou Street: t.11).

During the period of the city-state, the definition of age through mortuary practice became even more distinct and specific. Differential disposal of the infant and child body meant that the three age-groups – infants, small children and older children – were often clearly expressed. In addition to the distinctive burial accorded to infants, the first true formalised burial rite for small children aged between 1 and 3–4 years emerged around 500 BC through the use of household terracotta basins which measured between 80 and 100 cm (*Kerameikos* IX: 29–30). This mode of burial for the small child was extremely common throughout the fifth and most of the fourth century. Previously, this age group had normally been inhumed in pits, cist graves, or wooden coffins. In comparison to the urn and basin burials given to infants and small children respectively, older children aged between 3–4 and 8–10 years remained a more indistinct, although recognisable, group in terms of grave type. The main distinguishing criteria are the use of inhumation as the accepted ritual and the size of the pit or coffin, which was fitted to contain the body. Cremation, however, appears also to have been used in rare cases, such as in the Archaic and Classical cemetery in Kerameikos (Schlörb-Vierneisel 1966: 23/hS 181, 54/hS 170, 79/hS 151, 104/hS 156, 158/hS 87; *Kerameikos* VII.1 nos. 106, 141). In the period 300–0 BC, infants and small children continued to be buried in vessels and household basins, but it also seems that cremation was now more frequently used for children than before (*Kerameikos* XIV: enclosure VIII grave 40; *Kerameikos* VII.1. nos 154, 231, 233, 500, 568).

Grave goods

Identification of the most common categories of grave goods found in relation to child burials indicates that an unambiguous awareness of age pervaded the choice of children's grave goods for almost 1,000 years (Figure 12.1) although this pattern was somewhat more consistent in the city-state period than in the preceding or succeeding periods (compare the dotted and the full lines in Figure 12.1). In general, the number of pieces of jewellery, terracotta, toys, and items that were gender-laden in the adult world gradually increased with the age of the child. Examples of such gender-laden objects include *pyxides*, swords, belly- and neck-handled *amphorae*, *aryballoi*, strigils, mirrors, pieces of soap, make-up, *lebetes*, *kalathoi*, spindle-whorls, needles, arrowheads and cauldrons. On the other hand, the provision of the infant or child with vases for drinking and eating tended to decrease with age. In the Classical period, infants and small children were also provided with many more small and miniature jugs than older children and adults (Houby-Nielsen 1995: 149).Thus, artefacts in children's graves were selected with a view to their appropriateness for particular age groups of children.

The degree to which the age of the child at death influenced the choice of its grave goods is particularly illuminating in the Classical period. In addition to the examples given in Figure

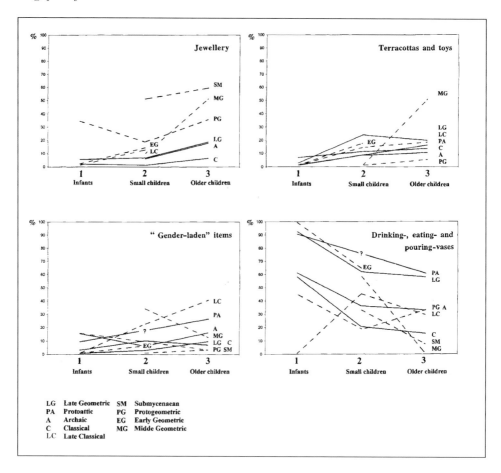

Figure 12.1   The frequency of categories of grave goods in relation to children's age in Athens from 1100 to 300 BC. Hellenistic grave goods are not included since the number of grave goods from this period is too low to be statistically meaningful

12.1, the *lekythos*, a special type of perfume container, is a useful illustration. *Lekythoi* are known both from written and archaeological sources to have been placed around the corpse of the adult when lying in state, probably as means of purification (Aristophanes, *Ecclesiazusae*: 1030). They were then carried to the grave and placed evenly around the corpse, again as a purifying device (Houby-Nielsen, in press; *Kerameikos* IX, 15; Kurtz and Boardman 1971: 207–9; Parker 1983: 35–6). However, when looking at the number of *lekythoi* in relation to the age of the deceased it is evident that notions of pollution were intimately tied to the age of the deceased. Thus, the number of *lekythoi* deposited as grave goods increased steadily with the person's age; almost none are found in infant graves, while they are somewhat more common in burials of small children, common in burials of older children and frequent in adult graves (Houby-Nielsen 1995: table 7).

Concepts regarding the needs of children at death and burial remained more or less unchanged over a period of 700 years, the main development being that these concepts became especially formalised during the period of the city-state. Throughout most of Athens' long history, the infant was provided with vases for food, the small and older child with toys, and the older child with items relating to its unattained adult gender role.

THE GEOGRAPHY OF CHILD BURIAL

In contrast to the deep continuity in the selection of burial types and grave goods for children, the frequency and spatial distribution of infant and child burials changed significantly over the course of Athens' history. There were periods in which Athenians chose to dispose of small infant and child corpses by such simple means that they escape us archaeologically. Conversely, there were periods when large areas at the city gates were reserved for the formal disposal of masses of such burials. Despite the gradual and consistent development of concepts of age in mortuary settings, a sudden rise in the formal burial of children in the city-state period indicates that the act of burying children attained special significance. This significance bore little relationship to understandings of the needs of dead children.

The changing number of child burials in cemeteries and burial plots in prehistoric to Early Archaic Attica, and its significance for the formation of the Athenian city-state, was first dealt with at length by Morris (1987). He saw the inclusion of children in formal cemeteries and in burial plots in the Late Geometric period as an indication of early democracy (ibid.). However, he treated child burials as a single undifferentiated group. Furthermore, temporal changes in the spatial distribution of child burials in Athens were not addressed. It is therefore worth looking at changes in the frequency of age groups among child burials since this shifted markedly over time. Moreover, early choice of burial location for children significantly influenced the layout of the Classical city.

The frequency of age groups in child burial

Infant burials were relatively rare throughout the period preceding the city-state. In the Submycenaean period, burials of older children were much more frequent than those of infants, while in the Protogeometric–Middle Geometric periods, the overall number of child burials declined leading to a further reduction in the number of infant burials. However, at the end of the eighth century in the Late Geometric period when profound social transformations began to take place (Morris 1987; Polignac 1995a, 1995b), a new pattern was suddenly established which lasted until the end of the fifth century. During these three centuries, the number of infant burials rose dramatically, forming the overwhelming majority of child burials. Burials of small children formed the second most frequent group. Burials of older children were least frequent by far. In the fourth century, the overall number of child burials dropped again. It remained low throughout the Hellenistic period, no age group being buried more frequently than any other.

Thus, the city-state period was characterised by a particularly high frequency of infant burials, and to a lesser extent those of small children. In view of the high infant mortality that no doubt existed, such a demographic pattern may at first sight appear 'natural'. However, the total number of graves is far too low to represent any kind of demographic reality. In the Classical and Hellenistic periods alone, several hundred thousand inhabitants lived in Athens. Rather, the proportionally high frequency of infant and small-child burials reflected a change in attitude towards infants and small children in the city-state period.

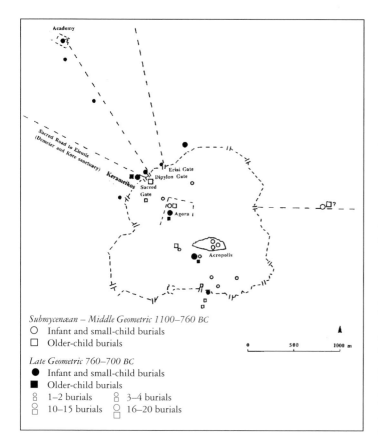

Academy

*Sacred Road to Eleusis
(Demeter and Kore sanctuary)*

Kerameikos   Eriai Gate
            Dipylon Gate
Sacred
Gate

Agora

Acropolis

Submycenaean – Middle Geometric 1100–760 BC
○ Infant and small-child burials
□ Older-child burials

Late Geometric 760–700 BC
● Infant and small-child burials
■ Older-child burials
1–2 burials   3–4 burials
10–15 burials   16–20 burials

0   500   1000 m

Figure 12.2   The distribution of infant and child burials in Submycenaean-Late Geometric Athens in relation to the Classical city wall and main roads

The spatial distribution of child burial

This impression of a change in attitude towards the burial of infants and small children is further strengthened by temporal variation in the spatial distribution of child burials in Athens.

Figure 12.2 shows the distribution of infant and child burials in Submycenaean–Middle Geometric Athens (1100–760 BC) in relation to the Classical city wall and main roads. From the Submycenaean to the Middle Geometric periods there were almost no burials of infants and small children in the cemeteries on the banks of the Eridanos river near the areas which later became the Sacred Gate and Dipylon Gate (*Kerameikos* I: 257–61; Krause 1975: 41). The only possible exceptions are graves 3, 81 and 70 in Kerameikos I. In the Submycenaean period, only older children were buried here. In the Pompeion cemetery, older children were buried between adults (Krause 1975: figure 6). Burials of infants and small children were kept close to habitation on the Acropolis. In the Protogeometric period, small and older children were buried together with adults in the Kolonos Agoraios, on the south slope of the Acropolis and the Areopagus, and in an area to the south and south-west of the Acropolis.

This picture changed in the Late Geometric period (Figure 12.2) with the beginning of the formation of the city-state and the sudden increase in the burial of infants and small children. Among the many burial grounds that now included infants and small children, three had particularly high frequencies of infant and child burials. One of these lay south of the Acropolis, thereby continuing the tradition of burying children in this area. The other two, however, appeared in new locations which were to become significant infant and small-child cemeteries in the Classical city; the Kerameikos cemetery located on either side of the Sacred Road, and the cemetery both at the Eriai gate itself and to the north of the gate.

In the Kerameikos cemetery, the area in and around the so-called 'Plattenbau' held a particularly dense concentration of small-child burials. This area, near what was later to become the Sacred Gate, continued to be used for infants and small children in the seventh and sixth centuries. In the last decade of the sixth century, an enormous neighbouring grave mound was also turned into an infant and small-child burial ground. Together, these two burial plots became the most frequently used burial ground for infants and small children in the fifth century (see Figures 12.2–12.4) (Krause 1975: 99, figures 24, 26, tables 25, 1–6 and 26, 1–9; *Kerameikos* V.1: plan 1; *Kerameikos* VII.1: area of grave mound G; *Kerameikos* IX: the south mound; Houby-Nielsen 1995: figures 1–7). Throughout the Archaic and Classical periods, the number of private burial plots along the Sacred Road increased steadily, extending outside Kerameikos and further towards Eleusis. Some of these burial plots also included an extraordinarily high proportion of child burials (Figures 12.2–12.4) (Houby-Nielsen 1995).

Kübler, the former excavator of Kerameikos, noted that the burials in the Kerameikos demonstrated a marked tendency in orientation, such that the deceased looked towards the Sacred Road or towards cross-

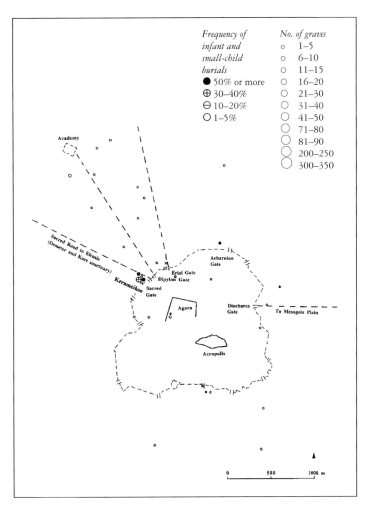

Figure 12.3   The distribution of child and adult burials in Athens in relation to the Classical city wall and main roads in the sixth century BC.

Note: The percentage frequency divisions of infant and child burials are based on actual proportions of infant and child burials in cemeteries

roads leading to it. According to Kübler, this pattern was visible from the Submycenaean period until as late as the fifth century BC (*Kerameikos* V.1: 14–15; *Kerameikos* VII.1: 194–97). Therefore both the choice of burial location and the orientation of the burials point to a strong wish to bury children and adults within view of the Sacred Road. This was undoubtedly linked to the ancient cults of Demeter and Kore in Eleusis, both of which had powerful chthonic and fertility elements. Eleusis had belonged to Athens since at least the sixth century BC, but its cults originated in the Bronze Age. In Classical times, the fame of the sanctuary of Demeter extended far beyond Greece. For the Athenians, initiation into the Eleusinian mysteries meant happiness and comfort in the afterlife. Each year a procession took place along the Sacred Road from Athens to

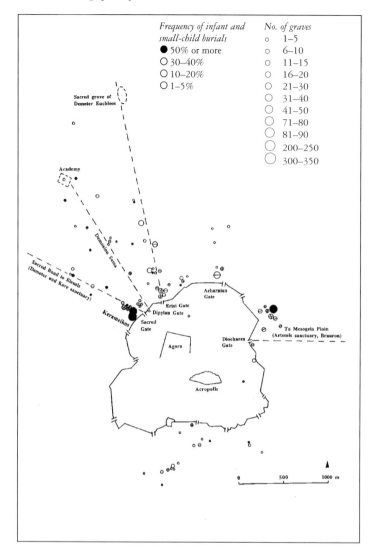

Frequency of infant and small-child burials
● 50% or more
○ 30–40%
○ 10–20%
○ 1–5%

No. of graves
○ 1–5
○ 6–10
○ 11–15
○ 16–20
○ 21–30
○ 31–40
○ 41–50
○ 71–80
○ 81–90
○ 200–250
○ 300–350

Figure 12.4   The distribution of child and adult burials in Athens in relation to the Classical city wall and main roads in the fifth century BC.

Note: The percentage frequency divisions of infant and child burials are based on actual proportions of infant and child burials in cemeteries

Eleusis in which all Athenians, including women and children, could participate (Burkert 1987). Women also frequently participated in decisively female festivals held in Eleusis – the *Chloia*, *Haloa* and *Thesmophorion* (Brumfield 1981; Burkert 1987; Foxhall 1995; Clinton 1996). Since women played an important role in burying close kin, infants and small children, it is significant that Athenian women were well acquainted with the Sacred Road through their participation in these religious activities (Houby-Nielsen, in press).

In the light of the close connection between private burials of adults and children and the Demeter sanctuary in Eleusis, it is interesting that the infant cemetery which appeared in the Late Geometric period in the vicinity of the later Eriai gate was situated on a road which – in later times, at least – also led to a Demeter sanctuary. The road emanating from here led towards Thebes. Not far from Athens it passed a grove sacred to Demeter *Euchloos*. This cult appears to have been linked to the cult of Demeter *Chloé* in Eleusis and thus to have been connected with fertility. It also appears to have been associated with the nursing of small boys (*Corpus Inscriptionum Atticarum* III:1, p. 70 no. 191; Pausanias I. 22, 3; *Paulys Realencyclopädie* IV, 2737). It is therefore no coincidence that women also turned this cemetery into an important burial ground for infants and small children in the Classical period (Figure 12.4).

By the sixth century, infant and small-child cemeteries had also become established near two of the other main city gates: the Archanes and Diochares gates (see Figures 12.3 and 12.4) (*Plateia Kotsia Archaeologikon Deltion* 43 B 1988 (1993): 22–9). More than 200 Classical burials have recently been excavated near the Syntagma Square in the vicinity of the ancient Diochares Gates (*Antike Welt* (1997) 28(2):161). Well over half of these were child burials. This cemetery at the Diochares gate therefore appears to have equalled, if not surpassed, that at the Sacred Gate with respect to size and the number of child burials. It is tempting once again to relate this growth of the Diochares cemetery to the fact that the road issuing from the Diochares Gate led towards the Mesogeia Plain, to *demes* known to have held important female religious festivals (*Thesmophoria*), and to the sanctuaries of Artemis and Iphigenia in Brauron. The latter sanctuary is particularly important since it is known to have held initiation rituals for small girls and, more significantly, to have played a special role for women during pregnancy and childbirth (Aristophanes, *Lysistrata*: 642–7; *Inscriptiones Graecae* 112, 1516 and 1522 line 30; Linders 1972; Garland 1990; Bruitt Zaidman and Schmitt Pantel 1994; Clinton 1996).

In parts of the Sacred Gate, Eriai Gate and Diochares Gate cemeteries, concentrations of infant and child burials often reached up to 100 per cent. In other areas of these cemeteries, they constituted 30–50 per cent. In sharp contrast, the proportion of infants and small children in the majority of minor burial plots, often placed at some distance from the city, only reached 1–5 per cent or 10–20 per cent (Figures 12.3 and 12.4). Therefore, the Sacred Gate, Eriai Gate and Diochares Gate cemeteries clearly had a distinctive function as centres in the city for infant and small-child burial, a function which finds close parallels in cemeteries in Eleusis (the west cemetery), Corinth (the north cemetery) and Olynthus (Mylonas 1975; Robinson 1942; Blegen *et al.* 1964).

Just as the tendency to reserve specific burial locations for infants and small children was rooted in the Late Geometric tradition, another important characteristic of the

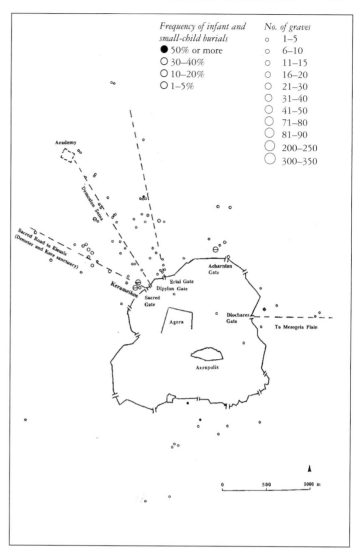

Figure 12.5 The distribution of child and adult burials in Athens in relation to the Classical city wall and major roads in the fourth century BC.

Note: The percentage frequency divisions of infant and child burials are based on actual proportions of infant and child burials in cemeteries

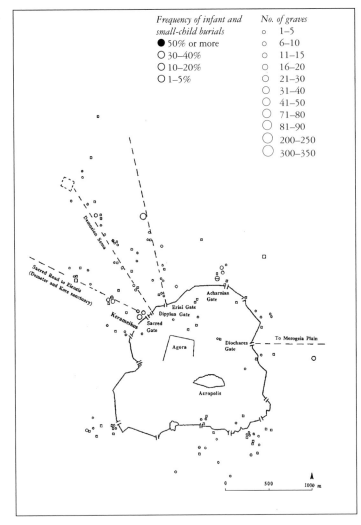

Figure 12.6 The distribution of child and adult burials in Athens in relation to the Classical city wall and major roads in the third to first centuries BC.

Note: The percentage frequency divisions of infant and child burials are based on actual proportions of infant and child burials in cemeteries

Classical Athenian city plan also began in the Late Geometric period. This was the use in burial practice of the road that in Classical and Hellenistic times became known as the *demosion sema*. It led from the Dipylon Gate in Kerameikos to the Academy of Plato. Importantly, however, the way in which the road was used in burial changed as the city developed.

In the Late Geometric period the road is likely to have connected Athens with a sanctuary for the hero Academus, the founder hero of Athens, situated in the area of the later Academy. A large, many-roomed Late Geometric house excavated in the Academy is probably related to a cult of a chthonic nature for Academus (Coldstream 1977; Travlos 1971). In this early period, burials of both adults and children first began to appear along the road, both inside the area of the Kerameikos and outside in the area of the Academy itself (see Figure 12.2) (Löringhoff 1974; *Ergon tis Archaeologikis Etaireias* 1958, 10; *Archaeologischer Anzeiger* 1934: 139; *Praktika tis en Athinais Archaeologikis Etaireias* 1956: 49, 1969: 5; *Archaeologikon Deltion* 33 B 1978 (1985): 24; *Archaeologikon Deltion* 42 B 1987 (1992): 21 no. 13).

In the centuries succeeding the Late Geometric period, infant and child burials disappeared from the Academus Road. By the beginning of the fifth century, the road had become reserved for public burials of warriors and statesmen (see D'Onofrio 1995: 63; Morris 1987: 228–33). It was here that the Classical city annually honoured its war dead through funerary speeches and games. The new status of the Academus Road as *demosion sema* meant that private burial activity was largely moved to other roads emanating from Athens (Figures 12.5 and 12.6). This also affected the Kerameikos cemetery at the Sacred Gate and the Dipylon Gate cemetery. As early as the sixth century BC, and certainly by the fifth century, Kerameikos had become divided into two halves. One consisted primarily of public burials of warriors, winners of public games and statesmen, constituting the *demosion sema* (issuing from the Dipylon Gate). The other half was centred along the Sacred Road and consisted primarily of private adult and child burials.[2]

While the importance of the cult of Demeter meant that private burials, not least those of children, clustered naturally along the road leading to the Demeter sanctuary in Eleusis, the institution of the *demosion sema* along the Academus Road is likely to have arisen from the increasingly masculine cultural and political significance which this road had attained. The Academus Road probably led to educational centres for the city's young men that predated Plato's academy. It also played a role in the most important religious event in Athens, the Panathenaean Festival, which celebrated the autochthony of Athens. A factor which may also have added to the masculine character of this road was the fact that women and children appear to have been excluded from participating in the aforementioned public funerary celebration of war dead (Loraux 1986, 1993). On the whole, it is therefore understandable that women, who bore the primary responsibility for the burial of infants and children, refrained from burying infants and children at a location which was so heavily embedded in the city's more masculine cultural and ceremonial life.

The Classical cemeteries with the highest concentrations of infants and children were situated very close to those city gates and roads which led to important chthonic and female cults, and which played a significant role in the commercial life of Athens. In recent years, scholars have increasingly stressed the mobility of women in ancient Athens with regard to their religious activities, duties and power in the household, rather than seeing them as confined to their homes (cf. Just 1991; Scheidel 1995 and Houby-Nielsen in press). No doubt women, no less than men, walked regularly on these roads on their way to work in the fields, to sanctuaries and family visits, or went to these roads to buy and sell fresh produce. Infant and small-child cemeteries were therefore situated at key places in the daily traffic to and from Athens, and in locations which must have been regarded as acceptable and natural for 'respectable' women to visit.

When the number of infant and child burials dropped dramatically in both larger cemeteries and minor burial plots in the fourth century and Hellenistic period, this was reflected in the comparatively abrupt abandonment of the Diochares Gate cemetery (Figure 12.5). A general shift in burial activity to the north-west of the city and the roads leading towards the Academy and Eleusis occurred at this time (Figure 12.6), marking a change in burial customs. The old state burials, noted by visitors to Athens in the second century AD along the road all the way to the Academy (Knigge 1988), mingled with private burials. Even extensive poor-man cemeteries were now situated along these roads (*Archaeologikon Deltion* 37 B 1982 (1989): 25 no. 12; *Archaeologikon Deltion* 40 B 1985 (1988): 29 no. 16).

In summary, infants and small children began to be emphasised in burial rites during a time of fundamental social and political change often taken to lead to the formation of the Athenian city-state. These age-groups continued to be emphasised throughout the Archaic and Classical period, finally resulting in extensive infant and small-child cemeteries at the major gates of Athens and along roads leading to, among other things, important sanctuaries with female or chthonic dimensions. At the beginning of the fourth century BC, and in the following centuries when Athens was no longer a politically independent city-state, the traditional formal infant and small-child cemeteries almost disappeared as part of a major change in the spatial distribution of burials.

THE CHANGING SYMBOLISM OF CHILD BURIAL IN ATHENIAN SOCIETY

Changes in the frequency and spatial distribution of child burials in Athens can be related to shifts in the symbolism of child burial within Athenian society. The emphasis on the formal burial of infants and small children in the period of the city-state suggests that children were promoted and regarded as necessary for the survival of the society, a notion common for many states and societies. As in Augustan Rome, the small child became a symbol of a political Golden Age (Manson 1983).

Nonetheless, although the emphasis on child burial may have been representative of a wider underlying ideology, it does not necessarily follow that child burial maintained exactly the same precise meaning throughout the period of the city-state. Many other mortuary customs and social and religious practices that appeared during the Late Geometric and Early Archaic periods changed in appearance, function and meaning in the later city-state (for instance, the use of writing, figurative decoration on pottery, the banquet, grave monuments with frontal pronunciation and temple architecture). It is not surprising, therefore, that the particular symbolism of child burials altered even within the city-state period.

Evidence for such a change stems primarily from those instances where infants and small children were buried in proximity to, or in the same grave as, adults. In the Late Geometric and Early Archaic periods this data comes from the 'Plattenbau' complex in the Kerameikos, a unique mortuary structure consisting of compartments divided by upright standing schist slabs. Here, burials of infants and small children were clustered around, or were buried together with, adults. The burial customs relating to these adults emphasise a male gender. Where available, anthropological analyses confirm that these adults were men (Kerameikos V.1: 17–19, G51–G63; cf. also Krause 1975: figures 24, 26, who regards Kerameikos V.1: G50 to be a boy; though see Strömberg 1993, 164 no. 343). Furthermore, the use of neck-handled *amphorae* as burial urns for the infants and small children may suggest that these individuals were male; neck-handled *amphorae* were traditionally used as containers for adult male cremations. As grave goods, neck-handled *amphorae* are more common in male than in female graves (Krause 1975: table 26; Strömberg 1993: 72, 81, 105). In the seventh century BC a man was buried up against two child burials not far from the 'Plattenbau' and, in the course of the following century, several children were buried close to his grave (D'Onofrio 1993: 144–47; Houby-Nielsen 1995: figures 1–3).

A shift in association seems to take place in the Classical and Hellenistic periods. Again, there are a number of cases, this time from a variety of locations in Athens, in which infants and small children were buried close to, or together with, adults. However, the anthropological determinations and associated grave goods suggest that all these adults are women (Kerameikos XIV: no. 55/Eck 46, no. 56/Eck 48; Archaeologikon Deltion 45 B 1990 (1995): 32 t. 17); Kerameikos VII.1: nos 465, 475). In other words, there appears to be a change over time in the relationship of the infant or small child to the sex of adult.

It is tempting to relate such a change to the gradual development from a 'big man' society in the early city-state, to a fully developed city-state known to have actively promoted an ideal of woman as mother or close kin to legitimate children (Loraux 1981; Vedder 1988). Demand (1994) has expressed reservations regarding this interpretation. However, it is well known that in the Classical period, the survival of the city-state was thought to depend on the birth of legitimate children, since laws limited citizenship rights to freeborn males of Athenian ancestry (Just 1991: 60–62; Patterson 1987). This growing legal conflation of legitimacy at birth with rights to citizenship no doubt increased the value placed on legitimate children and the significance of the early loss of a child. Furthermore, these laws cannot only have affected Athenian citizen families, but must have also changed attitudes to small children in Athenian society as a whole, including the huge number of resident non-Athenians without citizen rights (*metics*). Non-Athenians frequently imitated citizen burial customs (Bergemann 1997: 142–8).

Against this background, it is not difficult to imagine that female relatives of deceased children, from both Athenian and non-Athenian families, sought to express their ability to bear and give birth to children by formally burying their infants and small children. They naturally did so at those city gates of Athens with which they were most familiar and which led to cults of particular relevance to children, childbirth and death. This interpretation gains further weight if the new value system that arose in the fourth century and Hellenistic period is considered. This new system affected political life, gender roles and therefore also the attitude to children. Whereas female civic values formerly focused on the dutiful, child-bearing mother, they were now characterised by ideals of 'luxury', 'leisure', and time for body-care. These concepts clearly pervaded the choice of grave goods and grave monuments for adults of both sexes, and coincided with an ever-growing number of public baths in Athens, as well as elsewhere, in this period (Houby-Nielsen 1997, 1998; Zanker 1993). This set of fourth century and Hellenistic values may well have induced women to lose interest in the traditional burial customs for small children if, as suggested, these traditional customs served to highlight a woman's role as 'ideal' mother or kin to a child. Accordingly, cemeteries of infants and small children dwindled in size in the early fourth century BC.

The abandonment of traditional burial rites for infants and small children can therefore be related to the decline of a political ideology. However, a new relationship between the small child, society and close family arose in its place. Thus, the reduction in child burial actually coincided with the appearance of relief-decorated gravestones depicting, and sometimes even commemorating, babies and small children who do not appear to have been given a formal burial. Children could even be heroised (*IG* III: 1460). These changes in burial customs for children occurred at the same time as the depiction and description of children became refined in art and literature (Rühfel 1984).

CONCLUSION

The study of child burials highlights important continuity and links between periods in notions of age. Athenian women had a more or less common notion of children's age groups and their needs at death and burial over a period of almost a thousand years. This notion was current long before the significant social transformations in the late eighth century BC, which were directly related to the formation of the Athenian city-state, and persisted even after Athens lost her political independence. However, in terms of frequency and spatial distribution, burials of small children, and of infants in particular, came to play a highly significant role during the period of the city-state. The attention paid to the burial of children was related to an ideology that saw children as necessary for the survival of society and city-state. Yet, in accordance with the ever-changing face of Athens (from a 'big man' society to a fully developed state), the act of burying infants and small children nevertheless changed in its particular meaning, revealed through changes in the relationship between burials of infants and small children to the sex of deceased adults. The emphasis on the small child in mortuary practice during the city-state period resulted in extensive infant and child cemeteries at the major city gates of Athens. Indeed, attitudes to infant and child burials decisively influenced the plan and general rhythm of the Classical city, challenging established scholarly ideas regarding Athenians' disinterest in the small child before the fourth century BC.

ACKNOWLEDGEMENTS

I would like to thank Joanna Sofaer Derevenski most warmly for having invited me to contribute to the present anthology and for her efforts to revise my English. Leslie Beaumont kindly directed my attention towards the TAG conference on children and John Lund offered most helpful criticism on several parts of my paper. As usual, I cannot thank Anders Andrén enough for his many improvements on my arguments.

NOTES

1   The present study relies on a survey of the preliminary reports of rescue excavations published in *Archaeologikon Deltion* and *Archaeologika Analekta eks Athninon*, and for prehistoric Athens, on catalogues in Morris (1987) and Whitley (1991). The catalogue by Strömberg (1993) is more detailed but not all graves are listed. For additional references and corrections, see also D'Onofrio (1995) and d'Agostino and D'Onofrio (1993). Graves from the Classical and Hellenistic periods may be found in the catalogue in Houby-Nielsen (1995) (Kerameikos only) and Houby-Nielsen (1997).
2   Possible exceptions are two burials of envoys (Knigge 1972) and a group of Archaic warrior burials (Vierneisel 1964: 445; Houby-Nielsen 1995: 153 and figure 4 area C).

ABBREVIATIONS

IG	Inscriptiones Graecae (1873)
Kerameikos I	Kraiker, W., Kübler, K. and Breitinger, E. (1943) *Die Nekropolen des 12. bis 10. Jahrhunderts v. Chr. (Kerameikos, Ergebnisse der Ausgrabungen I)*, Berlin: de Gruyter.
Kerameikos V.1	Kübler, K. (1954) *Die Nekropole des späten 8. bis frühen 6. Jahrhunderts (Kerameikos, Ergebnisse der Ausgrabungen V.1)*, Berlin: de Gruyter.
Kerameikos VII.1	Kübler, K. (1976) *Die Nekropole der Mitte des 6. bis Ende des 5. Jahrhunderts (Kerameikos, Ergebnisse der Ausgrabungen VII.1)*, Berlin: de Gruyter.
Kerameikos IX	Knigge, U. (1976) *Der Südhügel. (Kerameikos, Ergebnisse der Ausgrabungen IX)*, Berlin: de Gruyter.
Kerameikos XIV	Kovacsovics, W. (1990) *Die Eckterrasse im Grabbezirk des Kerameikos (Kerameikos, Ergebnisse der Ausgrabungen XIV)*, Berlin: de Gruyter.

REFERENCES

Alexiou, M. (1974) *The Ritual Lament in Greek Tradition*, Cambridge: Cambridge University Press.
Bergemann, J. (1997) *Demos und Thanatos. Untersuchungen zum Wertesystem der Polis im Spiegel der attischen Grabreliefs des 4. Jahrhunderts v. Chr. Und zur Funktion der gleichzeitigen Grabbauten*, Biering & Brinkmann: München.
Blegen, C.W., Palmer, H. and Young, R.S. (1964) *The North Cemetery Results of Excavations Conducted by the American School of Classical Studies at Athens XIII*, Princeton and New Jersey: J.J. Augustin, Glückstadt.

Brouskari, M. (1980) 'A Dark Age cemetery in Erechteion Street, Athens', *Annual of the British School at Athens* 75: 13–31.

Bruit Zaidman, L. and Schmitt Pantel, P. (eds) (1994) *Religion in the Ancient Greek City*, trans. P. Cartledge, Cambridge: Cambridge University Press.

Brumfield, A. (1981) *The Attic Festivals of Demeter and their Relation to the Agricultural Year*, New York: Arno.

Burkert, W. (1987) *Greek Religion: Archaic and Classical*, Oxford: Blackwell.

Caraveli, A. (1986) 'The bitter wounding: the lament as social protest in rural Greece', in J. Dubisch (ed.) *Gender and Power in Rural Greece*, Princeton: Princeton University Press, pp. 167–94.

Cavvadias, P. and Kawerau, G. (1896) *Die Ausgrabung der Akropolis vom Jahre 1885 bis zum Jahre 1890*, Athens: 'Estia' K. Maïsner and N. Kargadouri.

Clinton, K. (1996) 'The Thesmophoria in Central Athens and the Celebration of the Thesmophoria in Attica', in R. Hägg (ed.) *The Role of Religion in the Early Greek Polis* (Proceedings of the Third International Seminar on Ancient Greek Cult, Swedish Institute at Athens, 16–18 October 1992), Stockholm: Paul Åström, pp. 111–25.

Coldstream, J.N. (1977) *Geometric Greece*, London: Methuen.

D'Agostino, B. and D'Onofrio, A.M. (1993) Review of I. Morris (1987) *Burial and Ancient Society: The Rise of the Greek City-State* (New Studies in Archaeology), Cambridge: Cambridge University Press, *Gnomon: Kritische Zeitschrift für die gesamte klassische Altertumswissenschaft* 65: 41–51.

Danforth, L.M. and Tsiaras, A. (1982) *The Death Rituals of Rural Greece*, Princeton: Princeton University Press.

Demand, N. (1994) *Birth, Death, and Motherhood in Classical Greece*, Baltimore: Johns Hopkins University Press.

D'Onofrio, A.M. (1993) 'Le trasformazioni del costume funerario ateniese nella necropoli pre-soloniana del Kerameikos', *Annali di Archeologia e Storia Antica* 15: 143–71.

—— (1995) 'Santuari "rurali" e dinamiche insediative in Attica tra il protogeometrico e l'orientalizzante (1050–600 A.C.)', *Annali di Archeologia e Storia Antica* (Nuova Serie N. 2): 57–88.

Foxhall, L. (1995) 'Women's ritual and men's work in Ancient Athens', in R. Hawley and B. Levick (eds) *Women in Antiquity: New Assessments*, London: Routledge, pp. 97–110.

Garland, R. (1985) *The Greek Way of Death*, Ithaca and New York: Cornell University Press.

—— (1990) *The Greek Way of Life*, London: Duckworth.

Golden, M. (1990) *Children and Childhood in Classical Athens*, Baltimore: Johns Hopkins University Press.

Holst-Warhaft, G. (1995) *Dangerous Voices: Women's Laments and Greek Literature*, London: Routledge.

Houby-Nielsen, S. (1995) '"Burial language" in archaic and classical Kerameikos', *Proceedings of the Danish Institute at Athens* 1: 129–91.

—— (1997) 'Grave gifts, women, and conventional values', in P. Bilde, T. Engberg-Pedersen, L. Hannestad and J. Zahle (eds) *Conventional Values of the Hellenistic Greeks* (Studies in Hellenistic Civilization 8), Aarhus: Aarhus University Press, pp. 220–62.

—— (1998) 'Revival of Archaic Funerary Practices in the Hellenistic and Roman Kerameikos', *Proceedings of the Danish Institute at Athens* 2: 127–45

—— (in press) 'Women and the formation of the Athenian city-state: the evidence of Burial customs', in F. de Polignac (ed.) *Rites et Société dans l'Athènes Archaïque (Métis)*.

Just, R. (1991) *Women in Athenian Law and Life*, London: Routledge.

Knigge, U. (1972) 'Untersuchungen bei den Gesandtenstelen im Kerameikos zu Athen', *Archäologischer Anzeiger*: 584–629.

—— (1988) *Der Kerameikos von Athen: Führung durch Ausgrabungen und Geschichte*, Athens.

Krause, G. (1975) *Untersuchungen zu den ältesten Nekropolen am Eridanos in Athen (Beiträge für Archäologie 3)*, Hamburg: Helmut Busche Verlag.

Kurtz, D. (1988) 'Mistress and maid', *Annali di Archeologia e Storia Antica* 10: 141–49.

Kurtz, D. and Boardman, J. (1971) *Greek Burial Customs*, London: Thames & Hudson.

Linders, T. (1972) *Studies in the Treasure Records of Artemis Brauronia found in Athens*, Stockholm: Paul Åström.

Lissarrague, F. (1992) 'Figures of women', in P. Schmitt Pantel (ed.) *A History of Women in the West: I. From Ancient Goddesses to Christian Saints*, Cambridge, Mass.: Harvard University Press, pp. 139–229.

Loraux, N. (1981) 'Le lit, la guerre', *L'Homme* 21: 37–57.

—— (1986) *The Invention of Athens: The Funeral Oration in the Classical City*, Cambridge, Mass.: Harvard University Press.

—— (1993) *The Children of Athena: Athenian Ideas about Citizenship and the Division between the Sexes*, Princeton: Princeton University Press.

Löringhoff, B. (1974) 'Ein spätgeometrisches Frauengrab vom Kerameikos', *Mitteilungen des Deutschen Archäologischen Instituts, Athenische Abteilung* 89: 1–25.

Manson, M. (1983) 'The emergence of the small child in Rome (Third century BC–First century AD)', *History of Education* 12(3): 149–59.

Morris, I. (1987) *Burial and Ancient Society: The Rise of the Greek City-State (New Studies in Archaeology)*, Cambridge: Cambridge University Press.

Mylonas, G. (1975) *To dytikon nekrotaphion tis Elefsinos*, Athens: Vivliothiki tis en Athinais arkhaiologikis etaireias 81.

Parker, R. (1983) *Pollution and Purification in Early Greek Religion*, Oxford: Clarendon Press.

Patterson, C. (1987) '*Hai Attikai*: the other Athenians', in M.B. Skinner (ed.) *Rescuing Creusa: New Methodological Approaches to Women in Antiquity* (Helios, New Series 13:2), Texas: Texas Tech. University Press, pp. 49–67.

Polignac, F. de (1995a) *Cults, Territory and the Origins of the Greek City-State*, Chicago: University of Chicago Press.

—— (1995b) 'Sanctuaires et société en Attique géométrique et archaïque: réflexion sur les critères d'analyse', in A. Verbanck-Piérard and Didier Viviers (eds) *Culture et Cité. L'avènement d'Athènes à l'époque archaïque*, Bruxelles: Fondation archéologique de l'Université Libre Bruxelles.

Pomeroy, S. B. (1975) *Goddesses, Whores, Wives and Slaves*, New York: Schocken.

Rehm, R. (1994) *Marriage to Death: The Conflation of Wedding and Funerary Rituals in Greek Tragedy*, Princeton: Princeton University Press.

Robinson, D.M. (1942) *Necrolynthia: A Study in Greek Burial Customs and Anthropology (Excavations at Olynthus XI)*, Baltimore: Johns Hopkins Press.

Rühfel, H. (1984) *Das Kind in der Griechischen Kunst: Von der minoisch-mykenischen Zeit bis zum Hellenismus*, Mainz: Philipp von Zabern.

Scheidel, W. (1995) 'The most silent women of Greece and Rome: rural labour and women's life in the ancient world (I)', *Greece and Rome* 42(2): 202–17.

Schlörb-Vierneisel, B. (1966) 'Eridanos – Nekropole I. Gräber und Opferstellen hS 1–204', *Mitteilungen des Deutschen Archäologischen Instituts, Athenische Abteilung* 81: 4–111.

Seremetakis, C.N. (1991) *The Last Word: Women, Death, and Divination in Inner Mani*, Chicago and London: University of Chicago Press.

Shapiro, A. (1991) 'The iconography of mourning in Athenian art', *American Journal of Archaeology* 95: 629–56.

Siurla-Theodoridou, V. (1989) *Die Familie in der Griechischen Kunst und Litteratur des 8. und 6. Jahrhunderts v. Chr.* (Quellen und Forschungen zur Antiken Welt 4), München: V. Florentz.

Stears, K. (1995) 'Dead women's society: constructing female gender in Classical Athenian funerary sculpture', in N. Spencer (ed.) *Time, Tradition and Society in Greek Archaeology*, London: Routledge, pp. 109–31.

Strömberg, A. (1993) *Male or Female? A Methodological Study of Grave Gifts as Sex-indicators in Iron Age Burials from Athens*, Jonsered: Paul Åströms Förlag.

Travlos, J. (1971) *Bildlexikon zur Topographie des antiken Athen*, Tübingen: Ernst Wasmuth.

Vedder, U. (1988) 'Frauentod-Kriegertod im Spiegel der attischen Grabkunst des 4. Jhr. v. Chr.', *Mitteilungen des Deutschen Archäologischen Instituts, Athenische Abteilung* 103: 161–91.

Whitley, J. (1991) *Style and Society in Dark Age Greece: The Changing Face of a Pre-literate Society 1100–700 BC (New Studies in Archaeology)*, Cambridge: Cambridge University Press, pp. 51–70.

Vierneisel , K. (1964) 'Die Ausgrabungen im Kerameikos', *Archäologischer Anzeiger*: 420–67.

Zanker, P. (1993) 'The Hellenistic grave *stelai* from Smyrna: identity and self-image in der Polis', in A. Bulloch, E.S. Gruen, A.A. Long and A. Stewart (eds) *Images and Ideologies: Self Definition in the Hellenistic World*, Berkeley/Los Angeles/London: Berkeley University of California Press, pp. 212–30.

Part VII

Children and value

Chapter 13

Children, grave goods and social status in Early Anglo-Saxon England

Sally Crawford

INTRODUCTION

The primary archaeological source material for information on fifth to seventh century Anglo-Saxon society and social structure, including the place of children within that society and attitudes of adults towards their offspring, comes from the excavated cemeteries. There are many known cemetery sites in England, and a proportion of these have been at least partially excavated. When Audrey Meaney published her invaluable catalogue of Anglo-Saxon cemeteries in 1964 she estimated that about 25,000 graves belonging to the Early Anglo-Saxon period had been excavated (Meaney 1964), and further sites have been investigated in the intervening years.

The pagan Anglo-Saxons had two main forms of burial ritual: cremation, where the body of the deceased was burnt and the ashes placed in the ground, often in special burial pots; and inhumation, where the body was placed in a grave in the ground. Both rituals included the use of grave goods. Often these items – necklaces, brooches, belt fittings – must have been part of the clothing worn by the dead person. Weaponry may also come into this category. Other objects such as pots and bottles must have been deliberately placed with the dead person before burial. Investigations into methods of interpreting Anglo-Saxon furnished burials have led to the conclusion that the burial reflected the age, social status and gender of the deceased (Pader 1982; Richards 1987; Arnold 1980), but the theoretical basis of these studies of the material remains of Anglo-Saxon populations has focused entirely on adults. While there is no doubt that the burial ritual, as a ritual, must reflect in some way the society that did the burying, the place of children within that society is obscure and little studied, to the extent that even defining children for comparison with adults within the archaeological record is beset by problems at the data dissemination stage (Crawford 1991b).

MISSING CHILDREN IN THE BURIAL RECORD

Cremation cemeteries tend to be the largest of known Anglo-Saxon burial grounds. The cemetery at Spong Hill, Norfolk, for example, contained the incinerated remains of an estimated 2,700 people (McKinley 1994). Inevitably, the process of cremation means that much of the evidence required by archaeologists to interpret a past society has been destroyed, not least the body of the dead person itself. It is possible to reconstruct the sex and age of the cremated person on the basis of the surviving fragments of burnt bone, but only a small proportion of cremated remains will be capable of this sort of analysis. To complicate matters, it appears that the same spot may have been used for several cremation pyres, and the retrieval of bones by the Anglo-Saxons was not thorough in all cases, so that ashes from previous cremations may have been collected with the most recent pyre. The ashes within cremation urns frequently contain the remains of more than one individual; the inclusion of ashes of other individuals may have been deliberate additions, but are more likely to represent contamination. In addition, it must be assumed that a significant proportion of the grave goods associated with the burial, in particular any organic material, would have been destroyed by the fire. Molten remains of beads and brooches, for example, are found in cremation urns, but they only serve to emphasise how much material must have been lost.

Items that were added to the cremated remains after the ashes of the dead person had been collected tend to be miniature or small items that would fit into a pot. In the nineteenth century, such miniature items were sometimes recorded as 'toys' (Meaney 1964), but where the age of the cremated individual associated with these items has been ascertained in modern excavations, it is clear that these tiny shears, knives and other items are part of the adult burial ritual. They undoubtedly had symbolic significance, but their meaning remains obscure and is indisputably adult-centred (Richards 1987: 130).

Inhumation cemeteries provide considerably more information for the researcher, including better survival of the skeletal evidence which allows closer ageing of juvenile skeletons, and more complete survival of the associated grave goods. Anglo-Saxon children, however, are conspicuous by their relative absence, both in inhumation and cremation cemeteries, and in modern interpretations of the pagan mortuary ritual with its associated social constructs. Children represent only 10–15 per cent of the total Anglo-Saxon mortuary population, when comparable juvenile mortality for non-industrial populations is closer to 50 per cent (Crawford 1991a; Richards 1987). Occasionally, commentators note the low numbers of children in the burial record (Evison 1987: 146; Richards 1987: 124), and writers such as Pader were drawing attention to the importance of distinguishing and discussing the place of children in assessments of mortuary populations as long ago as the early 1980s (Pader 1982). Some recently published site reports do take the place of children in the burial ritual seriously (Boyle *et al.* 1996), but this is by no means uniform. Many modern archaeological reports still persist in failing to recognise that children may not have been treated as 'little adults', that they may have possessed a specific subculture, that the threshold age of childhood/adulthood, defined by the artefacts associated with the burials, is one that needs to be given some consideration in mortuary studies, and that modern ideas as to what constitutes a 'child' may not necessarily have prevailed in the pagan Anglo-Saxon period.

IDENTIFYING THE AGE LIMITS OF CHILDHOOD IN THE BURIAL RITUAL

A contributory factor to the lack of work on children in the Anglo-Saxon burial ritual may be that, in a discipline dominated by the problems of interpreting the social meaning of artefacts deposited with burials, children's graves are relatively poorly furnished, and so fail to gain attention (Tables 13.1 and 13.2).[1] Children's burials, where they are included in the adult cemeteries, also include fewer of the immediately attractive precious metals

Table 13.1   Number of furnished and unfurnished Anglo-Saxon burials by age group

Age group	Furnished no. (%)	Unfurnished no. (%)
0–5	56 (37)	96 (63)
6–10	45 (49)	47 (51)
11–14	22 (58)	16 (42)
15–29	171 (75)	58 (25)
30–44	95 (69)	42 (31)
45+	112 (78)	32 (22)
Total	501 (63)	291 (37)

Source: Crawford 1991a

and stones of the richer assemblages, and tend not to include the glamorous artefacts that receive detailed interpretation. Great square-headed brooches, spears, shields and other selected artefacts considered worthy of detailed analysis and discussion by Anglo-Saxonists are never or rarely included within the juvenile burial ritual (cf. Hines 1997; Swanton 1973; Evison 1963). There is no class of inhumation grave good, no individual artefact, associated exclusively with children (Crawford 1991a). Within cremation burials, too, Richards noted that children have no representative artefact, and that their grave goods differ from adult ones in having a smaller range (Richards 1987: 130). The impression that children's graves can only offer a pale reflection of the adult ritual, and therefore can only be discussed within parameters of absence or poverty, if true, has important implications for interpretations of the child's place within Anglo-Saxon society.

Table 13.2   Number of grave goods in furnished graves by age group

Number of goods	Age group					
	0–5	*6–10*	*11–14*	*15–29*	*30–44*	*45+*
	(%)	(%)	(%)	(%)	(%)	(%)
1	31	15	6	37	14	19
	(55)	(33)	(27)	(22)	(15)	(17)
2	12	10	4	31	16	22
	(21)	(22)	(18)	(18)	(17)	(20)
3	7	8	1	19	19	19
	(13)	(18)	(5)	(11)	(20)	(17)
4	1	2	3	14	9	17
	(2)	(4)	(14)	(8)	(10)	(15)
5	2	3	1	13	10	12
	(4)	(7)	(5)	(8)	(11)	(11)
6	1	3	0	12	5	3
	(2)	(7)	(0)	(7)	(5)	(3)
7	0	0	3	9	6	6
	(0)	(0)	(14)	(5)	(6)	(5)
8	1	2	1	7	6	4
	(2)	(4)	(5)	(4)	(6)	(4)
9	0	1	1	7	3	4
	(0)	(2)	(5)	(4)	(3)	(4)
10	1	1	2	22	7	6
	(2)	(2)	(9)	(13)	(8)	(5)

Source: Crawford 1991a

There has been no consistent understanding of what a child may have been in the Anglo-Saxon period, even though it is suspected by some excavators that the artefacts buried with the bodies may be in some way age-related. However, because there has been little consideration of what the juvenile/adult age threshold may have been for the burying population, interpretations have often been frustrated (Crawford 1991b). The rare discussions that do exist in cemetery site reports regarding what criteria determine the labelling of 'children' and 'infants' often focus on age markers – objects within the burial, or aspects of the burial such as orientation of the body, presence or absence of grave furniture and layout of the body that are only associated with particular age groups. In the assessment of symbols within the burial ritual, excavators frequently relate their findings to age distinctions. At Portway, Hampshire, the occupant of grave 60, an 11–12 year old, is noted to have been buried with 'adult' grave features – a partially flint-lined grave with a wooden baulk (Cook and Dacre 1985). Two children aged 5 (grave 24) and 8–9 (grave 40) were observed to have had small spears, while the 'other' child, aged 15–16 was buried with a normal-sized spearhead. The excavator was looking for age-related artefacts, but was unable to find any convincing candidates. It may be that here the excavators' own categories of what constitutes an adult and what a juvenile have hindered them from considering that the evidence points to the age of 10–12 years as being the threshold from childhood to adulthood. If this were so, the fact that two juveniles are buried with small spearheads and the third 'child' is not, instantly becomes rational: the third child, as his adult-sized spearhead indicates, is in fact, in the burial ritual, an adult. If the evidence is read with sensitivity, the ritual of burial is rational and meaningful. Where the ritual pattern seems vague and uninterpretable, it may be because we do not understand the rules on which the pattern is based.

When a pattern emerges from one cemetery as clearly as at Portway, it is worth testing it against comparable cemeteries. The adult/juvenile threshold emerging at Portway both makes sense of, and is corroborated by, findings at Sewerby (Hirst 1985) and Buckland (Evison 1987) where 10–12 years also seems to have been a threshold age (Crawford 1991b). Even very recent cemetery reports continue to confuse the issue by failing to think within an Anglo-Saxon framework of child thresholds rather than a modern one. In the site report for Empingham II, Rutland, it is noted that there were three exceptions to the pattern of children being buried with fewer grave goods than adults. It is suggested that these exceptions represent 'inherited status or wealth' and that 'a direct correlation between age and number of possessions cannot be upheld' (Timby 1996: 93). Perhaps not, but these are not the examples on which to base such a statement: of the three, two are aged over twelve and have grave goods associated with skeletally mature females. The other, grave 105, is buried with the indisputably female grave goods of three brooches, eight beads and an iron chatelaine, yet is catalogued as a 'male child aged 9–10'. In a cemetery excavated under very difficult conditions, it seems likely that some confusion in identification has been made over the twenty years between excavation and publication! If age divisions, whether based on anthropological or biological assumptions, are not presumed in advance, then the divisions actually used by the populations may begin to emerge. Archaeologists might take into account that Anglo-Saxon law codes, written in the vernacular, indicate that an age of ten was regarded as an age of maturity: at this age, for example, a child could be regarded as a thief (Attenborough 1922: 39; Crawford 1991a: III).

THE STATUS OF CHILDREN

Having established that a threshold age between childhood and adulthood is represented within the burial ritual, we are then faced with the difficulty of explaining an apparent dichotomy in the symbolism of the artefacts associated with children. Status within the mortuary ritual is usually interpreted as indicated by the effort expended in the funeral, and that effort is directly related to the importance of the social persona of the individual. This interpretation poses problems in interpreting child burials. On the one hand, they are buried with grave goods that are also given to adults. On this basis, Richards argues that children in Early Anglo-Saxon England were ascribed their status at birth (Richards 1987: 130). On the other hand, that status does not quite seem to fit within the pattern of adult burials, because if children were ascribed the status of their family at birth, why were the majority of juveniles selected to be part of the burial ritual given the 'status' of poor adults? Were juveniles present within the ritual as children, a special group, missed and mourned by their bereaved parents, or as 'sub' adults – as children – but buried in a way to represent their incomplete social persona? Children are more meanly buried than adults – does this imply they had relatively little status? Boys in the inhumation cemeteries would seem to be at a particular status disadvantage because the weaponry associated with rank has clear age group correlations (Table 13.3). If nothing else, this example clearly indicates that some rank and status had to be earned during life before it could be represented in death. The age thresholds indicated in the burial ritual, though not clear-cut, are nonetheless present and affirm that, for the Anglo-Saxons, the grave assemblage did reflect a recognition that children were 'different' to adults. They are buried within the adult ritual, but they are identified as non-adult.

Does this imply that children were unimportant or less important to the adult buriers – that they had the same marginal status in life as they appear to have done in death? Perhaps the strongest evidence in support of this hypothesis is that some of the artefacts associated with their burials were clearly old and damaged adult items. At Wheatley, Oxfordshire, grave 12 of a 5–6 year old was accompanied by a damaged brooch (Leeds 1916), and the sub-adult in grave 210 from Finglesham, Kent was accompanied by an incomplete bracelet. The grave goods are unlikely to have been personal possessions, and the fact that they were broken indicates that it was their symbolic presence in the graves as part of the ritual that was important – the ritual dominated over the personal and reduced the individual to a place in the ritual social order. Added weight may be given to this argument by the utter absence of any artefact within the burial ritual that could be

Table 13.3 Number of Anglo-Saxon graves with weapons by age group

Weapon	Age group					
	0–5	*6–10*	*11–14*	*15–29*	*30–44*	*45+*
Spear	1	3	5	36	24	22
Shield	0	0	0	10	11	7
Sword	0	0	0	3	2	3
Seax	0	0	0	2	6	3

Source: Crawford 1991a

construed as a toy. Not only were children denied full adult status in the burial ritual, but the ritual emphatically rejects the notion of any child-based material culture. Whatever may have been precious or special to childhood in life (and we have no evidence at all for such artefacts) was not given similar value by the buriers.

Before the Anglo-Saxon parent is condemned out of hand for lack of emotional identification with the dead child, and for revealing an unsentimental or even callous disregard for the life-values of children, it should be noted that toys are one category of artefact unlikely to survive in the archaeological record, and, where they do survive, may not be recognised as such by the excavator. Later post-Conquest documentary sources quoted by Orme (1984: 34) describe children building houses and hobby-horses out of sticks, a sailing ship from bread, a sword from sedge and a doll from cloth and flowers. None of these playthings would survive in the archaeological record. Even where such springboards for a child's imaginative play-acting do survive, the purpose and function of childhood paraphernalia are unlikely to be meaningful to an adult observer. At Great Chesterford, Essex there was an infant in grave 98 aged between 0–2 months. Its diminutive grave contained a small, black burnished undecorated pot with a hobnail inside the pot (Evison 1994: 105). Could this have functioned as a rattle? It is not the only example. At Farthingdown in Surrey, Hope-Taylor's excavations in 1948 revealed the burial of a child with a small rouletted pot containing an unworked amber pebble (Meaney 1964: 241). If such objects within the pots were deliberate inclusions for the amusement of children, we must be aware that if the 'rattle' included a plainer stone it may not have been recovered or recorded by the archaeologist. Containers are among the most common artefacts included in furnished children's inhumations (Table 13.4).

It is clear from the later documentary sources of the Christian period that Anglo-Saxon children were observed by adults indulging in both group and solitary play – most famously, the juvenile St Cuthbert in the playground with other boys indulging in handstands and other gymnastics (Colgrave 1940: 65). What is interesting is that these games are never associated with recognisable, purpose-made toys, and that where Anglo-Saxon children do use material objects as a focus of play, these are items requisitioned from their environment or from the adult world. King Alfred added to his translation of *Boethius* the description of children riding on sticks (Sedgefield 1899: 108) and commented in his

Table 13.4   Number of grave goods found most frequently with Anglo-Saxon burials under the age of 15

Grave goods	Age group			
	0–5	*6–10*	*11–14*	*Total*
Knife	14	27	13	43
Beads	18	11	2	31
Buckle	5	14	8	27
Brooch	2	13	11	26
Container	13	4	6	23
Pin	7	8	6	21
Coin	4	2	12	18
Total number	63	79	58	189

Source: Crawford 1991a

'Pastoral Care' that children play with their parent's coins (Sweet 1871: 391). Such scanty evidence as there is from the Anglo-Saxon period, and the later mediaeval evidence, suggests that children would not have had toys manufactured for them by adults. Like children today who prefer to play with the wrapping paper rather than the expensive toy, Anglo-Saxon children made their own entertainment where they found it.

EXCEPTIONS TO THE RULE

Although children generally had a lower level of material wealth in their burials than adults, there were some dramatic exceptions to this picture. Young girls, in particular, seem to have occasionally been buried with extremes of wealth. The cemetery at Finglesham, Kent (Chadwick Hawkes 1982: 25) contained over 240 inhumations dating from the first quarter of the sixth century until the beginning of the eighth century. Grave 7, coin-dated to *c.* 675 AD (after the first phase of 'aristocratic' burials), contained the coffined remains of an individual aged between 2 and 5 years at time of death and a wealth of prestige goods, including a pottery bottle and a pottery flagon, a necklace made up of twenty-five beads (including silver and gold rings and two gold coins), a chatelaine, an iron knife, and a pouch with copper alloy fittings. Chatelaines are more usually associated with adult females and the overall nature of the assemblage contains more female items suggesting that this child was a girl. She is not an isolated case. At Buckland, also in Kent, the skeletal remains and grave goods indicate that the occupant of grave 20 was a girl aged not more than 6 years at time of death (Evison 1987: 220). She was buried with an iron weaving batten (again, an artefact more often associated with adult women and a rarity in Anglo-Saxon burials), a disc brooch including garnets and bronze, a silver pin, a gold bracteate, a necklace made up of fifty-four beads, two silver-gilt square-headed brooches, a silver wire bracelet, a bronze buckle, a bronze wire bracelet, a knife, key fragments (possibly making up a girdle hanger), a brown glass claw beaker, a spun bronze bowl and a wooden belt. She was among the most richly furnished burials at the site, and belongs to the earliest phase of burials (c.475–525 AD). Similarly, at Alton in Hampshire (Evison 1988: 73), grave 89 appears to be that of a female aged 7 buried with a necklace of sixteen beads, a knife, a purse with an iron mount and a ring, possibly part of a brooch or buckle.

How are such rich burials to be interpreted? Any hypotheses must be based on conjecture – there is nothing in the documentary sources to hint at an explanation. One hypothesis might be that the girls were buried with the wealth they would have inherited as their *morgengifu* or bridal gift had they lived. It is even possible to postulate that these children had already had matches or betrothals organised for them by their parents. Girls were betrothed at a very early age, even as young as 2 years old, in the later mediaeval period (Orme 1984: 37), but we cannot assume such practices took place in the earlier Anglo-Saxon period.

The documentary sources do tell us that boys, too, might escape the 'normal' rules of childhood if they belonged to the elite. Swords, the greatest male adult prestige symbol, could be conferred upon boys at a precocious age. Asser informs us that King Alfred was given a sword by his grandfather when he was only 4 years old, and the prince Æthelstan was recognised as Alfred's heir by a sword-giving ceremony when he was of a similar age (Ellis Davidson 1962: 109–10). Nonetheless, the archaeological evidence indicates that, if the elite child was granted exception from the normal adult age markers, he would rarely have taken these prized symbols with him to the grave. Weaponry, the cemeteries inform us, was accumulated with age, and boys hardly progressed beyond miniature spears until they were aged between 10 and 12 – the age at which the law codes suggest children became adults. Inevitably, there are extremely rare exceptions that prove the rule. The society burying their dead at Great Chesterford, Essex, operated outside the 'norms' of Anglo-Saxon mortuary ritual, including a high number of infant burials, two horse burials and the burial of a dog within the cemetery. The infant in grave 99 was furnished with a spear, a small knife and a small iron buckle and is one of the few securely attested Anglo-Saxon cemetery contexts in which a child under the age of 5 is buried with a weapon.

Some children were buried with scaled-down adult artefacts which must have been deliberately made for their wearers. These were items manufactured for, and in that sense belonging to, the children. The tiny brooches with burials 17 (aged 6) and 28 (aged 8) from Sewerby, East Yorkshire, are the only iron brooches on the site (Hirst 1985) and are smaller in size than the corresponding bronze brooches in adult graves. They may also have been cheaper than the bronze brooches. The iron brooches would seem to have been tailored to fit the diminutive wearers, and these can reasonably be regarded, I think, as part of their personal equipment. The skeleton in grave 28 was also accompanied by a large number of miniature beads of a type not found in any other grave, which may possibly have been, the excavator speculates, particularly suitable for a child (ibid.: 101). Similarly, the skeleton of an 11–12 year old in grave 35A, Abingdon, thought by the excavator to be female, is buried with a spearhead, which appears to have been ground down from one much larger (Leeds and Harden 1936).

At Barton-on-Humber, a unique artefact with an infant burial dating to *c.* 550–675 AD was discovered – a mammiform pot with a teat (Nenk *et al.* 1991: 168). The pot may represent a doomed attempt to feed a child that could not or would not breast feed. A boar's tooth was found in the nearby burial of a woman, and it is possible that there may have been a relationship between this grave and that of the infant. A link between animal teeth, children and their female carers has been postulated by Meaney, who drew attention to the beaver teeth in the graves of an 8-year-old child and a baby of under 1 year at Marina Drive, Dunstable, Bedfordshire, and a woman buried with an infant at Burwell in Cambridgeshire, who was also buried with a beaver's tooth (Meaney 1981: 136). A boar's tusk was found with an infant (grave 31) at Great Chesterford (Evison 1994: 35). Also at Great Chesterford, a case for a relationship between the grave of a child and an adult seems to have been indicated by the grave goods – the woman in grave 37 is buried by the side of the child aged 4–6 years in grave 118, and they were both given identical pots to accompany their burials (Evison 1994: 21).

Among the commonest grave goods at many sites was the knife, which appears to have been a vital part of the adult dress kit. Knives should not be regarded as weapons – they were buried with women and children as well as men – but rather as useful tools, probably used for all purposes, including as eating utensils. The ubiquitous nature of the knife emphasises its absolute necessity as a 'must' for life in Anglo-Saxon England, but at first glance the thought of children buried with knives only serves to emphasise either the lack of interest parents took in the safety of their offspring, or the strong influence of the adult ritual on children's burials once more. However, a comparison of knife lengths in children's and adults' graves shows that there is something of a correlation between knife length and age (Table 13.5). The knives cannot have been simply a requirement of the burial ritual because, under those circumstances, any knife would have done for a dead child. Far from being adult equipment foisted indiscriminately on children, like pots and brooches, these smaller knives would appear to be the personal possessions of the children, and were smaller in recognition of the child's relative lack of dexterity and size. While we would not normally like to see our own children playing with knives, these Anglo-Saxon versions were often no more dangerous than the modern butter knife, and, if the child was to be integrated into Anglo-Saxon life, it was obviously important that they learned how to handle these items from the earliest possible age.

Table 13.5   Knife lengths by age group

Age group	Mean length of blade (cms)
0–5	96.3
6–10	94.3
11–14	127.8
15–29	112.2
30–44	115.9
45+	135.6

Source: Crawford 1991a

These cases of 'personal selection' within children's burials require explanation. They suggest that we should be cautious in assuming that, because the majority of children are buried with artefacts indicating 'poor' adult status, children had an equivalent status in Anglo-Saxon society. Children are under-represented in the mortuary population, so that the children in the burial sample may not be typical of the Anglo-Saxon child, or may have held some particular and special place in their society (Crawford 1993). No 'model' of childhood or picture of the 'average' child should be postulated on the basis of this select group. Furthermore, sufficient numbers of children fall outside the normal patterns of mortuary ritual to suggest that it might be inappropriate to apply usual mortuary methodology to identify their roles.

CONCLUSION

If children were 'outsiders' within the adult mortuary ritual, then individual, non-ritual, personal behaviour, may sometimes apply. It is a dangerous and attractive thing to use a spectacular 'singleton' as an example for drawing wider conclusions, an attraction to which historians of childhood have often succumbed. Use of isolated tales from history often provide sensational material, while what the archaeologist should be about is discovering the continuity and consistency of past behaviour.

Anglo-Saxon burial was the ritual expression of a world from which children were largely excluded, not, perhaps, because they were unimportant, but because their place lay within other realms of social expression. 'What sight is more intolerable than the death of a child before its father's eyes?' asked King Alfred in his translation of 'Pastoral Care' (Sweet 1871: 342). We should not doubt that Anglo-Saxon parents cared about their lost children. The burial of children with few artefacts should not necessarily be equated with a low status for children in life. Their mortuary material culture may be poor, but exceptions and deviations from the 'normal' picture imply that there was a personal desire by grieving adults to express the importance of the child, indicating that, even within a child-excluded ritual, the desire to articulate the loss of an individual was too powerful to resist.

NOTES

1 Statistics in the tables are drawn from a database of over 1,000 burials representing a sample of excavated sites from Anglo-Saxon England (Crawford 1991a): Abingdon, Berkshire (Leeds and Harden 1936; Polhill, Kent (Philp 1973); Berinsfield, Oxfordshire (Boyle *et al.*1996); Sewerby, Yorkshire (Hirst 1985); Finglesham, Kent and Worthy Park, Hampshire (with thanks to the late Sonia Hawkes for access to the unpublished material); Alton, Hampshire (Evison, 1988); Westgarth Gardens, Suffolk (West 1988); Winnall, Hampshire (Meaney and Hawkes 1970); Portway, Hampshire (Cook and Dacre 1985); Buckland, Kent (Evison 1987); Swaffham, Norfolk (Wade-Martins 1976); Morning Thorpe, Norfolk (Green *et al.* 1987); and Monkton, Kent (Chadwick Hawkes and Hogarth 1974). Age groups in the tables have been determined by the ages given in site reports and are organised to include the maximum number of aged inhumations, taking into account the fluid age parameters offered by different excavators. A fuller analysis of the database may be found in Crawford (1991a). Grateful thanks are due to Dr A.A.S. Randall for management of the database.

REFERENCES

Arnold, C. (1980) 'Wealth and social structure: a matter of life and death', in P. Rahtz, T. Dickinson and L. Watts (eds) *Anglo-Saxon Cemeteries: Fourth Anglo-Saxon Symposium, 1979*, Oxford: British Archaeological Report 82: 81–142.

Attenborough, F.L. (1922) *The Laws of the Earliest English Kings*, Cambridge: Cambridge University Press.

Boyle, A., Dodd, A., Miles, D. and Mudd, A. (1996) *Two Oxfordshire Anglo-Saxon Cemeteries: Berinsfield and Didcot*, Thames Valley Landscapes Monograph 8, Oxford Archaeological Unit.

Chadwick Hawkes, S. (1982) 'Finglesham, a cemetery in East Kent' in J. Campbell, (ed.) *The Anglo-Saxons*, Oxford: Phaidon, pp. 24–5.

Chadwick Hawkes, S. and Hogarth, A.C. (1974) 'The Anglo-Saxon cemetery at Monkton, Thanet', *Archaeolgia Cantiana* 89, 49–89.

Colgrave, B. (1940) *Two Lives of St Cuthbert*, Cambridge: Cambridge University Press.

Cook, A.M. and Dacre, M.W. (1985) *Excavations at Portway, Andover 1973–1975*, Oxford: Oxford University Committee for Archaeology Monograph 4.

Crawford, S.E.E. (1991a) 'Age differentiation and related social status: a study of earlier Anglo-Saxon childhood', unpublished D.Phil. thesis, University of Oxford.

—— (1991b) 'When do Anglo-Saxon children count?', *Journal of Theoretical Archaeology* 2: 17–24.

—— (1993) 'Children, death and the afterlife in Anglo-Saxon England', *Anglo-Saxon Studies in Archaeology and History* 6: 83–92.

Ellis Davidson, H.R. (1962) *The Sword in Anglo-Saxon England*, Oxford: Oxford University Press.

Evison, V. I. (1963) 'Sugar loaf shield bosses', *Antiquaries Journal* 43: 38–96.

—— (1987) *Dover: Buckland Anglo-Saxon Cemetery*, HBMC Archaeological Report 3.

—— (1988) *An Anglo-Saxon Cemetery at Alton, Hampshire*, Hampshire Field Club and Archaeological Society Monograph 4.

—— (1994) *An Anglo-Saxon Cemetery at Great Chesterford, Essex*, Council for British Archaeology Report 91.

Green, B., Rogerson, A. and White, S. (1987) *The Anglo-Saxon Cemetery at Morning Thorpe, Norfolk, Volume 1: The Catalogue*, Gressenhall: Norfolk Archaeological Unit: East Anglian Archaeology Reports 36.

Hines, J. (1997) *A New Corpus of Anglo-Saxon Great Square-headed Brooches, Woodbridge*, Boydell for the Society of Antiquaries of London: Reports of the Research Committee for the Society of Antiquaries of London, 51.

Hirst, S.M. (1985) *An Anglo-Saxon Inhumation Cemetery at Sewerby East Yorkshire*, York: York University Archaeological Publications 4.

Leeds, E.T. (1916–17) 'An Anglo-Saxon cemetery at Wheatley, Oxfordshire', *Proceedings of Society of Antiquaries* series 2, 29: 48–65.

Leeds, E.T. and Harden, D.B. (1936) *The Anglo-Saxon cemetery at Abingdon, Berks*, Oxford: Ashmolean Museum.

McKinley, J. I (1994) 'The Anglo-Saxon cemetery at Spong Hill, North Elmham Part VIII: the cremations', *East Anglian Archaeology* 69.

Meaney, A.L. (1964) *A Gazetteer of Early Anglo-Saxon Burial Sites,* London: Allen & Unwin.

—— (1981) *Anglo-Saxon Amulets and Curing Stones*, Oxford: British Archaeological Reports 96.

Meaney, A. and Hawkes, S. (1970) *The Anglo-Saxon Cemeteries at Winnall, Winchester, Hampshire*, Society for Medieval Archaeology Monograph 4

Nenk, B., Margeson, S. and Harley, M. (1991) 'Medieval Britain and Ireland in 1990', *Medieval Archaeology* 35.

Orme, N. (1984) *From Childhood to Chivalry: The Education of the English Kings and Aristocracy 1066–1530*, London: Methuen.

Pader, E.-J. (1982) *Symbolism, Social Relations and the Interpretation of Mortuary Remains*, Oxford: British Archaeological Reports, International Series 130.

Philp, B.J. (1973) 'The Anglo-Saxon cemetery at Polhill, Kent' in Philp, B.J. (ed) *Excavations in West Kent 1960–1970,* Dover: Kent Archaeological Rescue Unit for the West Kent Border Archaeological Group: Kent Archaeological research reports 20, 164–214.

Richards, J.D. (1987) *The Significance of Form and Decoration of Anglo-Saxon Cremation Urns*, Oxford: British Archaeological Reports, British Series 166.

Sedgefield, W. J. (ed.) (1899) *King Alfred's Old English Version of Boethius*, Oxford: Oxford University Press.

Swanton, M. (1974) *A Corpus of Pagan Anglo-Saxon Spear Types*, Oxford: British Archaeological Reports 7.

Sweet, H. (ed.) (1871) *King Alfred's West Saxon Version of Gregory's Pastoral Care,* London: Early English Text Society 45.

Timby, J. R. (1996) *The Anglo-Saxon Cemetery at Empingham II, Rutland*, Oxford: Oxbow Monograph 70.

Wade-Martins, P. (1976) *Swaffham, the Anglo-Saxon Cemetery,* East Anglian Archaeology Reports 2.

West, S. (1988) *Westgarth Gardens Anglo-Saxon cemetery, Suffolk: Catalogue*, Bury St Edmunds: Suffolk County Planning Department in conjunction with the Scole Archaeological Committee: East Anglian Archaeology Reports 38.

Chapter 14

The archaeology and history of infanticide, and its occurrence in earlier British populations

Simon Mays

INTRODUCTION

Infanticide is the killing of unwanted babies. It is generally carried out at or soon after birth and has been practised on all continents and at every level of social complexity from hunter-gatherer to urbanised industrial societies (Williamson 1978). The practice of infanticide in earlier human groups has been much studied by those working with historical sources (e.g. Brown 1991; Harris 1982, 1994; Coleman 1976; Kellum 1974; Hoffer and Hull 1981; Jackson 1996), but it is only recently that it has commanded significant attention from archaeologists. This increased interest on behalf of the archaeological community may to some extent reflect recent methodological innovations which have facilitated the recognition of infanticide in the archaeological record. However, it may also be viewed as part of a more general trend within archaeology toward the study of groups in earlier societies upon which little attention has hitherto been lavished. One manifestation of this trend is the rise of the archaeology of gender (e.g. Gero and Conkey 1991; Moore and Scott 1997; Gilchrist 1997). Another is the interest which has lately been shown in the study of children and childhood in the past (e.g. Sofaer Derevenski 1994; Moore and Scott 1997). The recent interest in infanticide can be seen as a corollary of this latter, as its study clearly has a major role to play in the archaeology of childhood. In addition, infanticide is, as we shall see, very often an act perpetrated by women. Furthermore, in some societies female babies are more often its victims. Therefore, its study may also be seen in terms of recent interest in the archaeology of gender (which, in practice, means the archaeology of women).

The identification of infanticide in the archaeological record has often relied on examining aspects of burial treatment afforded the infant dead. For example, clusters of infant burials outside recognisable cemetery areas have been taken to be suggestive of infanticide, with surreptitious disposal of the bodies (e.g. Cocks 1921). However, since ethnographic evidence (e.g. Ucko 1969) shows that infants may routinely be afforded differential mortuary treatment from the rest of the community, care is needed when using this sort of evidence to infer infanticide. We can, nonetheless, occasionally recognise a particular form of infanticide, the sacrifice of infants for ritual or religious purposes, from the circumstances under which the remains are found. For example, at Springhead Roman temple in Kent, England, an infant burial was found at each of four corners of a small shrine; two had been decapitated. It seems likely that these represented foundation sacrifices (Penn 1960).

Finds of infant remains under circumstances which suggest human sacrifice are rare. However, we may be able to recognise when infanticide was practised as a regular method of population control in an earlier human group by demographic analysis of age at death of perinatal burials. Specifically, it has been argued that a perinatal age distribution showing a strong peak at about the age corresponding to a full-term baby is suggestive of infanticide, given that the deed is generally done at around the time of birth (Smith and Kahila 1992; Mays 1993); natural deaths generally give a rather flatter distribution. Although this technique is reliant on having fairly large numbers of well-preserved perinatal infant bones in order to reconstruct age-at-death profiles, it does mean that we are not solely reliant on chance finds of unusual deposits of infant remains, like the Springhead example above, to identify infanticide archaeologically. By using this technique to study infant skeletons excavated from cemeteries or other sites we can attempt to infer whether infanticide was practised routinely.

INFANTICIDE IN HUMAN SOCIETIES

Present-day Westerners generally regard infanticide as morally wrong. However, this view is exceptional. The majority of human societies in the recent past have openly accepted infanticide and have not regarded it as morally problematic (Warren 1985; Williamson 1978). Indeed, until recently it must have been one of the few means of controlling family size that was both effective and did not endanger the mother. Divale and Harris (1976) analysed data on 393 recent human societies, and found that infanticide was practised to some degree in nearly 80 per cent of them. Indeed, studies of living populations probably under-estimate the frequency of the practice as, by its very nature, it is a 'secret' act, easily concealed.

In a recent review, Hrdy (1992) noted that societies in which the newborn are considered fully-fledged social beings are much less likely to tolerate infanticide than those in which they are not; the withholding of full 'personhood' until some time after birth is a mechanism by which infanticide may be rendered socially acceptable. This generalisation is also echoed in debates among philosophers over the morality of infanticide. These debates often centre on defining certain attributes which are associated with having a right to life and whether infants possess such properties.

Michael Tooley's (1983) treatment of the problem has been highly influential in the philosophical debate. He contends that infants do not possess a right to life, and therefore that infanticide is not intrinsically wrong. He reasons that if rights may be considered as constraints upon the actions of others which are designed to safeguard the interests of the rights-holder, then those not capable of having interests cannot be said to have rights. Although interests and desires are only indirectly related, Tooley argues that interests in a morally relevant sense presuppose desires. Foetuses or neonates cannot be considered to have a concept of self or of temporal order, and so can have no desires or preferences concerning their own futures. Therefore, he contends, newborn infants cannot be said to have the right to life.

Some have disputed Tooley's analysis of rights in this context. Carter (1997) suggests that if an individual has a right to something, this means that unless that individual specifically waives that right, others should restrain themselves from actions which would infringe it. Murder is in most instances morally wrong. Since a newborn infant does not possess a concept of self or of temporal order he is not capable of releasing others from any duties they may have not to harm him. Consequently, infanticide may be morally impermissible.

Montague (1989) contends that arrogating decisions to oneself which are rightly the dominion of another is immoral. Whether the individual has the capacity to make such decisions at the time is irrelevant, they are still his to make when (and if) he is in a position to do so. The killing of an infant is therefore as wrong as the killing of an adult. The fact that the infant is incapable of formulating desires over its future at the time the deed is done is irrelevant.

Others have simply rejected the dichotomy between biological humanity and moral personhood which underlies Tooley's analysis, and indeed much of the philosophical debate on infanticide. Taking a theological perspective, Ramsey (1978) holds that, since human life is a gift from God, searching for some 'index of personhood' as a guide to moral action is futile – all human life possesses an inviolability flowing from its divine origin. It is invidious to speak of some lives, such as those of infants, being of lesser moral worth than others (see also Long 1988).

For Tooley, cognitive development determines when infants become persons; he suggests that about 3 months old is the time when infants start to assume personhood and so begin to have the right to life (Tooley 1983). In current English law, a defining moment is birth itself, it is at this point that the infant is recognised as having a separate existence and its life comes under the protection of the laws on homicide (Kellett 1992). In some societies cultural definitions of when life begins may vary between days, weeks and even years after birth (Scrimshaw 1984). Definitions of when life begins may also depend upon the attainment of some particular landmark of development. For Tooley, above, this was defined in terms of cognitive development, but in other cultures a variety of factors have been considered important, including the age at which the child first takes solid food, begins walking, teething or talking, or takes a name (Williamson 1978). For example, Pliny, writing in Classical Rome, considered that a child did not possess a soul until the age of teething (Nat. Hist. VII, 15, cited in Philpott 1991: 101). Whether a child has passed this sort of milestone may have an effect on the permissibility of infanticide. This is illustrated by the story from early mediaeval Europe of Liafburga, mother of Saint Liudger. Liafburga was born in Friesia towards the middle of the eighth century AD. Her parents had had several daughters, but no surviving son and it was decided that she must die. This was permissible by Friesian custom if the child had not tasted 'earthly' food, but Liafburga was saved by a servant who put some food in her mouth (Coleman 1976: 58).

In many societies children of one sex are valued more than the other. It is usually male offspring which are preferred. When such societies practice infanticide, more girls than boys are likely to be victims (Nordborg 1992). Placing a higher value on male work, assigning ritual authority or political power to men, and having customs that men inherit to the exclusion of females, may all encourage the preservation of male infants and the devaluation of female infants (Scrimshaw 1984). This may lead to skewed sex ratios in human populations who regularly practice infanticide. For example, in some parts of India boys are reported as outnumbering girls 5 : 1 (ibid.), and in China, where male offspring are traditionally preferred, males outnumbered females, both in the historic era (Langer 1974a; Lee et al. 1994) and more recently (Hesketh and Zhu 1997; Judson 1994). Looking at evidence relating to eighty-six hunter-gatherer societies, Divale (1972) found that among those known to practice infanticide the average sex ratio was 1.38 : 1 in favour of males, whereas in those which did not, the ratio was approximately 1 : 1.

Although rarer, instances of selective male infanticide have been reported. The Rendille are Kenyan pastoralists. The cattle herds upon which they depend increase only very slowly due to the harsh environment, and indeed the people look upon the herds as a static resource. Male infanticide is practised to limit the numbers of (male) cattle owners (Douglas 1966). Interestingly, modern data show that both in England and Wales, and in Scotland, male babies are more often victims of infanticide (Marks and Kumar 1993, 1996). There appears to be no conscious sex selection in these cases; why more male than female babies are killed is unclear.

Sex ratios derived from historical sources or archaeological evidence have on occasion been used to suggest the existence of female infanticide in earlier populations. For example, Russell (1948) analysed British evidence relating to the families of mediaeval serfs. Sons outnumbered daughters 1.7 : 1. He suggested that female infanticide might be one possible explanation. Coleman (1976) examined ninth century documents relating to dependants of the Abbey of St Germain des Pres, near Paris. She found an excess of males generally, and this was more pronounced in large families. She discussed a variety of factors which might be responsible and concluded that female infanticide was one. Divale (1972) noted that the adult sex ratio among more than 300 burials excavated from Palaeolithic and Mesolithic sites in Europe was 1.25 : 1 in favour of males, rising to 1.48 : 1 if only Palaeolithic material was considered. He interpreted this as suggesting that preferential female infanticide may have been practised as far back as Palaeolithic times.

A problem with using adult sex ratios to infer sex-specific infanticide is clearly that other factors may also be responsible for sex imbalances. In archaeological material, burial practices whereby one sex is more often accorded burial treatment which leaves surviving traces in the archaeological record is one obvious possibility. Another is migrations selectively involving one sex more than the other. In addition, greater devotion to nurturing of children of one sex may lead to differential mortality during childhood. Johansson (1984) has argued that excess female mortality during childhood may frequently have occurred in early modern Europe and European-settled countries, because of preferential care of male offspring when a child fell ill or there was economic pressure on material resources such as food or clothing. She refers to this pattern as the 'deferred infanticide' of females.

In order to make a more secure inference of sex-specific infanticide from archaeological evidence we would need to determine the sex of infants which have been identified as likely infanticide victims. Sex determination in infant skeletal remains by traditional morphological methods is problematic, but it is sometimes possible to sex infant remains using analysis of ancient DNA. At archaeological excavations at Ashkelon, Israel, remains of more than 100 newborn infants were discovered in a Roman sewer which ran beneath a bathhouse. The fact that the bodies had been disposed of in this way at a time when careful burial of infants was the norm, and that all were about the same age when they died (about neonatal), suggested infanticide (Smith and Kahila 1992). Faerman *et al.* (1997, 1998) analysed DNA from these infant bones. They attempted to extract DNA from forty-three individuals and were successful in nineteen cases, of which fourteen proved to be male and five female, a statistically valid sex imbalance. In the late Roman Empire, bathhouses were often dens of vice, and the one excavated in Ashkelon was situated in part of what was an established 'red-light' district. Faerman and co-workers argue that this may explain the preferential male infanticide. In the Roman period, both male and female prostitutes were recruited, but the greater demand was for the latter. The courtesans at Ashkelon may have selectively reared some offspring (mostly females) into the profession, discarding the others.

INFANTICIDE IN BRITAIN, PAST AND PRESENT

Documentary sources indicate that infanticide was practised in classical Roman society (Harris 1982; Wiedermann 1989), and archaeological evidence, in the form of demographic analysis of age distributions of perinatal burials, suggests that it also occurred in Britain when it was a province of the Roman Empire. In a study of the age-at-death distributions of infants excavated from Roman and mediaeval sites in England, I noted a difference between the two groups (Mays 1993). The Roman infants showed a strong peak at about 38–40 weeks, the gestational age corresponding to about a full-term baby. By contrast, the mediaeval perinatal burials (from the churchyard at the deserted village of Wharram Percy, North Yorkshire) showed a much flatter age distribution with no strong peak. Comparison with recent data showed that the mediaeval distribution was as expected if the perinatal burials here represented some combination of stillbirths and natural deaths in the immediate post-natal period. By contrast, the Roman distribution of perinatal ages was dissimilar to that expected from infants dying of natural causes. Instead it resembled the modern distribution of gestational ages of total live births. This might be expected if many of the Roman burials were of infanticide victims, given that infanticide generally takes place at or immediately after birth. The same age-at-death distribution was found to hold for Roman cemetery sites as well as non-cemetery sites suggesting that victims of infanticide in Roman Britain were not always denied regular burial.

It is interesting to note that most Roman cemetery sites in England show imbalanced adult sex ratios, with an excess of males. Combining data from about 2,400 adult burials from a number of large burial grounds reveals a sex ratio of 1.46 : 1 in favour of males (Mays 1995). Factors which might account for this pattern at individual sites include migration of males to towns in search of work, or a military presence increasing the number of males (Warwick 1968). Given that most of the large Roman cemetery sites which have been excavated are urban, these explanations are plausible; however, in light of the evidence that infanticide was regularly practised in Roman Britain, the sex imbalance can be viewed as consistent with selective infanticide for females. This will remain speculative, however, until Romano-British infant remains can be successfully sexed using DNA analysis.

There is also a suggestion that infanticide may have been a regular practice during the Anglo-Saxon period in Britain. Molleson (1991) studied the infant (under 2 years) to juvenile (2–19 years) ratios in assemblages excavated from cemetery sites. Using a demographic modelling approach she found that, in contrast to the pattern in the Roman period, at most Saxon sites the ratios of infant to juvenile deaths fell outside those expected for human groups in antiquity, with a deficiency of infants. Infant burials are rarely found on non-settlement sites in the Anglo-Saxon period, so that their bodies must have been disposed of in some way as to leave no trace in the archaeological record. Citing documentary evidence, Molleson notes that Germanic tribes in continental Europe subjected newborn infants to rigorous 'fitness' tests by immersion in running water. If the infant survived it was kept, if not the body was simply left in the river. Because of the lack of infant burials on British Anglo-Saxon sites, Molleson suggests that Germanic tribes may have brought this custom with them to England. If this suggestion is correct, then similar numbers of boys and girls would seem to have been subjected to such treatment, as there is no evidence of a sex imbalance among adult burials (Molleson 1991). Other evidence for the practice of infanticide in Saxon Britain comes from documentary sources. Theodore's Penitential (late seventh century) details penances to be performed by women guilty of the act (Cayton 1980). In the mid-eighth century, Boniface and seven other missionary bishops wrote a letter to King Æthelbald of Mercia admonishing him for, amongst other things, his fornication. Boniface noted that this vice was common in England, and that when women 'bring forth an offspring conceived in evil, they for the most part kill them' (quoted in Cayton 1980: 311).

Turning to the mediaeval period, historians have noted that legal records of infanticide are few. Nevertheless, there is reason to believe that this stems from the ease with which the deed might be concealed, rather than its genuine rarity (Kellum 1974; Damme 1978). Christianity preached sanctity of life for all those made in God's image, and hence abhorred infanticide, but its regular occurrence in mediaeval times can be inferred from the church's repeated censuring of the practice (Shahar 1990). One favoured method was suffocation, and there were warnings by the church against 'overlying' – that is taking the infant to one's bed and suffocating it with one's body (Kellett 1992). Another was abandonment. In the mediaeval period folk belief in the idea of the changeling was widespread (Shahar 1990). An unwanted, sickly, mewling child was sometimes thought to be a changeling, an infant exchanged for the true child by the agents of Satan. In order to obtain the true child's return, the infant might be tormented to make it scream or cry, or else abandoned at a remote spot in the countryside (for example, at the confluence of three rivers or the junction of three roads) for the mother to return to later in the hope that the true child had been restored. This treatment would of course, in many cases have led to the death of the infant (Shahar 1990). The idea of the changeling originated in pre-Christian times, the agents of the devil replacing the role of fairies in earlier versions of the legend. In the mediaeval period, its persistence appears to represent a subversion of orthodox Christian teaching on infanticide, the practice being facilitated and legitimised by explicit denial of the infant's humanity.

As mentioned above, the age at death distribution of perinatal infants excavated from the mediaeval churchyard at Wharram Percy is consistent with natural deaths, rather than infanticide. While this may suggest that infanticide was not practised at this site, it does not definitively exclude the possibility. Should infants have been the victims of infanticide they have may not have been accorded churchyard burial. This would be equally consistent with the archaeological data, and also with the likelihood that abandonment was a favoured method of causing infant death at this time. At Wharram Percy, the adult sex ratio was 1.58 :1 in favour of males. This might be viewed as consistent with female infanticide; however, I have elsewhere favoured a different explanation (Mays 1997). Documentary evidence shows that mediaeval towns often showed a sex imbalance in favour of females – for example, at York the sex ratio was 0.91 : 1 (Goldberg 1986). Goldberg connects this with female-led migration from surrounding rural areas. Wharram Percy lies about 20 miles from York, and there is documentary evidence (Russell 1948) which shows that many probably migrated this sort of distance to become resident in the city. Taking the York and Wharram Percy evidence together, it would seem that the best explanation for the shortage of females at Wharram was that female-led emigration left a rural sex ratio dominated by males – the sex imbalance cannot be taken as evidence of female infanticide.

By the mediaeval period, it is clear that infanticide was regarded as a feminine crime

(Shahar 1990), the offender typically being the child's mother. Motives are difficult to discern given the sparse legal records for the practice, but in some instances poverty and, particularly, the shame of bearing an illegitimate child were important factors (Kellum 1974). The limited documentary sources for the Saxon period (see above) may suggest that the pattern whereby infanticide was committed by the mother on an unwanted illegitimate child may obtain from early Christian times in England. It is certainly a theme which continues right through the mediaeval and post-mediaeval periods.

In mediaeval times, maternal infanticide was dealt with by ecclesiastical courts, as it was considered a sin against the church rather than a crime against the state (Kellett 1992). However, by the Reformation, the powers of these courts had declined and infanticide became a matter for the secular judiciary (Langer 1974b). Evidence for infanticide in the Tudor period is much more frequent than for mediaeval times, although the degree to which this reflects a genuine increase in its occurrence rather than simply more frequent recording is unclear. Nonetheless, by late Tudor times there are fairly regular references to it in coroners' inquests and court records (Emmison 1970). At this time society was re-examining its attitude towards children. For example, Thomas Phaire's *The Boke of Chyldrun* was published in 1544 with the intention of introducing more 'humanitarian' methods of childcare (Damme 1978). Despite concern in this period over the rate of newborn-child murder, it was very difficult to secure conviction of suspects. The usual defence of women suspected of having murdered their newborn babies was that the infant had been born dead. Under common law, the prosecution had to prove that the infant was in fact alive when delivered before they could hope to prosecute the mother for its murder. Suspects generally gave birth alone and in secret, and so there were no witnesses. Courts were forced to rely on circumstantial and forensic evidence which was normally inconclusive (Jackson 1996). In 1624 these problems led to a statute being passed which held that if a mother was found to have concealed the death of her illegitimate infant then she would be presumed guilty of its murder. The burden was now on the mother to prove that the child had been born dead, not as before on the prosecution to show that it had been alive. In mediaeval times, the penalties for infanticide were not in general severe – it seems that in practice an infant's life was not regarded as of the same worth as that of an older child or adult (Kellett 1992). However, the 1624 legislation clearly equated the death of an infant with that of an adult as it stated that a mother offending against the statute should 'suffer Death as in Case of Murther' (Jackson 1996: 32).

Shifting the burden of proof onto the defendant, coupled with the death penalty for offenders, meant that the statute was widely viewed as draconian and out of tune with popular opinion. As a consequence, juries were very reluctant to convict: for example, Jackson, studying evidence from the north of England in the eighteenth century, states that juries acquitted more than 95 per cent of women sent to trial accused of murdering their newborn offspring (Jackson 1996). The law dealing with the murder of illegitimate newborn children by their mothers was reformed in 1803, making it once more incumbent upon the prosecution to prove that the child had been born alive before it could hope to obtain a conviction for murder, although capital punishment was retained. However, conviction rates for infanticide were still very low and, when conviction was secured, the Crown was reluctant to seek the death penalty (Kellett 1992). Even when prosecutions were successful, offenders were normally spared the death sentence on the grounds of 'temporary insanity' (Behlmer 1979). By 1864 it had become standard practice for the Home Secretary to advise commutation (Damme 1978).

Despite continuing judicial leniency, public concern over the perceived high rate of infanticide in the mid-nineteenth century reached a greater intensity than seen in previous eras. In the anonymity of burgeoning industrial towns tiny bodies could easily be thrown in canals or abandoned in parks or alleyways. Reports of 150 dead infants being found in London streets during 1862 led *The Times* to lament that 'infancy in London has to creep into life in the midst of foes' (quoted in Higginbotham 1989: 319). In the same year, Dr Lankester, a Middlesex coroner, charged that the police thought no more of finding a dead infant than a dead dog or cat (Langer 1974b). There are a variety of possible reasons for the apparent rise in infanticide during the mid-Victorian period. Increasing urbanisation, and the greater mobility of all classes consequent on the rise of the railways, meant that infanticide and disposal of the body was easier than in the more tightly-knit communities of earlier times. In 1834, changes in the Poor Law relating to illegitimate children made maintenance proceedings against putative fathers more difficult, shifting responsibility onto the mother in the vain hope that this would reduce the number of illegitimate births by making women guard their chastity more carefully (Rose 1986). In addition, there was no requirement to register stillbirths; this opened the door to infanticide, as with collusion of the gravedigger, victims could be buried as stillborn (Behlmer 1979).

Although there was much public concern over the rate of infanticide, and the mother's deed was deplored, much blame was laid at the door of the father who had deserted her; both mother and child were to some extent seen as victims (Higginbotham 1989). This sympathetic attitude to the mother, by both the courts and the public at large, echoed that expressed in earlier times (Jackson 1996), but it was perhaps amplified by the 1834 Poor Law which was widely seen as an inhumane Act, and one which tilted the balance unfairly against women regarding responsibility for illegitimate children (Rose 1986). Juries continued to be reluctant to convict in cases of infanticide, particularly as it remained a capital offence.

Agitation over the problem of infanticide in the mid-Victorian period came from a variety of sources, the most vocal of which was probably the medical profession. A committee set up by the Harveian Society recommended, among other things, the revision of the Poor Laws, compulsory registration of all births including stillbirths, and the registration of foster nurses who took in illegitimate children (these last made no small contribution to the rate of infant murder). They also recommended the creation of infanticide as a crime distinct from murder that would not be a capital offence. Maternal infanticide was popularly viewed as distinct from other homicides, both because of the special nature of the mother–child relationship and because of the young age of the victims. This latter point was stated most clearly by James Fitzjames Stephens when he testified before a parliamentary commission that 'the crime itself is less serious than other kinds of murder. You cannot estimate the loss to the child itself, you know nothing about it' (Commission Report, cited in Higginbotham 1989: 331).

During the 1870s, references to infanticide become rarer. The rate of newborn child murder may have been reduced by success in moving some of the changes in the law recommended by the Harveian Society and others; the increasing availability of effective contraceptives may also have played a part, rendering recourse to infanticide unnecessary (Behlmer 1979). However, legal recognition of infanticide as a crime distinct from murder did not come in in England until the Infanticide Bill was passed in 1922. This reduced the offence of infanticide from murder to manslaughter if the woman was mentally disturbed at the time of the killing through the effects of having just given birth. It applied only to the mother who killed her newborn child. Present legislation in England and Wales dates to 1938. It specifies that the mother who kills her child within twelve months of birth while the balance of her mind is disturbed through 'not having fully recovered from the effect of giving birth' or as a result of 'the effects of lactation' may be dealt with as if guilty of manslaughter and not murder (Marks and Kumar 1993). The maximum penalty under the 1938 Act is life imprisonment, but in practice sentences are light, the most frequent being probation (ibid.).

The decline in infanticide appears to have continued during the first half of the twentieth century. Since the 1950s, the rate has stayed fairly constant at about 45 per million per annum of children aged under one year in England and Wales (Marks and Kumar 1993), despite changes in social mores (for example, the fading of stigma attached to illegitimate births), and the greater availability of contraception and safe abortion. The rate of infanticide in Scotland is similar, despite a markedly higher overall rate of homicide (Marks and Kumar 1996). Although infanticide is not common in Britain, infants are still about four times as likely to be victims of homicide as are older individuals (Rose 1986). As in the past, the overwhelming majority of perpetrators of this crime are the infants' parents. Of those killed in the first day of life, most are murdered by their mothers, but for older infants the killer is equally likely to be the father (Marks and Kumar 1993, 1996). Although the proportion of women among offenders does not appear to be as great as in the past, there is still a contrast here with other murders, in which the overwhelming majority of offenders are male.

In Britain it would appear that, since at least the mediaeval period, maternal infanticide has been viewed as a lesser crime than murder of an older individual or the homicide of an infant by someone other than the child's mother. It would seem that, despite the teachings of the Christian church, infant life has traditionally been accorded lesser worth than that of an older child or adult. Damme (1978) argues that the lesser penalties for infanticide than for other homicides, coupled with a very liberal insanity defence, have currently institutionalised this position under English law. That the 1938 Act remains in force may also be viewed as a continuation of the sympathetic attitude traditionally shown to mothers who kill their newborn children. This attitude has not extended to fathers, as illustrated by the studies of Marks and Kumar using recent data on infanticides. They found that in England and Wales, mothers who kill their infants receive less severe sentences than fathers who are found guilty of the same crime. The severity of sentences was a function of the sex of the perpetrator and was not related to the overt violence of the crime (Marks and Kumar 1993). In Scotland, there is no special legal provision for maternal infanticide, the mother being charged as for any other homicide. Nevertheless, here, too, penalties appear to be related to the sex of the offender, with fathers receiving heavier sentences than mothers (Marks and Kumar 1996).

REFERENCES

Behlmer, G.K. (1979) 'Infanticide and medical opinion in mid-Victorian England', *Journal of History of Medicine and Allied Sciences* 34: 403–27.

Brown, S. (1991) *Late Carthaginian Child Sacrifice*, Sheffield: Sheffield University Press.

Carter, A. (1997) 'Infanticide and the right to life', *Ratio* 10: 1–9.

Cayton, H. (1980) 'Some contributions from the written sources', in P. Wade-Martins (ed.) *Excavations in North Elmham Park, 1967–72*, East Anglian Archaeology Report No. 9, Gressenhall: Norfolk Museums Service, pp. 303–13.

Cocks, A.H. (1921) 'A Romano-British homestead in the Hambleden Valley, Bucks', *Archaeologia* 71: 141–98.

Coleman, E. (1976) 'Infanticide in the Early Middle Ages', in S.M. Stuard (ed.) *Women in Mediaeval Society*, Philadelphia: University of Pennsylvania Press, pp. 47–70.

Damme, C. (1978) 'Infanticide: the worth of an infant under law', *Medical History* 22: 1–24.

Divale, W.T. (1972) 'Systematic population control in the Middle and Upper Palaeolithic: inferences based on contemporary hunter-gatherers', *World Archaeology* 4: 222–43.

Divale, W.T. and Harris, M. (1976) 'Population, warfare and the male supremacist complex', *American Anthropologist* 78: 521–38.

Douglas, M. (1966) 'Population control in primitive groups', *British Journal of Sociology* 17: 263–73.

Emmison, F. C. (1970) *Elizabethan Life: Disorder*, Chelmsford: Essex County Council.

Faerman, M., Kahila, G., Smith, P., Greenblatt, C., Stager, L., Filon, D. and Oppenheim, A. (1997) 'DNA analysis reveals the sex of infanticide victims', *Nature* 385: 212–13.

Faerman, M., Bar-Gal, G.K., Filon, D., Greenblatt, C.L., Stager, L., Oppenheim, A. and Smith, P. (1998) 'Determining the sex of infanticide victims from the Late Roman era through ancient DNA Analysis', *Journal of Archaeological Science* 25: 861–5.

Gero, J.M. and Conkey, M., (eds) (1991) *Engendering Archaeology: Women and Prehistory*, Oxford: Blackwell.

Gilchrist, R. (1997) *Gender and Material Culture: The Archaeology of Religious Women*, London: Routledge.

Goldberg, P.J.P. (1986) 'Female labour, service and marriage in the late mediaeval urban north', *Northern History* 22: 18–38.

Harris, W.V. (1982) 'The theoretical possibility of extensive infanticide in the Graeco-Roman world', *Classical Quarterly* 32: 114–16.

—— (1994) 'Child exposure in the Roman Empire', *Journal of Roman Studies* 84: 1–22.

Hesketh, T. and Zhu, W.X. (1997) 'The one-child family policy: the good, the bad and the ugly', *British Medical Journal* 314: 1685–7.

Higginbotham, A.R. (1989) '"Sin of the Age": infanticide and illegitimacy in Victorian London' *Victorian Studies* 32: 319–37.

Hoffer, P.C. and Hull, N.E.H. (1981) *Murdering Mothers: Infanticide in England and New England 1558–1803*, New York: New York University Press.

Hrdy, S.B. (1992) 'Fitness tradeoffs in the history and evolution of delegated mothering with special reference to wet-nursing, abandonment and infanticide', *Ethology and Sociobiology* 13: 409–42.

Jackson, M. (1996) *New-Born Child Murder*, Manchester: Manchester University Press.

Johansson, S.R. (1984) 'Deferred infanticide: excess female mortality during childhood', in G. Hausfater and S.B. Hrdy (eds) *Infanticide*, Hawthorne: Aldine, pp. 463–85.

Judson, O.P. (1994) 'Killing the sex ratio', *Nature* 372: 503–4.

Kellett, R.J. (1992) 'Infanticide and child destruction: the historical, legal and pathological aspects', *Forensic Science International* 53: 1–28.

Kellum, B. (1974) 'Infanticide in England in the Later Middle Ages', *History of Childhood Quarterly* 1(3): 367–88.

Langer, W.L. (1974a) 'Further notes on the history of infanticide', *History of Childhood Quarterly* 1(4): 129–34.

—— (1974b) 'Infanticide: a historical survey', *History of Childhood Quarterly* 1(3): 353–65.

Lee, J., Feng, W. and Campbell, C. (1994) 'Infant and child mortality among the Qing nobility: implications for two types of population check', *Population Studies* 48: 395–411.

Long, T.A. (1988) 'Infanticide for handicapped infants: sometimes it's a metaphysical dispute', *Journal of Medical Ethics* 14: 79–81.

Marks, M.N. and Kumar, R. (1993) 'Infanticide in England and Wales', *Medicine, Science and the Law* 33: 329–39.

—— (1996) 'Infanticide in Scotland', *Medicine, Science and the Law* 36: 299–305.

Mays, S. (1993) 'Infanticide in Roman Britain', *Antiquity* 67: 883–8.

—— (1995) 'Child killing through the ages', *British Archaeology* 2: 8–9.

—— (1997) 'Life and death in the mediaeval village', in G. De Boe and F. Verhaege (eds) *Death and Burial in Mediaeval Europe*, Zellik: IAP Rapporten 2, pp. 121–5.

Molleson, T. (1991) 'Demographic implications of the age structure of early English cemetery samples', *Actes des Journées Anthropologiques* 5: 113–21.

Montague, P. (1989) 'Infant rights and the morality of infanticide', *Nous* 23: 63–81.

Moore, J. and Scott, E. (eds) (1997) *Invisible People and Processes: Writing Gender and Childhood into European Archaeology*, London: Leicester University Press.

Nordborg, M. (1992) 'Female infanticide and human sex ratio evolution', *Journal of Theoretical Biology* 158: 195–8.

Penn, W.S. (1960) 'Springhead: Temples III and IV', *Archaeologia Cantiana* 74: 113–40.

Philpott, R. (1991) *Burial Practices in Roman Britain*, British Archaeological Reports, British Series 219, Oxford.

Ramsey, P. (1978) *Ethics at the Edges of Life*, New Haven: Yale University Press.

Rose, L. (1986) *The Massacre of the Innocents: Infanticide in Britain 1800–1939*, London: Routledge & Kegan Paul.

Russell, J.C. (1948), *British Mediaeval Population*, Albuquerque: University of New Mexico Press.

Scrimshaw, S.C.M. (1984) 'Infanticide in human populations: societal and individual concerns', in G. Hausfater and S.B. Hrdy (eds) *Infanticide*, Hawthorne: Aldine, pp. 439–62.

Shahar, S. (1990) *Childhood in the Middle Ages*, London: Routledge.

Smith, P. and Kahila, G. (1992) 'Identification of infanticide in archaeological sites: a case study from the Late Roman–Early Byzantine periods at Ashkelon, Israel', *Journal of Archaeological Science* 19: 667–75.

Sofaer Derevenski, J. (1994) 'Where are the children? Accessing children in the past', *Archaeological Review from Cambridge* 13(2): 7–20.

Tooley, M. (1983) *Abortion and Infanticide*, Oxford: Clarendon Press.

Ucko, P.J. (1969) 'Ethnography and the archaeological study of funerary remains', *World Archaeology* 1: 262–80.

Warren, M.A. (1985) 'Reconsidering the ethics of infanticide', *Philosophical Books* 26: 1–9.

Warwick, R. (1968) 'The skeletal remains' in L. P. Wenham (ed.) *The Romano-British Cemetery at Trentholme Drive, York*, London: HMSO, pp. 113–76.

Wiedermann, T. (1989) *Adults and Children in the Roman Empire*, Routledge: London.

Williamson, L. (1978) 'Infanticide: an anthropological analysis', in M. Kohl (ed.) *Infanticide and the Value of Life*, Buffalo: Prometheus pp. 61–75.

Part VIII

Demography and growth of children

Chapter 15

Interpretation of the growth of past populations

Louise Humphrey

INTRODUCTION

Recent decades have seen a substantial increase in studies concerning the skeletal and dental remains of children from archaeological sites. It is now widely recognised that these provide a sensitive barometer of the state of health of past populations. This chapter will focus on the interpretation of skeletal growth from archaeological material. The first part of the chapter discusses some of the methodological problems and assumptions associated with growth studies of past populations and the second part reviews the types of growth study that can be undertaken using archaeological material.

The effect of stress on the developing skeleton and dentition

An underlying assumption of many growth studies of past populations is that large size relative to chronological age is indicative of a good standard of living in a population and poor growth attainment reflects impoverished environmental circumstances. This assumption is to a large extent borne out by studies of living populations. These demonstrate that growth can be disrupted by poor nutrition and disease, and is negatively influenced by other factors including poor maternal health and psychological stress (Bogin 1988). These factors can result in reduced size for chronological age. In order to evaluate growth in a sample of unknown chronological age, age must be estimated on the basis of maturation. Skeletal and dental maturation can be delayed by the same factors that disrupt growth, but the effect of nutritional and disease stress on skeletal maturation and dental development is less severe than its effect on skeletal growth (Demirjian 1986). We can therefore assume that small average size relative to dental or skeletal maturity is a reflection of a poor quality environment, provided that other factors involved in the comparison have been standardised.

METHODOLOGICAL CONCERNS
Mortality bias

A potential bias in any study of skeletal material is that a skeletal sample may not be fully representative of the living population from which it was drawn, and the development of the children represented in a skeletal sample may not be typical of the population as a whole (Johnston 1968). Non-survivors may have endured a prolonged period of illness and associated developmental retardation prior to death and are likely, in this case, to have been smaller than their healthy contemporaries at their time of death. Sundick (1978) argued that the majority of infant and juvenile deaths are caused by acute illness or malnutrition, and that, under these circumstances, the interval between the onset of illness and death is too short for growth to be drastically affected. Other studies indicate that the immediate cause of death may not accurately reflect the amount of growth disruption experienced by individuals prior to death. Children who die suddenly from acute illness may already represent a biased sample of the population, because children who are stressed by previous disease or poor nutrition can be more susceptible to subsequent stress.

This point was demonstrated very clearly by a longitudinal study of growth and mortality in two Gambian villages (Billewicz and McGregor 1982). Childhood mortality in the villages was extremely high during the period of study, with 50 per cent of children dying between birth and the age of five years. The mean heights and weights of the children who died in each measurement interval were compared to the means for children who survived beyond the age of five years. Children who died below the age of five years were significantly smaller and lighter when they were last measured than the children who survived beyond five years. Since the period of illness prior to death was usually short, this difference cannot be accounted for by an interruption of growth resulting from the illness (ibid.). The Gambian population were suffering from chronic nutritional and disease stress on a seasonal basis. Under more favourable environmental circumstances, children can experience complete catch-up growth following an episode of growth disruption (Prader *et al.* 1963) and there is less likely to be an association between poor growth and subsequent mortality risk. In a recent review of biological mortality bias, Saunders and Hoppa (1993) concluded that its effects are relatively small. The extent to which the growth patterns inferred from a mortality sample can be considered typical of the population as a whole will depend on both the causes of death of non-survivors and the circumstances under which the population were living. The problem of mortality bias is likely to be of greater significance for comparisons between a skeletal sample and data collected on living children than for comparisons between skeletal samples.

Age estimation

Typically, in an archaeological sample, age at death is not known and must be estimated from the dentition or skeleton. Accurate estimation of the chronological age of each individual is fundamental to any study of skeletal growth from an archaeological sample. Age estimates are based on the observed relationships between skeletal or dental development and chronological age in a population of individuals of known age. Dental development shows less variation in relation to chronological age than skeletal development and the average difference in the timing of male and female development is lower (Garn *et al.* 1958; Lewis and Garn 1960; Roche 1992, see below). Furthermore, dental development is less sensitive to extrinsic stress factors and hormonal influences than skeletal development (Edler 1977; Demirjian 1986). Age estimates based on dental development are therefore expected to be more accurate than age estimates based on skeletal development. A test of the accuracy of skeletal and dental age estimates using a sample of subadult skeletons of known age at death confirmed this expectation (Bowman *et al.* 1992).

Dental development can be assessed using tooth eruption or the formation of individual tooth crowns and roots. Tooth formation is less variable relative to chronological age than tooth emergence (Lewis and Garn 1960) and is less influenced by local factors such as premature loss or extraction of the overlying deciduous teeth and by the space available in the mandible and maxillae (Posen 1965). Tooth eruption is a poorly defined concept since it covers the entire period in which a tooth is moving through the jaws and mouth in order to achieve and maintain occlusion (Demirjian 1986). Clinical emergence, which is generally reported for studies of living children, describes the actual piercing of the gum, whereas in archaeological material alveolar emergence, or piercing of the bone, is more readily recognisable. An unknown margin of error is introduced if comparisons are made between a living population scored on the basis of clinical emergence and an archaeological sample scored according to alveolar emergence. Unlike tooth formation, tooth emergence provides a discontinuous record of the process of dental development. The deciduous dentition erupts between the ages of 6 and 30 months and the permanent dentition (excluding the highly variable third molar) emerges between 6 and 12 years (Demirjian 1986).

Tooth formation describes a series of stages that take place in each developing tooth, starting with the appearance of a bony crypt and initial cusp formation and ending with closure of the apex of the roots. Each of these stages can be observed directly on loose teeth or visualised radiographically if the teeth are in the jaws. Tooth formation provides continuous record of dental development between approximately 15 weeks after conception and 20 years (Hillson 1996). Various compilations of the age of occurrence of tooth formation stages are available for estimating the age at death of unknown children (Gleiser and Hunt 1955; Moorrees, Fanning and Hunt 1963a,1963b; Gustafson and Koch 1974; Anderson, Thompson and Popovich 1976; Smith 1991). Comparative studies of different dental ageing techniques demonstrate that estimates of age at death can vary quite markedly according to the method applied (Merchant and Ubelaker 1977; Saunders *et al.* 1993; Liversidge 1994). Saunders *et al.* (1993) and Liversidge (1994) have tested the accuracy and repeatability of dental standards for estimating age at death using samples of known-age children. Saunders *et al.* (1993) found that the standards of Moorrees, Fanning and Hunt were more reliable than those of Anderson, Thompson and Popovich (1976) in children from the Belleville sample aged between birth and 8 years. Liversidge (1994) found that the standards of Gustafson and Koch and the reworked version of the Moorrees, Fanning and Hunt data provided by Smith (1991) were more accurate than their original data for children from the Spitalfields sample aged between birth and 5.4 years.

Age at death can also be determined by counting incremental growth structures in the tooth enamel, starting from the neonatal line and following through a sequence of tooth crown sections to cover the whole period of crown formation (Hillson 1996). A major advantage of this technique is that it is independent of population, sex and other causes of developmental variation, but it has not yet been widely applied to archaeological material because it is a lengthy and invasive procedure.

Sexual dimorphism in growth

On average, males and females differ in their developmental schedules, with females being advanced over males in the timing of their skeletal growth and maturation, dental development and sexual maturation. These differences develop prenatally and become most visible at the time of the adolescent growth spurt, which occurs on average two years earlier in girls than boys. The developmental difference between boys and girls is more pronounced in the skeleton than in the dentition. Girls in the Fels study (Roche 1992) were advanced over boys by an average 0.3 years in the formation and eruption of their permanent teeth. This difference represents about 3 per cent of mean age of occurrence of each recorded event. Boys and girls from the Fels sample differed by between 8 and 25 per cent in the timing of identifiable stages of skeletal maturation (Garn *et al.* 1958).

Studies of the differences in male and female growth are rarely undertaken using archaeological samples (an exception is Y'Edynak 1976) because of the difficulties associated with determining the sex of juvenile skeletons. The sex determination of skeletal material is commonly based on the expression of secondary sexual characteristics, generally a visual evaluation of shape differences. In juveniles, the secondary sexual characters are poorly developed and sex determination is notoriously difficult. Despite these difficulties there have been numerous attempts to develop criteria that can be used to determine the sex of juveniles from the skeleton or dentition (e.g. Ditch and Rose 1972; Black 1978; Weaver 1980; Rosing 1983; Schutkowski 1993). Published methods generally have a success rate of between 70 and 95 per cent, although several studies have reported that boys can be more reliably identified than girls (Black 1978; Weaver 1980; Schutkowski 1993) and most techniques are only applicable within a limited age range. Many methods for determining the sex of juvenile specimens have been developed and tested on a single sample, and as with methods developed for adults, they may produce less reliable results if applied to a different collection. Techniques that are both independent of and potentially more accurate than morphological sex differences for determining the sex of juveniles from archaeological samples are becoming available through the application of molecular techniques (Stone *et al.* 1996).

It will not be possible to obtain an unbiased study of male and female differences in growth in an archaeological sample until the entire sample can be reliably sexed from skeletal and dental morphology, or the sample to be used in a growth study can be reliably sexed using a technique that is independent of morphology. When sex determination is based on morphology, inaccuracy in a proportion of the sample is likely to result in the overestimation of sexual differences, because this causes an artificial polarisation of the male and female groups. Exclusion of individuals of uncertain sex from an analysis would have the same effect because these individuals are likely to be those exhibiting an intermediate morphology. By contrast, if sex determination is independent of morphology, inaccuracy will be random with respect to morphology and is more likely to result in underestimation of sexual differences. A further problem stems from the fact that the chronological age of each individual must be estimated from skeletal or dental maturation. Since females show advanced dental and skeletal maturation compared to males of the same chronological age, a sample of equivalent biological age will tend to include males of an older chronological age than females, and this will result in an overestimation of sexual differences (Humphrey 1994).

Analysis

The first stage of analysis for most growth studies is to place each skeleton in one of a series of groups comprising individuals showing a particular range of dental or osseous ages (Johnston 1962; Armelagos *et al.* 1972; Y'Edynak 1976; Merchant and Ubelaker

1977; Sundick 1978; Hummert and Van Gerven 1983; Hoppa 1992). The mean size of individuals belonging to a particular age class is then plotted against the midpoint of the age range represented by the group, and growth is evaluated from the values of successive age classes. A problem with this approach is that sample sizes may be small, particularly for individuals over 5 years (Johnston 1968). As a result, age ranges may have to be broad and individuals may be unevenly distributed within each age range. One way of reducing this problem is to calculate the mean age of the individuals in each group instead of using the mid-point of the age range (Saunders, Hoppa and Southern 1993). This will reduce the incidence of erratic changes in size between successive age groups but not entirely elimi-nate the problem if the samples are very small or biased.

An alternative approach is to treat each individual as an independent data point and fit a linear or curvilinear line to size plotted against age (Cook 1984; Jantz and Owsley 1984; Mensforth 1985; Humphrey 1994, 1998). The use of a standardised equation for this type of comparison allows for an objective description of the differences between the samples under study, based on the mathematical descriptions of the fitted lines. It is important to ensure that the equation being fitted to the data is appropriate for the purpose of the study and the age range under consideration. In order to select an appropriate mathematical model both goodness of fit and theoretical considerations need to be taken into account (Humphrey 1994, 1998). A suitable growth model should accurately describe the distri-bution of the data and be appropriate for the underlying biological principles. An equation that is too simple will fail to provide an accurate description of growth, and one that is too complex may introduce artefacts into the growth model that are biologically meaningless. It would, for example, be inappropriate to fit an equation which incorporates a change in growth rate at adolescence to archaeological data since cross-sectional data disguise the individual growth spurts within the generalised population model.

Appropriate measurements

Most studies of archaeological material have been restricted to the long bones. The long bones tend to survive well and are easily identified and measured. Comparative data for modern children and archaeological groups are readily available. There is potential for considerably more information to be gained by examining growth patterns throughout the skeleton. However, many standard anthropological measurements cannot be made on juve-niles from archaeological samples since the bones are incompletely formed and disarticulated. In addition, bones from archaeological sites may be damaged or distorted and skeletal material may be incompletely recovered. Nonetheless, with carefully selected variables it is possible to measure the growth of most individual bones from birth to maturity (Humphrey 1994, 1998).

Humphrey (ibid.) described a series of growth patterns for different parts of the cranial and post-cranial skeleton. These demonstrate that there is considerable variation in the developmental schedules of different parts of the skeleton. The earliest growing parts of the skeleton follow an extremely rapid neural growth pattern, with growth complete by around 6 years. The mandible and palate show fairly rapid early growth followed by the more gradual attainment of adult size. The face and parts of the cranial base follow a pattern that is intermediate between that of the mandibular and neural patterns. The growth of the post-cranial skeleton is delayed relative to that of the cranial skeleton. The long bones achieve their adult length during the late teens, but the growth of the long bone diameters continues into adult life. Given this variability, it is recommended that future growth studies increase their scope, since the growth of different parts of the skeleton may be more or less sensitive to the factors being examined.

TYPES OF GROWTH STUDY

A common approach to understanding the health of children from an archaeological sample is to assess their growth by comparison with other groups (e.g. Johnston 1962; Armelagos *et al.* 1972; Y'Edynak 1976; Merchant and Ubelaker 1977; Sundick 1978; Hummert and Van Gerven 1983; Mensforth 1984; Hoppa 1992; Saunders, Hoppa and Southern 1993). Interpretation of the skeletal growth of an archaeological sample may involve an evaluation of changes in growth patterns through time at a single site, or more frequently comparison between sites or with a modern sample. Comparisons can also be made between sub-samples within a single site in order to address specific questions relating to the variation within the sample. This approach has been used to compare the growth of individuals with or without stress indicators (Mays 1985, 1995; Ribot and Roberts 1996), and to evaluate the development of sexual dimorphism in different parts of the human skeleton (Humphrey 1994, 1998).

Comparisons between archaeological samples or between an archaeological sample and a modern group are frequently made under the assumption that a lower level of growth attainment relative to age in one of the groups is an indicator of a higher level of stress in that group. In order to justify this assumption, it is important to standardise as many as possible of the factors which could influence either growth or the evaluation of growth. The aim of any comparative analysis is to be able to interpret differences between the two samples in terms of a single differentiating factor or as small a number of factors as possible. While this is widely acknowledged, it is rarely explicitly stated and any survey of the literature will show that it has not always been possible to work within these constraints. The groups being compared should, if possible, be sampled from genetically similar populations, since part of the variation observed in the growth of modern populations can be attributed to genetic differences (Eveleth and Tanner 1990). This constraint should be applied both to comparisons between archaeological samples and to those between an archaeological sample and a modern group. Unfortunately, modern comparative samples are not available for most of the world's populations (Johnston 1968; Saunders 1992) and many researchers have had to use inappropriate modern samples for age estimation and comparative purposes.

Comparison of archaeological and modern groups

Comparisons of archaeological samples and modern groups are helpful because they enable the growth of an archaeological population to be evaluated in terms of modern expectations, but it is important to remember that data for archaeological and modern samples are collected using different techniques. A major difference between modern comparative samples and archaeological samples is that the individuals incorporated into the modern sample are of known chronological age whereas the age at death of the individuals in the archaeological samples must usually be estimated from dental or skeletal development. An in-built assumption of this approach is that the error introduced by estimating age at death is randomly distributed relative to real (chronological) age throughout the age range used in the analysis. In fact, comparisons relying on dental or skeletal age estimates will tend to slightly overestimate growth achievement since the chronological age of the most severely stressed individuals in the archaeological sample is likely to be underestimated. Allowance should be made for these potential biases when comparisons are made with modern data.

Growth studies of living children, and indeed the type of study with which most people are familiar, are generally longitudinal in design, whereas growth studies of archaeological samples are by necessity cross-sectional. A longitudinal growth study follows a single child through his or her growth period. Changes in growth velocity, such as the onset of the adolescent growth spurt, can normally be detected on a graph of size plotted against age, and will be clearly visible on a velocity curve (increase in size per unit time plotted against age). In a cross-sectional growth analysis each child contributes a single data point to the overall evaluation of growth in a population. Growth is generally evaluated from the mean values of successive age classes, each composed of groups of individuals showing a particular range of dental or osseous ages. A major disadvantage of this kind of study is that particular growth events, such as the onset of the adolescent growth spurt, which are imperfectly synchronised between individuals, cannot be modelled. This was clearly illustrated by Tanner and colleagues (1966) who showed the effect of superimposing the growth spurts of five children. The increase in growth velocity is barely perceptible in the average height velocity curve because it is smoothed out across a period of several years. Studies of modern children commonly used for comparison with archaeological samples are mixed longitudinal (Maresh 1955; Gindhart 1973). Each child will probably have been measured on several occasions, although not necessarily for the whole duration of the study. However, since the data are presented as means or percentiles calculated for successive chronological age ranges, this type of analysis incorporates the same loss of information regarding changes in growth velocity as cross-sectional growth studies.

A further difference between studies of living and skeletal samples is that the measurements for living children are derived from radiographs, whereas the data for a skeletal sample are based on direct measurement of the bones. Measurements from radiographs incorporate a degree of distortion or enlargement caused by X-ray diffusion. The amount of distortion is affected by the distance of the tube from the object and the distance between the object and the film (Aiello 1981), and will therefore vary according to the set-up of the equipment and the position of the child when the image is made. A correction of about 3 per cent should be made to allow for this enlargement (Gindhart 1973; Aiello 1981).

The most frequently used modern comparative sample is based on a radiographic study of long bone lengths in North American children (Maresh 1955). The data are presented as percentiles and comparisons are usually made on the basis of the 50th percentile (Johnston 1962; Armelagos *et al.* 1972; Y'Edynak 1976; Merchant and Ubelaker 1977; Saunders, Hoppa and Southern 1993). Comparisons with a modern sample could be more valuable if the 10th and 90th percentiles were shown so as to give a better indication of the range of possible values in the comparative sample.

Comparison between archaeological samples

Comparison between archaeological samples involves fewer potential biases than comparison of an archaeological sample with data collected on a living population, since all of the samples represent non-survivors and all of the data are collected from osteological material. With this type of comparison it is important to ensure that the same ageing criteria are applied to all of the samples. Several studies have demonstrated that the estimated age at death can vary systematically according to the technique used for age estimation (Merchant and Ubelaker 1977; Saunders, Hoppa and Southern 1993; Liversidge 1994) and may even be affected by which teeth are present in each specimen (Jantz and Owsley 1984). It may not be possible to standardise the methodology if comparative data are culled from the literature since some of the early growth studies do not give sufficient detail about the technique used for age estimation and some use a combination of osseous and dental criteria. Under these circumstances, it is important to make allowance for any error that may be introduced (Merchant and Ubelaker 1977). It is also important to standardise the statistical treatment of the data if this is possible.

An example of an ideal experimental set-up for a comparative growth study is to evaluate secular changes in the growth patterns of two or more samples from a geographically restricted region that has been continuously or repeatedly occupied by people from the same population. Variation in growth attainment relative to biological age can be used as an indicator of differential levels of stress through time, since all of the other factors that influence growth can be standardised. This type of study has been used to assess the effects of changes in subsistence or socio-political circumstances on the health of a population (Hummert and Van Gerven 1983; Cook 1984; Jantz and Owsley 1984; Mensforth 1985). A variation on this type of study is to compare the growth of genetically similar groups inhabiting different regions or continents as a result of migration (Saunders, Hoppa and Southern 1993).

Comparison of the growth of archaeological samples from different populations should be undertaken with caution because there may be too many differences between the samples to draw any useful conclusions in terms of the direct or indirect influence of genetic and environmental factors on growth. If the aim of a comparative study is to evaluate population differences in growth, it is important to ensure that all of the other circumstances that may affect growth are equivalent. This is problematic with archaeological material.

Comparison of sub-groups within an archaeological sample

Comparisons between the growth of different groups within an archaeological sample can be undertaken if these groups can be clearly distinguished and sample size is adequate for all of the groups throughout the age range under investigation. This approach has been used to investigate the relationship between variation in growth attainment and social status within a site. Cook (1984) investigated the relationship between skeletal size and social status in a Middle Woodland sample from the Illinois Valley series by inferring the social status of each child from their burial treatment. The children who received the most elaborate types of burial did not differ significantly in size from those who received less elaborate burials, suggesting that size variation in children was not related to social status during this period.

A further application of this approach is shown by recent studies that have examined whether individuals with clear stress indicators in the skeleton and dentition were smaller than individuals of the same age without stress markers. Mays (1985, 1995) has argued that a combined study of stress indicators (specifically, Harris lines) and skeletal size can be used to determine whether the stress to which a population was subjected was chronic or acute. This issue is relevant to the ongoing debate (Wood *et al.* 1992; Saunders and Hoppa 1993) about the extent to which juveniles represented in a skeletal sample are typical of the population as a whole, or, more specifically, to what extent they differed from children who survived until adulthood. If a population is shown to have been suffering from chronic stress, mortality bias is likely to be more pronounced than otherwise. Mays (1985) compared the growth of the femur diaphysis (length and cortical thickness) in samples of subadults with and without Harris lines from the skeletal collection from the Romano-British site of Poundbury. In this collection, there was no discernible difference between the regression lines describing the growth of the children with and without Harris lines. Mays argued that the Harris lines present in children from the Poundbury population reflected episodes of acute stress followed by a full recovery and complete catch-up growth. In juveniles from the mediaeval site of Wharram Percy, a significant relationship between the occurrence of Harris lines on the femur and cortical thickness could be demonstrated, although the relationship was not significant for diaphysis length (Mays 1995). These results indicate that the stress suffered by children at Wharram Percy was more chronic than that suffered at Poundbury, and they reflect a difference in socio-economic status between the two sites (Mays 1995).

Ribot and Roberts (1996) carried out a similar study of long bone growth and stress indicators using two mediaeval populations from Britain. Each individual was examined for Harris lines, enamel hypoplasia, porosity on the external surfaces of the skull (orbit and cranial vault) and subperiostial bone formation on the long bones. Their study showed that individuals with more than one stress indicator were not systematically smaller than those individuals with only one or no stress indicators present. Cook (1984) investigated the relationship between the growth of the femur and the occurrence of stress indicators in eight skeletal series from the Lower Illinois Valley. In each of the groups, individuals who were small for their dental age had higher frequencies of cribra orbitalia and circular caries, suggesting an association between poor growth and other childhood stress indicators.

There is potential to develop this kind of analysis in order to investigate more subtle variation in stress levels. The extent to which different parts of the human body are affected by stress-induced developmental disruption is variable. As discussed above, dental development appears to be better buffered against environmental stress than skeletal development. Within the skeleton, maturation appears to be less affected than growth, and, within the dentition, formation appears to be better protected than eruption (Demirjian 1986). When nutrition is inadequate, the growth of the post-cranial skeletal system is maintained at the expense of the surrounding soft tissues, and increase in the length and width of the long bones is maintained at the expense of cortical thickness (Huss-Ashmore 1981). It is also possible that different functional regions of the cranial skeleton may be differentially buffered against stress. Appropriate comparisons of the relative development of the skeletal and dental systems and the relative growth of different parts of the skeleton could therefore be used as a means of comparing stress levels between skeletal samples.

A third type of within-site comparative growth study is the investigation of growth differences between males and females. Such a study should only be undertaken for a collection in which the sex and preferably the age of death of each child are known independently of their morphology. Collections of identified individuals are ideal for this purpose and in recent years several such collections have been made available for long- or short-term study (Molleson and Cox 1993; Saunders, Hoppa and Southern 1993; Scheuer and Bowman 1995). One of the most important identified skeletal samples available for study was derived from excavations carried out at the crypts of St Bride's Church on Fleet Street, St Barnabus Church and Christ Church, Spitalfields in London (Molleson and Cox 1993; Scheuer and Bowman 1995). The interments within the three churches took place during the eighteenth and nineteenth centuries and represent a comparatively recent British urban population. Each skeleton could be identified from an associated coffin plate and the sex and age at death of each individual could be established from the information on the coffin plate and supporting documentary evidence.

This London crypt sample has provided a unique opportunity for a detailed analysis of skeletal growth in males and females. Humphrey (1994, 1998) investigated the development of sexual dimorphism throughout the human skeleton using this collection. Differences between the growth of males and females were analysed by fitting separate curves to the male and female data. The results show that the developmental basis of sexual dimorphism in the human skeleton is extremely variable. Sexual dimorphism in long bone length develops during adolescence and is the result of differences in both the overall duration of growth (males grow for longer) and growth rate (males grow faster). In contrast, sexual dimorphism in long bone diameter develops prior to adolescence and is largely (in some cases almost exclusively) the result of differences in male and female growth rates. This study clearly demonstrates that the development of sexual dimorphism in a species should not be regarded as a uniform phenomenon (Humphrey 1994, 1998).

CONCLUSION

The investigation of subadult skeletons from archaeological assemblages can be used to help understand complex biological and social issues, and the comparative analysis of skeletal growth provides an important and relatively straightforward means of investigating such issues. The type of questions that can be addressed using this technique include the investigation of subtle differences in the type and degree of environmental stress experienced during different periods or by contemporary occupants of a single site. This variation can be interpreted in terms of changing socio-economic and political circumstances, and may incorporate changes in subsistence basis and population density, differential levels of social inequality or political instability and warfare. Collections of identified individuals can be used to examine more subtle patterns of growth variation, including differences between males and females. A comparative growth study should ideally aim to investigate the effect of a single differentiating factor on the growth of the groups being studied. In order to do this, it is necessary to standardise other factors that could influence growth, including population affinity, and to apply the same techniques for data collection, age estimation and growth analysis to each sample.

ACKNOWLEDGEMENTS

I would like to thank Joanna Sofaer Derevenski for inviting me to contribute to this volume and Theya Molleson for helpful discussions.

REFERENCES

Aiello, L.C. (1981) 'On analysis of shape and strength in the long bones of higher primates', unpublished PhD thesis, University of London.

Anderson, D.L., Thompson, G.W. and Popovitch, F. (1976) 'Age of attainment of mineralisation stages of the permanent dentition', *Journal of Forensic Sciences* 21: 191–200.

Armelagos, G.J., Mielke, J.H., Owen, K.H., Van Gervan, D.P., Dewey, J.R. and Mahler, P.E. (1972) 'Bone growth and development in prehistoric populations from Sudanese Nubia', *Journal of Human Evolution* 1: 89–119.

Billewicz, W.Z. and McGregor, I.A. (1982) 'A birth-to-maturity longitudinal study of heights in two West African (Gambian) villages 1951–1975', *Annals of Human Biology* 9: 309–20.

Black, T.K. (1978) 'Sexual dimorphism in the tooth-crown diameters of the deciduous teeth', *American Journal of Physical Anthropology* 48: 77–82.

Bogin, B. (1988) *Patterns of Human Growth*, Cambridge: Cambridge University Press.

Bowman, J.E., MacLaughlin, S.M. and Scheuer, J.L. (1992) 'The relationship between biological and chronological age in the juvenile remains from St Bride's Church, Fleet Street', *Annals of Human Biology* 19: 216.

Cook, D.C. (1984) 'Subsistence and health in the Lower Illinois Valley: osteological evidence', in M.N. Cohen and G.J. Armelagos (eds.) *Palaeopathology at the Origins of Agriculture*, Orlando: Academic Press, pp. 235–69.

Demirjian, A. (1986) 'Dentition', in F. Falkner and J.M. Tanner (eds.) *Human Growth 2: Postnatal Growth and Neurobiology*, second edition, New York: Plenum Press, pp. 269–98

Ditch, L.E. and Rose, J.C. (1972) 'A multivariate dental sexing technique', *American Journal of Physical Anthropology* 37: 61–4.

Edler, R.J. (1977) 'Dental and skeletal ages in hypopituitary patients', *Journal of Dental Research* 56: 1145–53.

Eveleth, P.B. and Tanner, J.M. (1990) *Worldwide Variation in Human Growth*, 2nd edn, Cambridge: Cambridge University Press.

Garn, S.M., Lewis, A.B., Koski, K. and Polacheck, D.L. (1958) 'The sex difference in tooth calcification', *Journal of Dental Research* 33: 561–7.

Gindhart, P.S. (1973) 'Growth standards for the tibia and radius in children aged one month through eighteen years', *American Journal of Physical Anthropology* 39: 41–8.

Gleiser, I. and Hunt, E.E. (1955) 'The permanent first molar: its calcification, eruption and decay', *American Journal of Physical Anthropology* 13: 253–84.

Gustafson, G. and Koch, G. (1974) 'Age estimation up to 16 years of age based on dental development', *Odontologisk Revy* 25: 297–306.

Hillson, S. (1996) *Dental Anthropology*, Cambridge: Cambridge University Press

Hoppa, R.D. (1992) 'Evaluating human skeletal growth: an Anglo-Saxon example', *International Journal of Human Osteoarchaeology* 2: 275–88.

Hummert, J.R. and Van Gerven, D.P. (1983) 'Skeletal growth in a medieval population from Sudanese Nubia', *American Journal of Physical Anthropology* 60: 471–8.

Humphrey, L.T. (1994) ' Sexual dimorphism in humans and other catarrhine primates', unpublished PhD thesis, University of Cambridge.

—— (1998) 'Patterns of growth in the modern human skeleton', *American Journal of Physical Anthropology* 105: 57–72.

Huss-Ashmore, R. (1981) 'Bone growth and remodelling as a model of nutritional stress', in D.L. Martin and M.P. Bumstead (eds) *Biocultural Adaptation Comprehensive Approaches to Skeletal Analysis*,

Research Reports Number 20, Department of Anthropology, University of Massachusetts at Amherst.

Jantz, R.L. and Owsley, D.W. (1984) 'Long bone growth variation among Arikara skeletal populations', *American Journal of Physical Anthropology* 63: 13–20.

Johnston, F.E. (1962) 'Growth of the long bones of infants and young children at Indian Knoll', *American Journal of Physical Anthropology* 20: 249–54.

—— (1968) 'The growth of the skeleton in earlier peoples', in D.R. Brothwell (ed.) *The Skeletal Biology of Earlier Human Populations*, Oxford: Pergamon Press, pp. 57–66.

Lewis, A.B. and Garn, S.M. (1960) 'The relationship between tooth formation and other maturational factors', *Angle Orthodontist* 30: 70–7.

Liversidge, H.M. (1994) 'Accuracy of age estimation from developing teeth of a population of known age (0–5.4 years)', *International Journal of Osteoarchaeology* 4: 37–45.

Maresh, M.M. (1955) 'Linear growth of long bones of extremities from infancy through adolescence', *American Journal of Diseases in Childhood* 89: 725–42.

Mays, S.A. (1985) 'The relationship between Harris line formation and bone growth and development', *Journal of Archaeological Science* 12: 207–20.

—— (1995) 'The relationship between Harris lines and other aspects of skeletal development in adults and juveniles', *Journal of Archaeological Science* 22: 511–20.

Mensforth, R.P. (1985) 'Relative tibia long bone growth in the Libben and Bt-5 prehistoric skeletal populations', *American Journal of Physical Anthropology* 68: 247–62.

Merchant, V.L. and Ubelaker, D.H. (1977) 'Skeletal growth of the protohistoric Arikara', *American Journal of Physical Anthropology* 46: 61–72.

Molleson, T. and Cox, M. (1993) *The Spitalfields Project: Vol. 2 The Middling Sort*, Council for British Archaeology Research Report 86.

Moorrees, C.F.A., Fanning, E.A. and Hunt, E.E. (1963a) 'Age variation of formation for ten permanent teeth', *Journal of Dental Research* 42: 1490–1502.

—— (1963b) 'Formation and resorption of three deciduous teeth in children', *American Journal of Physical Anthropology* 21: 205–13.

Posen, A.L. (1965)' The effect of premature loss of the deciduous teeth on premolar eruption', *Angle Orthodontist*, 35: 249–52.

Prader, A. Tanner, J.M. and von Harnack, G.A. (1963) 'Catch-up growth following illness or starvation', *Journal of Pediatrics* 62: 645–59.

Ribot, I. and Roberts, C. (1996) 'A study of non-specific stress indicators and skeletal growth in two mediaeval subadult populations', *Journal of Archaeological Science* 23: 67–79.

Roche, A.F. (1992) *Growth, Maturation and Body Composition: The Fels Longitudinal Study 1929–1991*, Cambridge: Cambridge University Press.

Rosing, F.W. (1983) 'Sexing immature human skeletons', *Journal of Human Evolution* 12: 149–55.

Saunders, S.R. (1992) 'Subadult skeletons and growth related studies', in S.R. Saunders and M.A. Katzenberg (eds.) *Skeletal Biology of Past peoples: Research Methods*, New York: Wiley Liss, pp. 1–19.

Saunders, S.R., Hoppa, R.D. (1993) 'Growth deficit in survivors and non-survivors: biological mortality bias in subadult skeletal samples', *Yearbook of Physical Anthropology* 36: 127–51.

Saunders, S., Hoppa, R. and Southern, R. (1993) 'Diaphyseal growth in a nineteenth century skeletal sample of subadults from St Thomas' Church, Belleville, Ontario', *International Journal of Osteoarchaeology* 3: 265–81.

Saunders, S., DeVito, C., Herring, A., Southern, R., and Hoppa, R. (1993) 'Accuracy tests of tooth formation age estimations for human skeletal remains', *American Journal of Physical Anthropology* 92: 173–88.

Scheuer, J.L. and Bowman, J.E. (1995) 'Correlation of documentary and skeletal evidence in the St Brides' Crypt Population', in S.R. Saunders and A. Herring (eds) *Grave Reflections*, Toronto: Canadian Scholars Press, pp. 49–70.

Schutkowski, H. (1993) 'Sex determination of infant and juvenile skeletons: 1. Morphognostic features', *American Journal of Physical Anthropology* 90: 199–205.

Smith, B.H. (1991) 'Standards of human tooth formation and dental age assessment', in M.A. Kelley and C.S. Larsen (eds) *Advances in Dental Anthropology*, New York: Wiley Liss, pp. 143–68.

Stone, A.C., Milner, G.R., Pääbo, S. and Stoneking, M. (1996) 'Sex determination of ancient human skeletons using DNA', *American Journal of Physical Anthropology* 99: 231–34.

Sundick, R.I. (1978) 'Human skeletal growth and age determination', *Homo* 29: 228–48.

Tanner, J.M., Whitehouse, R.H. and Takaishi, M. (1966) 'Standards from growth to maturity for height, weight, height velocity and weight velocity: British children 1965', *Archives of Disease in Childhood* 41: 454–71.

Weaver, D.S. (1980) 'Sex differences in the ilia of a known sex and age sample of fetal and infant skeletons', *American Journal of Physical Anthropology* 52: 191–5.

Wood, J.W., Milner, G.R., Harpending, H.C. and Weiss, K.M. (1992) 'The osteological paradox: problems of inferring prehistoric health from skeletal samples', *Current Anthropology* 33: 343–370.

Y'Edynak, G. (1976) 'Long bone growth in Western Eskimo and Aleut skeletons', *American Journal of Physical Anthropology* 45: 569–74.

Chapter 16

Minor concerns: a demographic perspective on children in past societies

Andrew Chamberlain

INTRODUCTION

My intention in this contribution is to explore some of the ways in which demographic modelling may have implications for our reconstructions of the place and role of children in past societies. As Sofaer Derevenski (1997: 193) has emphasised, it is imperative to develop robust theoretical frameworks that establish the importance of children in past societies *precisely because* the historical and archaeological records appear to be deficient as a testament to their presence and agency. In particular, there is a requirement for objective models that are not biased by modern Western preconceptions concerning past demographic structures, the economic value of children's labour, and the relative importance of the social and political roles of adults and children (see also Chamberlain 1997: 250). This chapter argues that demographic analysis can inform our understanding of children in past societies, although it should be noted that the sub-discipline of palaeodemography is by no means free of theoretical and methodological problems, some of which are highlighted below.

POPULATION STRUCTURE

Demographic studies of historical populations often utilise data on individual vital events (births, marriages and deaths), but these data were only sporadically recorded before the modern era and records are particularly deficient in the case of the deaths of young children. Samples of human skeletal remains from archaeological sites can provide data on age-specific mortality, but excavated assemblages of human remains often show markedly biased age and sex distributions as a result of selective burial, incomplete preservation in the burial context and partial recovery of the burial sample on excavation. Fortunately, human populations exhibit a degree of regularity in population structure, and demographers have constructed model stable populations that encompass much of the variation observed in living populations in different regions of the world (Coale and Demeny 1983). These model populations provide a reliable benchmark against which we can compare our reconstructions of population structure in the past. Perhaps the least 'Westernised' populations for which data are available are those foraging communities studied ethnographically prior to their assimilation or extinction following contact with colonising Western populations. The age structure and mortality levels observed in carefully censused foraging communities match the model stable populations (Figure 16.1), thereby giving confidence to the belief that these population models might also be applicable to human societies known only through the archaeological record.

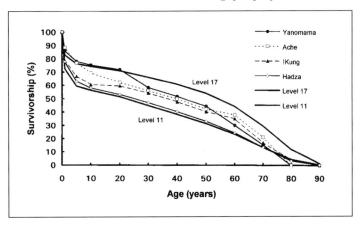

Figure 16.1   Survivorship in four foraging populations (Ache, Hadza, !Kung and Yanomama) compared to survivorship in the Coale and Demeny 'West' model stable populations. Average age at death in the model populations are 30 years (Level 11) and 45 years (Level 17). The stable populations have annual growth rates of 1.5 per cent, while annual growth rates in the foraging populations range from 0.3 per cent (!Kung) to 2.7 per cent (Yanomama)

The main parameters that determine the age structure of a living population are the age-specific probability of death (especially the infant death rate) and the rate of intrinsic population growth (the difference between the birth rate and the overall death rate). Higher infant and childhood death rates result in a smaller proportion of the population reaching adulthood and, paradoxically, a greater proportion of the population's total person-years are lived in childhood. High rates of population growth also result in proportionately more children in the total population because, in an expanding population, the most recent birth cohorts will always be numerically larger than those born several years earlier. The age structure of the living population, in turn, determines the age distribution of the deaths that occur in the population, but the relationship between the age structure of the living and the dead is not straightforward.

CHILDHOOD MORTALITY IN RELATION TO POPULATION STRUCTURE

Childhood, in a broad sense, can be defined as the period of physical and social development from birth to maturity. A demographic convention is to define children as individuals less than 15 years of age. This convention recognises that at least in traditional societies, individuals of about 15 years of age have the potential for economic and reproductive self-sufficiency, whereas prior to that age they are, to a greater or lesser extent, dependants of their parents and other adult kin.

In stable population models the proportion of the population made up by children varies inversely with life expectancy at birth (average age at death). The segment of the total population constituted by children varies from about 36 per cent in a low life expectancy population to about 19 per cent in the highest life expectancy populations (these figures assume zero rates of population growth, and take slightly higher values in expanding populations). In a population with low life expectancy the high risk of death in childhood, coupled with the relatively high proportion of children in the population,

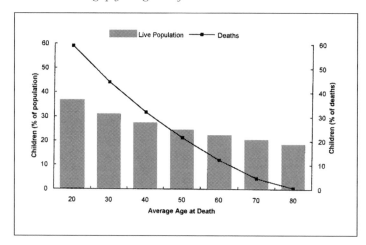

Figure 16.2 The effect of overall levels of mortality on the proportion of children among the live population (shaded histogram) and among the deaths (points along line) in model stable populations at different levels of mortality. Overall mortality is indicated by the average age at death, with lower average age at death signifying higher mortality

Note: Children are defined here as individuals less than 15 years of age

combine to result in 50 per cent or more of total deaths occurring to children (ethnographic studies have shown that childhood mortality in pre-industrial societies varies from 20 to 56 per cent (Hewlett 1991: 8)). At the other extreme, populations with high life expectancy (such as those predominating in contemporary Western Europe) have very low rates of childhood mortality, often with much less than 10 per cent of the people dying in childhood (Figure 16.2). Thus the variation in the rate of childhood mortality is considerably greater than the variation in the proportion of children in the living population, and in most pre-industrial populations children are proportionately over-represented among the deaths occurring in the population.

Communities with strongly contrasting experiences of the impact of childhood mortality might be expected to have very different attitudes towards the likely survival of children, which may have consequences for the level of care and attention that is directed by parents and adult kin towards an individual child. Ethnography provides some evidence that adult care-giving varies in response to perceived risks of childhood mortality. Levine *et al.* (1994) observed that in the Gusii agro-pastoralists of south-west Kenya, a population with moderate levels of infant mortality, maternal care of infants is closely attuned to the infant's prospects of survival with 'indulgent' care being a direct response to elevated mortality risk. Hill and Hurtado (1996) note that in the Ache, a hunter-gatherer community in eastern Paraguay with high levels of childhood mortality, increased parental and kin investment in offspring alleviates some of the risks of infant and childhood mortality, although many of the hazards to Ache children are unavoidable given the nature of the environment occupied and the resources available to the population.

THE ECONOMIC CONSEQUENCES OF CHILDHOOD MORTALITY

Child mortality rates also have implications for economic models of the value of children to families. As Nieuwenhuys (1996: 237) has recently pointed out, the notion of valuing children's work is problematic for modern Western societies in which childhood is held to be a period of dependency while the child undergoes instruction and socialisation through the media of education and play. In contrast to modern Western ideology which denies children agency in the economic sphere (Sofaer Derevenski 1994: 9), in many pre-industrial societies children participate in the production of value both in the household and in the wider community. In strictly economic terms, children contribute to household economies, but their contribution is usually more than offset by their consumption of resources so that they often impose a net economic cost on families well into adolescence (Reher 1995: 520; Hawkes *et al*. 1997: 552). In hunter-gatherer communities, children's contribution to production does not exceed their consumption of resources until 18 to 20 years of age (Kaplan 1996: 102). Thus the real 'value' of children to parents primarily lies in their potential as an 'investment' in the future. In genetic terms, they embody their parents' share in the future collective gene pool, while, in socio-economic terms, surviving children can provide political and economic support when they are mature as well as being an 'insurance' for when their parents reach old age.

The economic concept of the 'future' or 'investment' value of children can be extended to explain the practice of pledging children's work in exchange for a financial loan (Nieuwenhuys 1995: 244), and 'future' value is also realised when adult kin actively negotiate the marriage potential of children. Pursuing this logic, deaths that occur in childhood can be viewed in economic terms as representing a 'wasted' parental investment, with the loss of investment being much greater if the child is older (because of the cumulative net cost of child-raising), and correspondingly less burdensome if the child dies at or shortly after birth (Reher 1995: 522). This latter point enables a clearer understanding of the practice of infanticide (homicide or fatal neglect of infants, often perpetrated by parents or other close kin). Infanticide is widespread among ethnographically documented human cultures and occurs at an estimated rate of between 5 per cent and 50 per cent of all live births in foragers, horticulturalists and traditional agrarian societies (Dickeman 1975: 130). In some instances, infanticide is the most common cause of death among infants and anthropologists have increasingly cited domestic economic reasons to explain its occurrence (ibid.: 133; Harris 1994: 13).

HOW CHILDREN DISAPPEAR FROM THE ARCHAEOLOGICAL RECORD

Turning to the archaeological record, it is possible to estimate the age structure of past populations from palaeodemographic data but it is well established that there are considerable problems of sampling bias and in the accuracy of age determination if the estimates are based solely and uncritically on the available skeletal evidence. There are sometimes corresponding difficulties with historical data as deaths in certain age classes may be under-enumerated in primary historical records, and the self-reported ages of adults might be exaggerated in situations where individuals accumulate status and authority with increasing age. Departures from expected distributions of deaths in historical datasets and archaeological samples can be detected and characterised by 'pattern matching' (Milner *et al*. 1989; Paine 1989) using data from appropriate model life tables as the basis for comparison.

Under-representation of infants is very common in assemblages of human skeletal remains from archaeological contexts (Acsádi and Nemeskéri 1970). The shortfall in numbers of children, particularly infants and young children, is manifest even when large samples of skeletons are recovered from the cemeteries of communities in which deceased individuals of all ages are expected to receive normative funerary rites (Lucy 1994: 26).

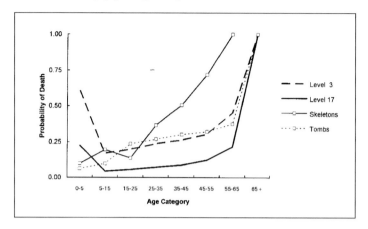

Figure 16.3   Age-specific probability of death calculated from the distribution of deaths in a skeletal sample from a later mediaeval British Christian cemetery and from inscriptions on Roman tombstones

Source: Grauer 1991: 75; Durand 1960: 368

Note: The archaeological and historical data are compared to the probabilities of death in model populations with different mortality experiences (Level 3: average age at death 16 years; Level 17: average age at death 47 years; both model populations with growth rates of 1.5 per cent per annum)

Figure 16.3 shows age-specific probability of death calculated for a later mediaeval British urban cemetery sample (Grauer 1991: 75) compared to the probability of death in stable model populations with high (Level 3) and low (Level 17) mortality and moderate (1.5 per cent per annum) rates of population growth. Also shown are comparable data calculated from ages at death given on Roman tombstone inscriptions (Durand 1960: 368). Both the skeletal sample and the tombstone inscriptions show abnormally low apparent rates of mortality in infants and young children – the direct effects of under-representation of these age classes in the data sets. In the skeletal sample there is an additional anomaly because the adult ages of death have been systematically underestimated, leading to inflated estimates of rates of mortality in the young and middle adult categories. Howell (1982) has pointed out that underestimating adult ages at death leads to unrealistically high estimates of the rates of orphanage amongst children.

There are a variety of factors that may contribute to the under-representation of children's skeletons in archaeological samples. Quite apart from cultural practices which may have excluded children from normative mortuary rituals in the past, their skeletons also may have lower preservation potential; their bones are less robust and, because children's graves may be shallower than those of adults, they are more liable to damage or loss through subsequent disturbance to surface layers, whether through natural processes of soil erosion or through land usage such as ploughing, drainage or building. Furthermore, even when children's graves are preserved, they are less likely to be recovered; children's skeletons are smaller and less easily recognised, they may have less elaborate graves, or they may be overlooked when commingled with the remains of adults. Several workers have drawn attention to cases where the deposition of the remains of children occurs in contexts separate from those of adults. In Neolithic central and southern Italy, for example, children's remains are under-represented in cemeteries associated with settlements, whereas they are over-represented in mortuary deposits in caves (Skeates 1991: 126, 1997: 81; Robb 1994: 36). At a later period, the extensive literary evidence for the extent of child exposure and infanticide in the Roman Empire (Harris 1994) is corroborated by the recovery from late Roman 'non-cemetery' sites of assemblages of infants' remains with maturational age distributions characteristic of neonatal deaths (Smith and Kahila 1992; Mays 1993). These examples suggest the need for care in interpreting cemetery samples, particularly those of past communities in which a range of alternative mortuary practices may have been followed. While each type of archaeological context merits its own analysis, only a consideration of *all* categories of mortuary deposit is likely to provide an accurate basis for the demographic study of archaeological populations.

CONCLUSION

The extensive documentation of age structures and patterns of mortality in present-day globally distributed populations (albeit stimulated by current Western concerns with macroeconomic development and the impact of population growth on natural resources) provides a fertile source of models and baselines against which reconstructions of past populations can be evaluated. Stable population models are particularly useful for prehistorians because of the difficulties caused by selective archaeological sampling and the tendency for demographic estimators to be inaccurate when applied to archaeological data.

The wide variation between human populations in rates of childhood mortality is predicted to have a significant effect, both on the nature and intensity of parental care and on the ideological perception within a given community of the economic value and social role of children. Where the net economic costs to a family of raising children are high, the child's value may lie mainly in its future potential, but this potential is likely to be discounted unless the child has a reasonable chance of survival to adulthood.

REFERENCES

Acsádi, G. and Nemeskéri, J. (1970) *History of Human Life Span and Mortality*, Budapest: Akadémiai Kiadó.

Chamberlain, A.T. (1997) 'Missing stages of life: towards the perception of children in archaeology', in J. Moore and E. Scott (eds) *Invisible People and Processes: Writing Gender and Childhood into European Archaeology*, London: Leicester University Press, 248–50.

Coale, A.J. and Demeny, P. (1983) *Regional Model Life Tables and Stable Populations*, 2nd edn, New York: Academic Press.

Dickeman, M. (1975) 'Demographic consequences of infanticide in man', *Annual Review of Ecology and Systematics* 6: 107–37.

Durand, J.D. (1960) 'Mortality estimates from Roman tombstone inscriptions', *American Journal of Sociology* 65: 365–73.

Grauer, A. (1991) 'Patterns of life and death: the palaeodemography of mediaeval York', in H. Bush and M. Zvelebil (eds) *Health in Past Societies*, British Archaeological Reports International Series 567, Oxford: BAR, 67–80.

Harris, W.V. (1994) 'Child-exposure in the Roman Empire', *Journal of Roman Studies* 84: 1–22.

Hawkes, K., O'Connell, J.F. and Blurton Jones, N.G. (1997) 'Hadza women's time allocation, offspring provisioning, and the evolution of long postmenopausal life spans', *Current Anthropology* 38: 551–77.

Hewlett, B.S. (1991) 'Demography and childcare in preindustrial societies', *Journal of Anthropological Research* 47: 1–37.

Hill, K. & Hurtado, A.M. (1996) *Ache Life History. The Ecology and Demography of a Foraging People*. New York: Aldine de Gruyter.

Howell, N. (1982) 'Village composition implied by a paleodemographic life table: the Libben site', *American Journal of Physical Anthropology* 59: 263–9.

Kaplan, H. (1996) 'A theory of fertility and parental investment in traditional and modern human societies', *Yearbook of Physical Anthropology* 39: 91–135.

Levine, R.A., Levine, S., Dixon, S., Richman, A., Leiderman, P.H. and Keefer, C. (1994) *Child Care and Culture: Lessons from Africa*. Cambridge: Cambridge University Press.

Lucy, S. (1994) 'Children in early mediaeval cemeteries', *Archaeological Review from Cambridge* 13: 21–34.

Mays, S. (1993) 'Infanticide in Roman Britain', *Antiquity* 67: 883–8.

Milner, G.R., Humpf, D.A. and Harpending, H.C. (1989) 'Pattern matching of age-at-death distributions in palaeodemographic analysis', *American Journal of Physical Anthropology* 80: 49–58.

Nieuwenhuys, O. (1996) 'The paradox of child labor and anthropology', *Annual Review of Anthropology* 25: 237–51.

Paine, R.R. (1989) 'Model life table fitting by maximum likelihood estimation: a procedure to reconstruct paleodemographic characteristics from skeletal age distributions', *American Journal of Physical Anthropology* 79: 51–61.

Reher, D. (1995) 'Wasted investments: some economic implications of childhood mortality patterns', *Population Studies* 49: 519–536.

Robb, J. (1994) 'Burial and social reproduction in the peninsular Italian Neolithic', *Journal of Mediterranean Archaeology* 7: 27–71.

Skeates, R. (1991) 'Caves, cult and children in Neolithic Abruzzo, central Italy', in P. Garwood *et al.* (eds) *Sacred and Profane*. Oxford, OUCA, 122–34.

—— (1997) 'The human use of caves in east-central Italy during the Mesolithic, Neolithic and Copper Age', in C. Bonsall and C. Tolan-Smith (eds) *The Human Use of Caves, British Archaeological Reports International Series,* 667. Oxford: BAR, 79–86.

Smith, P. and Kahila, G. (1992) 'Identification of infanticide in archaeological sites: a case study from the late Roman-early Byzantine periods at Ashkelon, Israel', *Journal of Archaeological Science* 19: 667–675.

Sofaer Derevenski, J. (1994) 'Where are the children? Accessing children in the past', *Archaeological Review from Cambridge* 13: 7–20.

—— (1997) 'Engendering children, engendering archaeology', in J. Moore and E. Scott (eds) *Invisible People and Processes. Writing Gender and Childhood into European Archaeology*, London: Leicester University Press, 192–202.

Name index

Subject index